Wakefield Press

MOOD

Roz Bellamy is a writer, editor and researcher living in Naarm/Melbourne. Their work has been published in *The Big Issue, Crikey, the Guardian, Huffington Post, Island Magazine, Kill Your Darlings, Meanjin, Overland* and SBS, and in anthologies *Growing Up Queer in Australia* (Black Inc.) and *Living and Loving in Diversity* (Wakefield Press). An excerpt of *Mood* was longlisted for the 2020 Kill Your Darlings Unpublished Manuscript Award. Roz recently completed a PhD at La Trobe University exploring the impact of life writing on young LGBTQ+ people's mental wellbeing. *Mood* is Roz's first book.

MOOD

A Memoir of Love, Identity and
Mental Health

Roz Bellamy

Wakefield
Press

Wakefield Press
16 Rose Street
Mile End
South Australia 5031
www.wakefieldpress.com.au

First published 2023

Copyright © Roz Bellamy, 2023

All rights reserved. This book is copyright. Apart from any fair dealing for the purposes of private study, research, criticism or review, as permitted under the Copyright Act, no part may be reproduced without written permission. Enquiries should be addressed to the publisher.

Some names and identifying characteristics have been changed out of respect for those involved.

Edited by Jo Case
Text designed and typeset by Jesse Pollard, Wakefield Press

ISBN 978 1 74305 870 1

A catalogue record for this book is available from the National Library of Australia

Wakefield Press thanks Coriole Vineyards for continued support

'Time is what makes everything OK. How it flows forward and circles round itself, both; how life, suspended, zero gravity, in time consists of so many things repeating . . .
In the benign repetition of daily acts an invisible net is cast, holding people up, protecting them.'

Maria Tumarkin, *Axiomatic*

Prologue

Rachel calls while I'm driving and asks me where I am. I peer around in the darkness, trying to make out details, but the lights from oncoming cars overwhelm and distract me. I tell her I'm nearly home and she sounds reassured. It's a lie.

When Rachel next calls me, I'm on Rathdowne Street in Carlton, heading in the direction of the city. I'm evasive when she asks where I am. As Rathdowne Street becomes Exhibition Street, and I see the bright lights, I say, 'I think I'm in the city.'

'What do you mean "you think"?' she asks, sounding frightened. 'Rozy, come home!'

I don't have control over my decision-making. I feel like there's someone else calling the shots behind the scenes. I'm letting that voice control my actions while I pretend that I'm still in charge, just slightly confused and disoriented.

It doesn't help that I've only been sleeping for a few hours each night. Each morning, I turn to caffeine and sugar to reanimate me and sustain me through the teaching day. I'm also drinking alcohol more than usual, and I want to take drugs but don't know where to buy them.

Sleep deprivation, I've discovered, leads me down the path to disassociation and psychosis. In this state, I wouldn't be able to resist, say no, push back or fight back if someone did something to me. I've become gummy; my muscles and bones no longer work the way I expect them to and I don't have any strength left in me.

I don't go home.

Chapter 1

Like many shy people, I find it easier to communicate in written form. I met my wife, Rachel, online. Some of my closest friends, too. In person, I become flustered and forget names, faces and pertinent details. After the Covid-19 lockdowns, I found it challenging to try to re-integrate people's physical bodies with their online selves.

The bio section of social media apps is a treasure trove. I dig into bios as though the 'secrets' they reveal will help me understand and click with people. Some bios have a witty one-liner, while others provide extensive information about identities, qualifications and health conditions.

My Twitter bio has changed many times over the years. Right now, it tells anyone who cares to look that as a non-binary person, I use they/them pronouns. It has shared that I am bisexual, queer and Jewish. For a while, it shared that I live with mental illness (though it didn't specify the diagnoses of bipolar disorder and borderline personality disorder it took me years to discover). I described myself as a leftie (which tends to be obvious from what I tweet and retweet). It mentioned my wife (whose account I tagged) and our two rescue greyhounds.

For many marginalised people, there's a strange balance to be achieved on these platforms. How do you indicate pride about aspects of your identity (perhaps when advocating for a related cause) while remaining aware of how critical people can be, and how personal information can be used against you?

At different times in my life, that information has meant different things to me. My sexuality, gender, religious background, political activism and mental health are all are intrinsic to who I am. But my willingness to share them with others varies wildly.

My relationship, which I no longer mention in my bio but continue to write and post about, has been one of the most stable things in my life, since I was eighteen.

I met Rachel on the internet, thanks to the TV show *Buffy the Vampire Slayer*. This fact elicits all sorts of strong reactions, from 'that's adorable!' to 'you nerds'.

It was after my one attempt at dating a cisgender man. The Kitten Board was my favourite queer space: an online forum for fans of one of television's first same-sex couples, *Buffy*'s Willow and Tara. It was a place where geeks and questioning queers fit right in.

It was on the Kitten board, on a thread titled 'When I Knew', that I had the strongest realisation yet about my own sexuality. I'd known for a long time that I was attracted to women as well as men, but I hadn't identified with any labels. Some on the thread told stories about their first crushes on someone of the same sex, while others shared lesbian stereotypes they recognised themselves in.

A few months after my revelation, I met Rachel while posting on a 'Word Association' thread. We shared a tendency to post quirky associations, and got carried away so often, the moderators got annoyed and closed down the thread.

I suggested we email each other instead. Many Kitten Board users were North American, so I was surprised to discover Rachel also lived in Australia. She was part of the Jewish community in Melbourne, comparatively close to mine in Sydney. We were two months apart in age. Her graduating class was one year below mine and she was in the middle of her Year 12 final exams. Rachel had also related to the 'When I Knew' thread, which made her think back on her crushes and come to her own realisations about her sexuality.

We started using *Buffy* quotes as our email subjects, quickly progressing from quirky episodes to poignant moments between Willow and Tara. In one, Tara tells Willow how much work they need to do to repair their relationship after a break-up. Then she asks: *Can we just skip it? Can you just be kissing me now?*

Mood

Our discussions moved from *Buffy* to our families, friendships, our sexuality and how glad we were to have met each other. Rachel and I were on the same wavelength: one that seemed different to everyone else's. We connected with humour other members of the site didn't understand. We were intrigued by each other's stories and created our own jokes, language and understanding of the world. I began to fall in love with her through words.

Our emails got longer and more involved. We started to sign off with *Love you*, then *I love you*. We called each other *baby*. I used these words intentionally, wanting us to be in a relationship like Willow and Tara's. But I was too scared to acknowledge that what was taking place between us was anything more than close friendship. I'd had close friendships with girls. Some had been all-consuming, but they'd never become explicitly romantic or sexual. I assumed my feelings for Rachel were unrequited – though I wanted to believe otherwise.

Chapter 2

Anxiety bubbles in my stomach and throat. I dip my head under the water and feel the ocean running through my curls and across my scalp. I'd hoped the cold water would clear my panic, but it doesn't. The ocean, particularly the Sydney beaches I grew up near, has always been a source of comfort, and it's a shock to feel anxious in the water in Hawaii.

There is something about being in the ocean that makes me feel embodied. Out of the water, I feel clumsy and bump into things or fall over. I miss things other people pick up easily. I forget to focus on my senses and have to catch up with other people who seem highly attuned to minor details. But I know how every part of my body feels in a cool body of water. In the ocean, I'm aware of every sensation.

As a child, no matter what I faced at school, an evening swim at Camp Cove in Watson's Bay transformed the way I was feeling. After the swim, Mum would present me with a plum and a nectarine that were just ripe enough to drizzle down my chin.

The ocean was never scary, even when the waves at Bondi or Coogee were big, even if they were so strong that I found myself scraped against the seabed, spiralling under the surface. When I came up again, the foam soothed my body. I always went back for more.

Sometimes, a weekend trip to Nielsen Park for a swim and a picnic provided a sense of comfort I hadn't known I needed. It was the beach where Mum took me as a newborn baby and it is a place I never stop missing, especially down in Melbourne, on Wurundjeri land, where the weather is often grey and grizzly.

The worst thing about anxiety is the disconnect it causes. My brain is wry, cynical and critical of my body. *You're at Hanauma Bay, fuckface. You are floating with your beloved wife in a Hawaiian volcanic crater filled with tropical fish. The heart palpitations need to stop. The chest pain needs to stop. The nausea needs to go away. Put the snorkel back on, hold Rachel's hand and go and see some damn fish while you can.*

My body ignores my brain. My anxiety about returning to Australia has intensified as we reach the end of our holiday, but this is the first panic attack I've had away from home. It feels the way I've always imagined a heart attack would. As I hold my hand to my chest, I think about how much an ambulance would cost in the United States. *Not worth it*, I tell myself. *Just find a way to calm down.*

I submerge and surface, over and over, each time blinking water out of my eyes and staring at the delicate palm trees close to the shoreline. Beyond them, I see mountains covered in lush greenery. I wish I could drape myself with something, too – maybe with the weighted blankets I keep adding to shopping carts and forgetting to purchase.

The bay is protected from nearby roads and the freneticism of Waikiki. I wonder what it looked like during the time when Hawaiian nobility, ali'i, used it for fishing and entertainment. I think of my late grandparents, Nana and Popsi, visiting Hawaii decades ago, and realise Hanauma Bay reminds me of their travel photographs. Nana looking radiant and peaceful, and Popsi leaning against a palm tree, wearing a kukui nut lei. I loved this photo for many reasons, but mostly because it was one of the few photos Nana hadn't defaced using blue pen, after she developed a habit of scribbling on photos to cross out her double chin. She must have liked this photo enough to leave her face as it was.

My anxiety starts to fade.

'Babe, do you want to go out a bit further and snorkel some more?' Rachel asks.

I nod and pull my mask down, kicking hard against the water as I follow her.

In the water, we look around in separate directions, using hand gestures or making sounds through the mouthpiece to alert each other to a particularly impressive fish. We see clown fish, reef fish, yellow tangs, triggerfish, butterflyfish and parrotfish exploring the coral. Sometimes, we hold hands, using our other hands to paddle against the water as the tide pushes us around.

It's a joy to be back in Hawaii, even as anxious as I am, nearly three years after our honeymoon in 2013. We got married ten years after we became a couple, delayed by unequal marriage laws and our own hesitations about how people in our life would react. Rachel grew up on a Pacific island nearby and spent a lot of time here during her childhood. We're both nurtured by being here, especially after a difficult few months.

When we make our way back to the shore, I stare at the trees and mountains again, hoping to burn the memory into my retinas. This might be my last sense of peace for a while.

As we wait for the bus after snorkelling, we wipe sand off our feet and pass a cold can of Sprite between us. We are tired and hungry; I take out a bunch of tangy apple-bananas to keep us going. I tell Rachel about the panic attack I had in the water. It's unusual for me. My anxiety spikes happen on public transport, at work or in university lecture theatres. Not by the beach.

'Are you okay now, love?' she asks. Her eyes are earnest, worried.

'Yeah, I think so. I'm a bit scared that I reacted like this while we're here. If my anxiety is bad on holidays, I'll probably have a breakdown by the time Term 1 starts.' Soon after we return to Melbourne, I'll be starting my first high school teaching position.

She touches my hand. 'You'll be amazing. Your students are going to love you.'

'Thanks, Boo. I hope so.' I'm already doubting whether teaching is the right job for me. I worry that I should get out of it while I can.

The flight attendants turn the lights on. People start waking up, putting their seats forward, shifting around and retrieving items that have fallen. Soon, they're accepting omelettes, sausages, tea and coffee. The smell takes over in the confined space. It's not breakfast time, no matter how you calculate it; at our destination that we're rapidly approaching, Sydney, the time is 7 pm, and in Honolulu, it is now 10 pm the previous night.

I turn on my screen and a map of the east coast of Australia comes into bright view, its shape fuzzy without my glasses.

Mood

The pilot's voice comes on over the passenger address system. There's something going on with the weather and we can't land yet, so we're going to hover. I watch us loop around parts of Sydney. The flight path looks like a neon dick and balls, which would normally strike me as funny, but I'm nauseous and the circling isn't helping.

Two days ago, it would have been my grandfather Deda's ninetieth birthday. We had originally timed this stopover for then, so we could celebrate with him. Instead, I sent his death certificate to the airline so we could delay the flight. I didn't want to land in Sydney on his birthday.

I'm still not ready to land. I like the fantasy plane travel promotes – a suspension of time and space – and I don't particularly like reality at the moment. Two months earlier, I lost two people I loved in the same week. The first was Deda, Mum's father, in Sydney. And then, a week after his death, my friend Jenny died suddenly. Days earlier, she had comforted me about losing Deda. Even though I've experienced grief and loss before – I lost my three other grandparents in my twenties – this time feels different. I'm reverberating with anxiety and anger, propelled into a dark and strange place. The shock of grief has made me brittle. I feel it in my jaw when I grind my teeth instead of sleeping, in my bones, through my hunched posture, and in my tight neck.

The captain announces we can land, finally, even though the rain is hitting the windows sideways, and the clouds are sharp grey and black. The plane hits the ground with a bump. As we wait to disembark, I realise I forgot to look out at beautiful Warrane – Sydney Cove – from the air. None of my grandparents are now alive, in this city where I grew up. It's wet, late and we've missed our connecting flight to Melbourne.

✳ ✳ ✳

Mum's parents, Baba and Deda, had to flee from their hometown of Odesa, Ukraine, when it was occupied by Nazi Germany and their Romanian allies. During the Holocaust in Odesa, Jewish people faced kidnappings, imprisonment, mass shootings, death marches, ghettos, starvation, concentration camps, forced labour and torture. Family members had been murdered. Baba and her family suffered through starvation, eating frozen dirt when they could find nothing else, before finding refuge in Tashkent, Uzbekistan.

Even after the war ended, antisemitism was rife in the Soviet Union, or USSR. Baba and Deda looked into any options available to them, and found a way to apply for residency in Australia for themselves, their two children and some of their family members. After migrating, Mum and her family had 'stateless' stamped on their arrival cards at Sydney airport. They added an 'e' to the end of their surname; they wanted to assimilate and to do so, they needed to sound less foreign.

Dad's parents, Nana and Popsi, were British Jews who had faced rations and bombing raids. Their parents before them had fled Romania and Ukraine in search of safety. Popsi joined the British Army to fight Hitler, after changing his name from Cohen in case he was captured by the Germans. Later, Nana and Popsi moved their family from London to Sydney as 'ten-pound Poms' on a ship.

My sister Jess and I, with our progressive parents, were different from many of the others whose families were from the Soviet Union – even those we were related to, like the cousins who participated in ballroom dancing and wanted to go into real estate. We hadn't been taught Russian, our grandparents' first language, apart from words for our favourite foods, the instruction to wash our hands and terms of endearment. (Mum wanted us to be fluent in English first and worried learning two languages would make things difficult for us.) But my parents sent us to a school that was deeply conservative, in order to learn about our religion and culture. Like many of our schoolmates, Jess and I shared a family history severely impacted by antisemitism and trauma.

My Modern Orthodox Jewish school strongly emphasised binaries. In the mornings, the boys and girls were split into different rooms for Shacharit, morning prayers. In the boys' room, they recited the line '*Shelo atzani isha*', or 'Blessed are you, God, that you did not make me a woman.' In the girls' room, we substituted that line for '*She'atzani kirtzono*', or 'Blessed are you, God, that you made me according to your will.' When we learnt about Shabbat, the girls in my class played the role of Ima, mother, lighting the candles, preparing the food and nurturing the family, while the boys played Abba, father, reciting Kiddush, the sacred blessings.

Mood

I had crushes on multiple people. One of the girls I liked was in my prayer group. She did not seem to fit the mould, and anyone who did not fit into that place fascinated me. I was far too shy to talk to her, but I observed her from a distance. She had dark blond hair that she kept tied back and tucked behind her ears, and seemed smart and cynical, which I admired. There was so much to be cynical about, though few of my classmates seemed to realise that.

At twelve, I chose to reject the Orthodox model of a girl's bat mitzvah. Instead, my bat mitzvah followed the model of a boy's bar mitzvah, which involved reading from the Torah – the most sacred Jewish text – and leading the prayers in parts of the service. This was normal at my family's progressive and egalitarian synagogue, but was considered unusual at my Orthodox school. There, a bat mitzvah for a girl involved reading a speech, tucked away in the separate women's section.

Afterwards, I continued to struggle with rigid binaries. They struck me as unfair and unequal, even though they seemed to be enforced widely and constantly.

* * *

Back home, I book my first psychology appointment for the year before we've even unpacked. I dread the appointment, but know that I need it.

I've been seeing Karyn for two years and feel comfortable around her, though I'm aware that I act a certain way for her. I crack jokes, determined to see her laugh, and try to entertain her throughout our appointments. But I hold back so much.

Today, she seems to be aware that I need to be handled with care. I don't know how. I'd straightened my posture when the session started and forced myself not to pick or bite at my nails and cuticles, even though I'm drawn to 'fix' the dry skin and jagged nail edges. I look at Karyn and she is smiling and asking about my trip to Hawaii, and maybe the awkwardness I feel – the sense that I'm doing therapy wrongly – is all in my head.

I enthuse about how great the trip was and then I tell her what is objectively good news, even if it scares me shitless. 'On the first night of the trip, one of the high schools I applied to work at called and offered me the position.'

Karyn is cautiously optimistic with whatever I tell her, and always gentle and patient. 'Congratulations, Roz!' she says. 'How do you feel?'

I pause, hesitant to talk about my fear of the role. When I was offered the job, my first teaching position, there was a sense of lightness and of possibility: the way things used to feel at the end of the school year when I was a child and a teenager.

But as Term 1 rapidly approaches, I've begun to feel terrified. I have been staying up until 3 am most nights, biting my nails and ripping at my cuticles, obsessively researching the government school as though the promotional materials on the website would tell me all its inner workings and secrets. When I go to bed, I struggle to fall asleep and have to remind myself to pay attention to my breathing, which speeds up when I'm anxious.

I don't know what to say, but the silence makes me uncomfortable so I reply, 'I'm nervous about it, but also relieved to have gotten it. It'll be the first job I've had where I actually use my qualifications. Also, it's a public school with a very different socioeconomic demographic to any of the schools I've attended or taught at on placement, so it will probably require some adjustment.'

She nods and I realise I've given her the same answer I'm using with family and friends. 'Nervous' and 'relieved' are accurate descriptors for how I am feeling, but they don't capture the terror I feel too. There's the belief that if I get this right I will have found my calling, changing my life and those of my students. But there's also the strong, unshakeable sense that I'm incapable of this, even before I step into my own classroom and face the students.

My role was advertised at the last minute, after a teacher resigned late in the school holidays, which tells me what I need to know: even though I had job interviews at multiple schools, I wasn't good enough to get a graduate teacher position at the end of the previous year. *You only have a job because the school is desperate*, my brain reminds me constantly.

'What else has been happening for you?' Karyn asks.

I tell her about my grief over Deda and Jenny's deaths. She asks some questions and I respond hesitantly, shyly. I segue into talking about my anxiety, which I find easier to talk about, and make blanket, generic statements about heart palpitations and stress. When I talk or think about anxiety, it is focused on my body, heavily disassociated from my feelings.

Karyn goes easy on me and doesn't turn the conversation back to grief or ask difficult questions. She asks what I'm doing to look after myself.

'I read in the bathtub. I go for walks. And I spend time with Rach.' I'm grateful that Rachel understands what anxiety is like. I feel an ease with her that I don't feel with anyone else; it's the lightness of existing as I am, and how I feel, without any need for justifications or fakery.

I've done a lot of reading about anxiety over the years. I know how to identify the symptoms. I know that while over two million Australians have anxiety disorders, there is stigma around them. A former boss once said, 'It's the latest buzzword – now apparently *everyone* has it. How convenient when there's something you don't want to do.'

'I'm very glad you have some forms of self-care that work for you,' Karyn says.

I nod, embarrassed by the term self-care, not sure that it fits with me lying in a bathtub eating chocolate.

'Let me know how you go in the new job,' she says. 'Don't be too hard on yourself.'

I nod, aware this is my default mode.

Chapter 3

Fast forward six months: July 2016
July. I introduce myself to my new Year 10 History class. It's the beginning of Term 3 – the second semester. Many Year 10 students don't want to study Humanities, but it's compulsory for them to do at least one Humanities subject per semester.

'What do you know about World War II?' I ask.

One of the students raises his hand and looks at me as he speaks. 'Hitler tried to kill the Jews. He should have killed all of them.'

Nearly six months into my first teaching job, I am a calm teacher now. Unflappable, for the most part. I am not calm hearing my student's remark about Jews. I explain to the student and the rest of the class why I find that comment deeply hurtful. And then, because I need a break, I send him out of my class. He ends up spending the next couple of weeks in the assistant principal's office, writing out short questions and answers from a textbook chapter on the Holocaust. I'm secretly pleased to hear this is his punishment.

A few weeks later, I enter my Year 10 History classroom at the unfortunate time of last period on a Friday. This is never an entirely successful period, as the students' minds are on their weekend plans. A group of students are bunched together, laughing and whispering. As I step forward, I see what they are working on: a large red swastika, in dripping red ink.

The ink has stained their hands and run onto the desks.

Mood

***

Rewind: January 2016
January. The school holds an induction session for the new graduate teachers, a day before Term 1 of the teaching year starts.

I'm relieved that I will know someone: my friend Lisa, who I studied teaching with, was offered a job there at the start of the previous year's recruitment rush. I've seen her teach. She knows exactly how to get the balance right between approachable and authoritative. She's good at sport, which can be a good way to connect with teenagers, and she is intelligent and funny. I know she probably makes mistakes, too, and she's told me about some of her insecurities, but I view her reverently, while I can't stop thinking harshly about myself. *You're a loser. Awkward weirdo. You can't do this. Why did you ever think you could?*

When I approach the school, I feel a pang of jealousy when I see her talking to another graduate teacher. The year ahead starts to come together in my mind. Lisa will be amazing at this and will become close friends with the other teachers. I'll fail, and I'll be on my own.

The first few days of term are pupil-free days for staff professional learning. I'm shy when I interact with my colleagues for an activity, but feel more confident as I listen to presentations about classroom management, different learning styles and students' various allergies. The presenters are high energy, clearly well-caffeinated, and make it sound achievable. In the break, I walk around the yard, imagining the tables and benches full of students in a few days. I peer into one of my classrooms and think about how to set it up. I start to think maybe I can do this.

On my first day, I realise the job is going to be even harder than I anticipated. There are 29 students in my Year 10 Economics class. Some of them look like fully grown adults. I'm physically intimidated, but try not to show it. The classroom that seemed big and full of promise is now at maximum capacity.

'Okay. Who knows the game Two Truths and a Lie?'

My students roll their eyes or ignore me.

'So here are three bits of information about me. Try to guess which one is a lie. I've travelled to Sri Lanka. I grew up in Sydney. I have four brothers.'

A group of boys sitting in the front row laughs loudly and shouts made-up answers. '100!' 'Two sisters!' 'You have a cat!'

I sigh, deciding not to try playing games again for a while.

In comparison, my Year 7 class is angelic. Fresh from primary school, they are softly spoken, respectful and interested in everything. They want to tell me random facts about Egypt and recycling. I try to focus on how attentively the Year 7s listen to me, how they cut out and stick in the little maps in Geography or rearrange timelines in the right order in History, the way they politely ask questions and share knowledge.

Wednesday, it turns out, is my worst day of the week. I have yard duty followed by my Year 9 class and then a double period with my Year 10 class. I spend yard duty panicking. I'm positioned at the sports oval and have to keep an eye on any fights, injuries and general rule breaking. While I stand there, shivering in the wind and staring out at the oval, I think about why I'm struggling in my new role.

It isn't possible to plan my lessons, assess learning and teach the way I hoped. I have an idea of how my classes should be planned and how they should run based on what I was taught in my Masters. My teaching isn't remotely like the 'best practice' I was taught. It's impossible to promote higher-order thinking skills when you're struggling with the basics of classroom management. I want to come across as capable and professional but feel the opposite. I constantly expect a student or parent to make a complaint about me, or to be found out as a fraud and then fired. And it hasn't even been a week.

In my Year 9 Humanities class that afternoon, I walk around and ask to see my students' exercise books. Flicking through one book, I see the words, *Fuck humanities*. She has used a lot of force to write the words and they go through to the other side of the page. I worry her intense hatred of the subject is because of something I've done.

In my Year 10 class, I try to give my PowerPoint presentation before they do an activity but it's too hard. They're so noisy, and I can't stop thinking about two of the hard-working students in my class who can't learn with the amount of talking and play-fighting around them. My brain reminds me, *You need self-belief to teach. It's not fair to them that they have a teacher like you. You should quit now, before you fuck up their learning entirely.*

Mood

I feel my initial cautious optimism draining away, replaced by fatalism and even fear. Only a week in, I'm certain I should quit my job. But I feel a sense of duty to keep going, for as long as I'm physically capable.

A few weeks later, I'm over at my parents' house in Northcote. They have been living in Melbourne for less than a year. Before the school term started, Mum told me she wouldn't be living in Melbourne for much longer. She had shared the information hesitantly. Her grief over Deda's death made her want to return to Northern New South Wales, where she and Dad lived for a decade before they moved to Melbourne: that was where she felt a sense of comfort and familiarity. They'd made an offer on a house, and Dad would follow soon after she left.

I love living in the same city as them. I long for closeness, even if proximity makes it harder to lie or omit the truth when I'm struggling. While it is possible to have a close relationship over the phone, it isn't the same.

I know Mum is experiencing grief and depression after losing her father, but I worry she's also leaving because she hasn't seen me and my sister as much as she'd expected to. Now, with my parents leaving, I can't help feeling like I'm being abandoned.

The weekend before Mum is due to leave, we share a home-cooked lunch. I'm trying to ignore my emotions and channel my energy into putting together PowerPoints for my classes. My laptop keeps warning me my storage drive is full, so I drag what I think is a back-up of my teaching folders to the recycling bin and delete them. Then I double-check their status. As my laptop syncs, I see all my files disappearing.

Mum tries to soothe me as I hyperventilate. 'It's okay, it's not the end of the world. You might be able to get them back. Even if you can't, you can try to remember what you had done and start again.'

'No, I can't. This is *everything*. All my uni assignments, all my lessons and PowerPoints. This is years of work.' I try unsuccessfully to control my distress. I berate myself. *What is wrong with you? God, look how pathetic you look in front of them. Way to seem like you have your shit together.*

'Can I give you a hug?' she asks, holding out her arms.

After a moment, I pull away. I know she means well, but I'm wound up too tightly to find a hug comforting. 'I have to contact Google and see if they can fix this.'

Hours later, I manage to retrieve my files. My parents keep looking at each other, but I don't feel I overreacted. If anything, I'm concerned about whatever caused me to delete them in the first place. I am usually the most careful, deliberate and obsessive person. I'm losing a sense of control – over my family, my work and even my inner thoughts.

I panic when I'm teaching most classes, but never more so than in my Economics classes, where I pinch my skin, press my fingernails into my palms and chant anything in my head that may calm me down. Sometimes, the words *You're okay, Rozy* are helpful.

At most, I have basic knowledge of the subject. At my job interview, I had been asked if I was willing to teach Economics, Business and Accounting. These subjects are part of Humanities, which is one of my two teaching specialisms, but my degree focused on History, Geography and Civics. I'd said yes: I wanted the job.

Some of the students won't stop talking to each other during my lesson, regardless of what I say or do. I catch another student checking out expensive sneakers online.

One of the textbook questions is about how gifts affect supply and demand. 'Why do you think some economists don't like gift giving?'

'Because they're Jews?'

I turn to look at the student who said it. He stretches, grins at me.

'No, that's not why.' I talk briefly about stereotypes and how they hurt people. I want to say more, and think I should, but I sense he's hoping to cause drama, so I leave it. It stays with me, though.

As a Jewish teacher, I've experienced plenty of casual antisemitism, especially after completing teaching placements at government schools and a Catholic school. During yard duty, I've seen a group of boys play Who's the Jew?, where they drop a twenty-cent coin on the ground and see who'll be the first to grab it. The first time I heard them mention the game, I told them not to play it anymore. They keep playing it, though. I wonder if other teachers bother to stop them when they're on duty.

Mood

My depression becomes more severe with each passing week. I'm not able to manage challenging behaviour in my classroom and I internalise all the associated feelings of failure, stress and guilt. My sense of failure as a teacher starts to extend to other areas of my life. I believe I'm not good enough at anything I try, that I miss things that come easily to others, that I am pathetic and hopeless. I know I shouldn't listen to this depressive inner voice, but I can't make the thoughts stop. Instead, I think about how it would be easier to be dead.

On my fifty-minute commute to school each day, I pray for something bad to happen. Anything, so long as it means I don't have to teach. I stare out the tram window as we get closer and closer to school, not even able to cry. I'm numb, suspended between the bed I haven't left inside my head and the busy, industrial streets near the school.

Some days, I hope to get sick, to be diagnosed with a terminal illness that will prevent me from continuing to work. When I'm feeling particularly dramatic, I hope for a terrorist attack to take place, or for an apocalypse to happen. This is always followed by strong feelings of guilt and self-loathing. I ramp up the self-hatred by thinking about people who are dying. I read a blog post by a woman with a terminal disease who would give anything for more time with her loved ones, and I see this as evidence of how pathetic I am for taking my life for granted and for wanting to end it.

Soon, these passive thoughts about suicide become more invasive and urgent. For the first time in my life, I start planning how to kill myself. This is a magic reprieve from my alternating feelings of fear, numbness or self-disgust. I don't have to think hard to choose a method. I ignore anything that contradicts my belief that suicide is the answer to my problems.

I haven't talked to Rachel about feeling suicidal, and it's far beyond anything I've told Karyn. I've only mentioned mild depression to her. I keep telling myself that if I can't work it out in therapy, there's no point trying with anyone else.

When I want to talk myself out of suicide, I reflect on a conversation Rachel and I had years earlier. We were driving at night with no destination, as we often liked to do. I mentioned someone from my high school who had died by suicide.

'I don't understand why people ever think that suicide is the only answer,' I'd said, flicking my eyes from the road to Rachel to see her reaction.

Rachel had nodded, running her fingers through her ponytail as she thought about it.

'I know,' she'd said after a pause. 'If it's ever getting that bad, leave the job, leave the relationship, even leave the country if you can. Just try something – anything – else first.'

But now that I am in that place, actively planning the end of my life, the alternatives we had discussed seem not only impossible but pointless. Maybe this is it, I think. Maybe there isn't enough reason to keep struggling. Why worry my wife, family, friends or psychologist by telling them how I feel? They will try to talk me out of it and I will do it anyway.

Rather than telling my family, friends or Rachel I am constantly thinking about suicide, I say, 'I'm not coping very well with teaching.'

When I say this to Karyn at a therapy session, she says, 'You feel as helpless as a teacher as you did as a student'. She's referring to the severe bullying I experienced from my best friend, Dara, which started when I was five years old.

* * *

Dara forced me to do certain things and punished me if I didn't comply. In class, she expected me to sit in my chair in one of two ways: with my legs folded or with my legs together and my feet pointing forward at angles. This was, she said, 'ladylike'. She gave me orders, like I was in a boot camp, including, 'Don't talk to anyone unless I give you permission.'

I had met Dara on my first day of school. She was taller than me and seemed far wiser. I admired her long, straight hair and thought she was beautiful. She had opinions on how I looked, too: she gave me the nickname 'Fuzzball' because of my frizzy hair.

She developed a system of punishments, which ranged in severity, for when I broke her rules. I developed ways to cope. When she forced my foot into a toilet at school, or belittled me, I went blank. When she pinched me as hard as she could, I tried to separate myself from my thoughts, feelings and pain receptors. It was the start of dissociation – though I only discovered the concept decades later.

My parents had both attended single-sex public schools, where they encountered bullying, antisemitism and racism. They wanted to protect their children by sending us to a Jewish private school. Our whole family had to work to fit into that community.

It worked to some extent. But there were numerous bullies and a generational set of cliques at my school, despite – or perhaps because of – most of our ancestors having experienced trauma. We shared history and culture. Our grandparents displayed similar neurotic behaviours. It was sad to realise I wasn't safe there.

The bullying lasted, undetected, for three years, because I acted the same as I always had at home. I talked to my family but didn't mention what was going on. Once my parents worked out what Dara was doing to me, they made it clear to the school leadership that they had to do something.

By the time the principal got involved, I had changed. I was silent and submissive at school. Whatever consequences Dara may have faced behind closed doors, she remained at my school. This reinforced something I had suspected: bullies were untouchable. Strangely, I missed her. Other than seeing her from a distance at school assemblies or in the corridors, she was gone from my life. I didn't feel confident on my own. I focused on what she had taught me about how to sit, and when to speak or keep quiet. Now, I enforced her strict rules on myself.

* * *

I tell Karyn I'm aware that being back in the school setting is triggering me. 'Can I ever overcome that?'

As a child and teenager, I didn't feel confident that seeking help at school would do anything, and I don't feel confident now about using the chain of command to seek help with my most unruly students, or telling my colleagues how much I'm struggling.

'You can learn to manage it. Recognise your unrelenting standards and stop looking for evidence of failure. You are capable. I know you can do this.' She looks at me closely. 'It's okay to feel a sense of dread; it's horrible sometimes!'

'Can you explain what you mean by "evidence of failure"? I don't have to seek evidence of failure; I find it everywhere.'

'Sure. You have a very intense failure narrative you tell yourself. You're convinced of your own failure and look for evidence. You need to develop techniques so you can observe yourself doing this. Don't try to stop it. When you start feeling panicked, worthless or critical of yourself, notice yourself letting this narrative play out.'

I nod. 'I try to put my fears and panic into perspective, but it's not easy.'

'You need to focus on the real world,' Karyn says, 'not what your mind is telling you about it.'

If I weren't so depressed, I would challenge her on this point. All the things my mind tell me feel real.

I speak to Mum two weeks before the end of Term 1. She has settled into the new house up north and tells me about it in detail. I try to respond enthusiastically.

'And how are you going, my darling?' she asks.

I start sobbing. Mum seems as shocked as I feel by my sudden tears. She is soothing and supportive throughout the conversation. She's also very self-deprecating, occasionally cutting into whatever advice she gives with 'But what do I know?'

After our call, she texts me. *I love you very much and wish I could help make you feel happier about life right now. You have so much going for you . . . you'll get through this difficult time. Whatever decision you make with regards to your job, I support you.* Later, she adds, *You'll find another job that doesn't make you hate your life, I'm sure of it!*

I thank her, and mean it, but I doubt her words. *Don't you see that it's me?* I think. *It's not the job. It doesn't matter where I go. I'm useless.*

My uncle calls to discuss my job. We don't talk often, apart from birthdays, so I assume Mum told him she's concerned about me.

'I hear from my sister that it's hard,' he says. 'Tough school, yeah?'

'There are lots of things I like about it,' I reply. 'But some of the kids . . .'

'. . . are little shits,' he says, finishing my sentence for me. 'I was a little shit at school, so I can give you some advice. Want to know what to do?'

'Sure.'

He pauses for effect. 'Get a stripper.'

I laugh, and he says, 'I mean it! They'll be interested for an hour or two. They'll be happy! What else is a fifteen-year-old boy interested in?'

'Ha. Thanks. I better go.'

'One more thing! Find the weakest link in that group and push on it until it breaks.'

'Okay.' His suggestions are not helpful or implementable. But I appreciate that he cares.

Somehow, I make it through Term 1, including parent-teacher conferences in the final week. Many parents don't attend, including those I need to talk to about their children's behaviour.

When I reach the long-awaited school holidays, I know it's an achievement. But I feel flat. All I want to do is watch TV, but Rachel and I have organised a trip with my parents to a regional town to see my sister. Jess is teaching theatre to young people there, helping them put on a show. Mum flies in from New South Wales so we can drive there together. She greets me with a big hug. 'You did it! Congratulations! How do you feel?'

I try to smile, but feel sad. I don't know how to explain it to her. 'Relieved. Thank you.'

On the four-hour drive, I notice my parents exchanging looks. It's nice they care about me, but I can't help worrying they're judging me.

'You're so quiet back there,' Mum says. 'I thought we'd be chatting the whole trip.'

We stop in Echuca and walk along the Murray River to stretch our legs. We decide to have lunch at a trendy pub and I sit there while the others talk. It's awkward. I head to the bathroom at one point, and when I come back I see Mum and Rachel leaning into each other. Their faces are drawn, concerned.

Later, I ask Rachel what they had said to each other.

'She's worried about you,' she says. 'You should try to talk to her.'

'Okay.'

But I don't know where to begin.

Chapter 4

A couple of months after Rachel and I started talking online, I went overseas to Europe: my first solo adventure, which I'd been planning for a year. I was eighteen. I had spent so long saving for the trip but when I arrived, I felt like something was missing. Rachel and I were used to spending hours talking to each other each day. I spent most of my time in internet cafes, despite being entranced by my surroundings.

Rachel finished her exams while I was away. She started looking for a summer job before university started. We wrote fan-fiction together about Willow and Tara from *Buffy*, including one story set at a cow farm they ran together. I cried with laughter as we wrote new chapters.

Everything I did in Europe was marked by this burgeoning love. While my new friends were partying and sleeping around, I was secretive. I hid my growing feelings for Rachel even from her. I didn't mention her to my travel buddies, nor my friends at home.

In one email, I reported to Rachel, *I met a girl on tour and she's Aussie, Wiccan and a* Buffy *fan. But she hates Tara! Argh! She likes Spike! Noooo!*

She replied, *This girl sounds cool. Apart from that huge whopping detail about the lack of Tara liking.*

I parsed every syllable and punctuation mark in her reply. She seemed less enthusiastic than usual. I doubted she had feelings for me, but wondered if she thought I was attracted to my new friend. I hoped this was why she seemed a bit down. I was quick to clarify, telling her, *The two friends I'm with are guy crazy. I always feel kind of uncomfortable when we're at a bar and some guys chat us up, and my friends never understand why I'm not interested.*

One day, my new friend had sex with a stranger on the front desk of our backpacker hostel. When she told me, I flushed, unsure what to say in response. I had the freedom to do whatever I wanted while I was away, but I felt scared and unprepared. I was evasive when my friends tried to find out who I thought was cute.

It was late December, and Europe was sinking into the depths of winter. It was getting dark earlier each day and it made sense to give up on sightseeing in the afternoon and move to an internet cafe where I watched the streetlights switch on and waited for Rachel to email me.

I parted ways with my friends in Ireland, and finally started looking up gay and lesbian bars and clubs, equally intrigued by and afraid of the idea of exploring my attraction to women. I'd never had any sort of physical relationship with a woman, and it felt like this was my chance.

In Dublin, I crossed the Liffey late at night to go to a lesbian bar. It wasn't crowded enough for me to be anonymous. I felt far too shy to go inside, and certain I wouldn't fit in. The women were at least twice my age and seemed to be there to drink and talk. I didn't know what I wanted. I couldn't work up the confidence to approach them, or dance.

I tried another lesbian bar when I visited Belfast, but only made it halfway up the wooden staircase before turning back. I heard party music and excited voices, and didn't have it in me to join in. I wondered what was wrong with me. Would I stay permanently single? I returned to my hostel outside the city and had an early night. The next morning, I heard a bomb threat had shut down the city overnight. I sank into my bunk bed, scared.

It was difficult to process my sexuality while I was away. At the hostels, the people I met talked openly about hooking up and had sex in the bunk beds around me. I didn't meet anyone who was openly queer.

My feelings for Rachel continued to grow despite the distance. Eventually, I realised that I didn't want to be away from home anymore. I wanted to be back, chatting with Rachel and working out where things between us were going. I had another month away but had used up most of my savings. I was living on dented tins of baked beans and stale bread from the sale section of the supermarket. I tried to change my return flight to Sydney but the airline didn't allow it. After telling my parents I was homesick, they offered to buy me a one-way ticket home. I felt very guilty about the cost but accepted.

Days before my return flight, Mum emailed me. She sent her best wishes for my safe flight home, then added her hopes I would be seated next to a *gorgeous, friendly and funny Jewish doctor or lawyer* around my age, who lived in the same suburb. She said it would be *love at first sight*. She didn't specify this person should be male, but it was assumed.

She didn't know I *was* falling madly in love with a gorgeous, friendly and funny Jewish person, only two months younger than me. I smiled at the email. At the time, coming out seemed impossibly distant: not something to worry about in the present. I was very good at compartmentalising my feelings and avoiding certain realities.

When I returned home, my parents, sister and grandparents met me at the airport. They called to me and cheered as I walked out of customs and into arrivals. We hugged and kissed, then left in separate cars and met back at my family home. Mum had asked what foods I'd missed and put on a feast, including a huge platter of mangos, grapes, watermelon and apricots. It felt nice to eat my favourite foods and tell my travel stories to a captive audience.

It felt like many other family meals, with my proud and loving grandparents and parents listening as Jess and I bantered, our miniature schnauzer cosy on my lap. Something was different, though. I was in a different place. I had come back to see what would happen with Rachel.

Our emails continued once I returned. We made plans to meet, and I booked a flight to Melbourne using my small amount of remaining money. My stomach was in knots. I didn't tell my family anything about Rachel; I lied, not ready to share, and said I was going to stay with a friend from my Jewish youth movement. They didn't ask many questions.

A few days after I turned nineteen, I flew to Melbourne. Rachel sent me directions to her house, which her mother had provided: I had to take a train and then a tram, and then it was a short walk to their house. I arrived in Melbourne on Friday evening. Observant families were walking home from Shabbat dinners and there were very few cars on the road.

Despite our similar demographics, Rachel and I lived remarkably different lives. I belonged to a progressive synagogue that offered a Mardi Gras Pride Shabbat. She belonged to an Orthodox synagogue, where women sat behind the men, separated by a curtain. I had one sibling, while Rachel was one of eight children. Her house was strictly kosher, while my family bought kosher meat but otherwise didn't worry about Kashrut.

I brought along a large box of Swiss chocolates as a gift to her parents for hosting me. Dad had taken me shopping the night before the trip to Melbourne and I had chosen the expensive box, wanting to make a good impression.

I walked towards Rachel's house feeling strangely confident, perhaps because I had disregarded anything she'd told me that was unfamiliar. I had grown up surrounded by Jewish families, and my friends' parents all seemed to like me. Any nerves I felt were about whether Rachel would like me.

I paused at the front door, looking down at my outfit. Like all my T-shirts at the time, I had cut off the sleeves and collar of the one I was wearing and stretched the material so it hung off one shoulder. This look was completed with short shorts and a stud in my nose. I held the box of chocolates.

The house was dark; her family had all gone to bed. I knocked quietly and stood outside, enjoying the cool night breeze after a hot summer's day. I took some deep breaths while I waited. I heard Rachel coming downstairs to let me in. When she opened the door, all we could do was grin and stare at each other. She was wearing a white lacy shirt and black skirt, her long hair falling over her shoulders. I felt a strong sense of relief; I hadn't invented my feelings for her. I knew all my pining had been worth it.

I hugged her and relished the feeling of holding her body in mine. I breathed in her scent, hoping my attraction wasn't too obvious. I felt like I finally understood the feeling of love at first sight. At school, I'd had many crushes that felt like love. But I had fallen for Rachel before I met her. That was new. So were my strong feelings of attraction, respect, care and protectiveness.

We walked upstairs, talking non-stop. I noticed her adorable laugh. It was bright and musical, which didn't surprise me as I knew she loved singing.

'You can put your stuff down here,' Rachel said. Her parents had arranged for me to have my own room. They had moved her sister into another room so I was alone in a room with twin beds. I put my bags in the room and quickly returned to Rachel.

She showed me around her bedroom. There was no awkwardness between us. We could, and did, talk all night. In the early hours of the morning, we were still sitting on her bed talking. We were both night owls, accustomed to staying up late chatting online.

'Maybe you should just sleep in here with me,' Rachel suggested, not long before the sun started to rise.

'Okay!' It still didn't feel awkward between us, even as I crawled into her bed. We were both used to having slumber parties with our girlfriends – platonic ones – at our houses.

Lying next to someone I had fallen in love with felt more intimate than I could have imagined. She fell asleep and I lay there, wide awake, aware of our proximity. *Imagine if I reached out and touched her hand,* I thought. *Or kissed her.* Maybe she wouldn't mind.

Thinking of ways to facilitate 'accidental', G-rated touching, I reflected on our interactions since my arrival. I was sure we'd been looking dreamily at each other, even if we hadn't talked about having feelings for each other and hadn't kissed. There was undeniable chemistry. But despite our intense connection, I worried my romantic feelings and sexual desire were one-sided.

The next day, I experienced what Shabbat was like for Rachel. Her family were very religiously observant, more than I'd realised – or perhaps I'd ignored any information that hadn't fit with my hopes and expectations. They didn't drive, use the stove or even turn on lights during Shabbat. I didn't interact with them much apart from during mealtimes, when her parents asked me questions about my studies.

Over the following days, Rachel guided me around her neighbourhood. We walked past Glicks, a kosher bakery, with its queue of religious Jewish people – men wearing head coverings, their tallit strings hanging from their shirts, and women wearing wigs and modest dresses – waiting to buy bagels and cakes. The smell was intoxicating. It was a new neighbourhood to me but intrinsically familiar, despite growing up near Sydney's equivalent area. We walked past shops with menorahs, Shabbat candlesticks and other Judaica in the windows, and saw groups of students whose uniforms displayed the names of local Jewish schools and a Magen David – the Star of David. I noticed many minivans like the one Rachel's parents owned, which fit their many children.

Rachel took me to her favourite falafel restaurant for lunch. 'Mmm, it's great,' I said. I was used to eating un-kosher food and superior falafel, but I loved wandering around with her, experiencing her life. We laughed constantly and never ran out of things to talk about.

At night, I lay in her bed, watching her at her computer. I stared at her profile as she chatted to our friends from the Kitten Board. As she smiled or laughed, I breathed in sharply. Oh dear, I thought, I have it *bad*.

Sometimes, we touched accidentally. We'd separate quickly. I wanted my hands to linger but made myself pull away.

Lost in my dreamy, romantic feelings, I didn't pick up on the tension in the house. I had shown up with only a vague departure date. That was how I did things. 'A few days' turned into almost a week. I didn't want to leave her and didn't have the budget to pay for accommodation in Melbourne. I hadn't realised her parents were ready for me to go.

'When are you planning on leaving, Roz?' Rachel's mother asked.

'Oh, I don't have a set plan.'

'I didn't expect you to stay so long,' she said. Her tone made it clear it was time to go.

'No problem.' I smiled. 'I'll pack up.'

Rachel looked sadly at me. As I left, I saw my box of chocolates in the bin. It hadn't occurred to me to buy kosher chocolates.

* * *

I often think back on what made me fall for Rachel. I met her at the end of my teenage years and she ticked all the items on my teenage checklist: she wasn't fake, she was kind, patient and gentle, she listened to my obscure stories, she was beautiful and she loved animals. I saw all of this in Rachel when we met, and again when we next spent time together – in a rural town in Wisconsin in the United States, in the height of summer. She was living with friends after finishing her Year 12 exams in Australia.

It was my first time visiting the US, and Rachel and I continued to fall in love as we went strawberry picking, ate meals on hay bales, listened to music under the steady hum of a ceiling fan, and ran into cold Lake Michigan.

Our friends had a husky who spent a lot of time in their large garden, and had a cat who'd just had a litter of kittens and absconded. We sat in the backyard and played with the kittens. They darted around on their tiny legs, occasionally getting cheeky with the husky. I watched Rachel, noticing how patiently and tenderly she interacted with the kittens as she helped them work out how to function. As she walked around our friends' property, they followed her in a line.

There's a difference between someone who finds animals cute and someone who will dart through traffic to rescue an injured bird, find a lost chicken's home, administer medication to a very displeased dog, or accept a dying rat from the neighbour who put out rat poison – all of which Rachel has done. I noticed and fell for her even harder.

Rachel was born in the Marshall Islands and spent a lot of time in Hawaii. She grew up with hermit crabs, sea cucumbers and sharks as part of her daily life. Later, when her family moved to Adelaide and she was trying to adapt to her new life, she spent her time with blue tongue lizards in her backyard.

I was born and raised in Sydney, close to the city. I'd grown up with pet bunnies, cats and a miniature schnauzer. The most exotic of my childhood pets were the snails my sister and I once relished keeping.

Despite our very different starts in life, we'd managed to find each other.

Over a decade later, we've survived obstacles, made sacrifices for our relationship and built a life together.

But I'll soon find myself testing exactly how much Rachel will put up with.

Chapter 5

The more I struggle with my new job, the more I realise how much I rely on Rachel. During the day, I accrue a list of worries and thoughts to run past her. When I get home, I know she will listen and calm my anxiety. As I spiral, she takes me back to things that make sense. She prompts me to return to these footholds rather than slip further.

At thirty-two, I think I should be able to rely on myself more than I do. Sometimes, when I think about quitting my teaching position, I wonder if I would regain a sense of agency, as well as self-belief and self-reliance. Maybe I wouldn't need therapy anymore.

It seems a particularly cruel twist that I need therapy to survive teaching, when it was therapy that led me into teaching.

* * *

I first started seeing a therapist at twenty-six. I had been sent to school counsellors as a child and teenager and hadn't found them helpful. Because of this, I avoided therapy as an adult until my emotions became so intense and hard to handle that I couldn't any longer

Both sides of my family have stigma around therapy. Mum's side didn't see a point in talking about problems, while Dad's side thought it was rude and embarrassing. I was nervous about being expected to talk about my emotions. I fastidiously avoided crying, sometimes making tight fists of my hands in a physical attempt to force my emotions away.

After graduating from high school, it dawned on me that I had social anxiety. It presented as twitching, obsessive finger tapping, hair twirling, fingernail and cuticle biting, and hiding in the bathroom. I had to force myself to walk through the door into new academic, professional and social situations.

I went to see my GP because I didn't feel well. I had been dealing with thyroid disease for a few years, but I was starting to think there was more going on. I couldn't talk about my emotions or mental health without crying. My doctor probably took one look at me and realised how desperate I was. She was calm and empathetic, and referred me to a psychologist.

I held off seeing the psychologist for a few weeks, then booked an appointment. It cost $220 a session, and I only received about $80 back from Medicare. Still, it was necessary, so I left work twenty minutes early and made my way to her city office.

The psychologist, Radhika, asked me questions to get a sense of what I was experiencing. Towards the end of the appointment, she moved her tissue box so it stuck out on her bookshelf at a 40-degree angle. 'Does that bother you?' she asked.

'Yes,' I said, not feeling the need to lie. She wrote something down on a notepad. Later, she told me she thought I had generalised anxiety disorder.

I often heard people describe themselves by saying 'I'm so depressed' or 'I'm anxious'. I had started to believe these were just adjectives, not possible symptoms, syndromes and disorders. In their softer adjective forms, words like 'depression' and 'anxiety' lose their potency.

Before starting therapy, I relied on my own systems for managing my issues. I attended free yoga sessions in the park, hosted by my local council; I ate chocolate and I drank. The yoga wasn't enough, and sugar and alcohol weren't sustainable as mood improvers, but I held out as long as possible.

My mental health had worsened considerably when I started to lose my grandparents. My family was small, close-knit. It was always just us four in my immediate family, and my four grandparents (there was drama with our extended family).

I was close to all four of my grandparents. Grieving their deaths – in some cases following severe deterioration – contributed to my own decline. Baba, Mum's mother, had died when I was twenty, followed by Nana, Dad's mother, when I was twenty-four. Nana died only a year

Mood

after Rachel and I moved to Melbourne from Sydney, and I was wracked with guilt over having left her. Soon after, I was diagnosed with Grave's Disease, lost a drastic amount of weight and started having terrible heart palpitations.

Popsi, Dad's father, only lasted at home for a few months after losing Nana, unable to continue functioning without her. He was moved into a Jewish nursing home.

I wondered if his last few energetic years had been forced for Nana's sake. As long as she was around, he was mobile and desperate to do things for her. Once she was gone, he could give up. When we went to visit him, he was distressed and weeping, angry, or apathetic. It was hard to believe he managed at home for so long. He always had such a sharp mind that he felt capable and refused help.

Popsi rarely remembered my visits, but I needed to see him. I continued to travel to Sydney regularly. I would rush and stress to get there, then arrive at the nursing home to find total stillness. The stillness made the activity of my regular life feel ridiculous.

I would leave Popsi's nursing home in a sad state and then head to Bondi to see Deda. Deda was younger, and in better shape, so visiting him felt uplifting. He would ask how Popsi was and shake his head sadly at the response, saying, 'Poor Popsi.' I agreed, still remembering the strong man who swam laps daily and called out to his grandchildren, 'Get in! It's warm as toast!'

Usually we couldn't afford for both Rachel and I to visit Sydney, so I did these trips alone. I would return to Melbourne late on a Sunday night, not in the best frame of mind to prepare for a week of work in my administration role.

On New Year's Eve, Dad received a phone call from his brother. I heard him say, 'Oh shit,' and knew it was the end. Gangrene in Popsi's foot had led to infection.

We booked the next available flight to Sydney.

At the nursing home, Popsi had been moved off the bed to a mat on the floor. There was a medical reason, related to the gangrene, but there was an absurd jungle-gym feel to the room, with its blue floor mats.

There was nothing more the medical and nursing staff could offer beyond morphine doses. I moved to the mat, beside Popsi. My dad watched me talk to Popsi and hold his hand for a long time. Eventually, Dad also took Popsi's wrinkled, almost translucent hand. There was something innocent in the gesture, possibly the first time they had held hands in decades; I imagined Popsi had been more likely to shake his son's hand than hold it.

I hadn't seen a person die before. There was something spiritual and pure about it, a sense of him leaving his painful body. It turned out that having views on heaven, souls or the afterlife was not important.

After Popsi's funeral, I felt my old worries returning. I was unsure how to process my grief, and glad that I had a therapist to see when I got back to Melbourne.

In therapy, Radhika encouraged me to talk about my grief over my grandparents' deaths. Over time, I told her about Dara, my school bully – mostly reluctantly.

I was more comfortable complaining about my job and expressing my desire for postgraduate study. Popsi had always been passionate about academic success and his grandchildren's future careers, so it seemed like a positive thing to focus on. I was ashamed I hadn't established a career: so many family members had made sacrifices for me.

'I'm thinking of studying something with a clear career trajectory at the end, unlike my degree in creative writing,' I said. 'I keep coming back to publishing, editing, teaching or library studies.'

'Look,' Radhika replied, 'based on everything you've told me, you won't be happy in your work unless it involves books.'

I raised an eyebrow, not sure that that was true, but I didn't argue.

'Interesting. I haven't thought of it like that before.'

'What if you became an English teacher?'

I liked having a therapist who told me what she thought I should do. Soon after, I applied to do a postgraduate teaching degree.

I struggled with indecision and general passivity. During one appointment, I told Radhika that on a recent trip I had walked back and forth between two airport terminals because I couldn't decide what to eat until I ran out of time and had to rush to the departure gate. Radhika listened and nodded when I told her that I had hoped the flight would be announced so I wouldn't have time to ruminate any longer. That it would force me into a decision.

She was direct about most topics and didn't hold back her thoughts. I appreciated this, but occasionally baulked at her bluntness.

Sometimes, when I told Rachel something that Radhika had said in an appointment, she was surprised. 'Really? I wouldn't go back to a therapist who worded things so bluntly.'

'But I think she's right,' I would say.

I didn't tell her all the blunt comments.

Once, Radhika argued it would have been better if a person in my life who had attempted suicide had died. 'Some people don't want to live,' she said.

I kept my rage inside, not even capturing it in the meticulous notes I kept about each session.

After starting my teaching degree, I found I enjoyed the theoretical side of my studies and being back at university. But during my first teaching placement, my anxiety returned, stronger than ever. I couldn't bear sitting in the staff room talking to the other teachers. I didn't understand how teaching was a normal part of their day, when for me it was more frightening than performing on stage. The size of the classes scared me, and my mentor teacher's presence was additional stress: I worried he was judging my incompetence.

When I started experiencing panic attacks at school, I began to think about trying an anti-anxiety medication. I went to see my GP.

'I'm scared to go on meds,' I said. 'There are fears and stigma around psychiatric medication in my family, but I thought I should talk to you about it.' It felt like if I could get over my fears, medication might be an easy solution.

'I understand that. I would absolutely support you taking medication, if that's what you think you should try next,' she replied. 'Sometimes talking therapy can only go so far. If you want to try medication, which may help alongside therapy, I'd like to refer you to a psychiatrist.'

I nodded. Radhika, as a psychologist, couldn't prescribe medication. I had expected I might be referred to a psychiatrist, based on the reading I'd done about antidepressants. 'I'm anxious about starting all over again with a psychiatrist,' I admitted. 'I have a good rapport with Radhika and she knows so much about my life.'

'I completely understand that and I'll make sure I refer you to someone suitable. You don't have to tell them everything at once. Start off with your immediate concerns.'

'Okay. I can try that.'

My doctor opened a database and scanned a list of names. 'Dr Sandra Manuel is meant to be good. I've heard great things about her from my patients.'

'I'll give it a go,' I said.

During my first appointment with Sandra, she wrinkled her brow when I said I'd been seeing Radhika for four years.

'Four years is too long not to have made progress,' she said.

'But I have made progress. I've come a long way. It's more that my current situation has made things flare up again.'

'Tell me more about your current situation.'

I thought about how to describe it. I was doing my teaching degree part-time, so my five-week placement blocks were split over May and September. We were allocated a mentor teacher each placement: a classroom teacher at the school who agreed to have a student-teacher observe them teaching and to observe the student-teacher's classes and provide feedback. Mine was a motorbike-riding, passionately left-wing Sicilian man who was late to most of my classes and didn't seem very interested in giving me feedback on my lessons.

'I started my postgraduate teaching course this year, and I'm finding my teaching placement very difficult. In my first week, a student ran out of the classroom without any warning, and later I found out she had gone to the bathroom to self-harm. I had no idea what to do, and my mentor teacher was dismissive, saying she acts up all the time.'

She nodded. 'What do you do when you find the situation challenging at school?'

Even though I found it very difficult to talk about, especially with a stranger, I forced myself to answer honestly. 'I go to the library whenever I can. It's quiet there. And I go to the bathroom in my breaks and basically sit there the whole time. I've even eaten my lunch in there before, which is disgusting. And I'm struggling to make it through each day of teaching.'

She didn't ask what I meant by struggling to make it through, and I didn't offer any more information.

'Based on what you've told me, it's clear you're still very anxious and possibly depressed,' Sandra said. 'If talking therapy alone was going to help, it would have done so by now. Your psychologist might not have been the right fit for you. Either way, I strongly recommend you start on an antidepressant medication. I would like to prescribe one. You will start on a low dose and go up in two weeks. Then we'll touch base to see if we need to raise the levels.'

I glanced at her, hoping my expression would convey my hesitation, but she was already typing notes. 'Actually, I haven't made up my mind about going on meds. I'm worried about the changes it might lead to. I'd hate to end up with side effects, especially if the meds don't do much to help.' I didn't tell her what I was afraid of – that my sex drive and my creativity would disappear – and she didn't ask, either.

Sandra reached for a pad of paper. 'Do you know much about how SSRIs work?' she asked.

'No.'

She drew a complicated diagram and began to explain the science behind SSRIs, using jargon I vaguely remembered from previous studies in biology, psychology and chemistry. I hadn't understood it back then, and things weren't much clearer now.

I know now that selective serotonin reuptake inhibitors (SSRIs) treat depression by increasing serotonin levels in the brain. Serotonin is a neurotransmitter, a chemical messenger that delivers signals between neurons (brain nerve cells). SSRIs work by stopping the neurons from reabsorbing the serotonin so more of it is available to improve the transmission of messages between neurons. SSRIs are also used to treat anxiety disorders and obsessive-compulsive disorder (OCD).

'Does that make sense?' she asked five minutes later, when she reached the end of her explanation.

'Uh, yeah. I guess so.' I had switched off.

'Okay, great.' She began to type rapidly on her laptop. 'I'll give you a script for Lovan, and I'll see you in two weeks to see how you go with it.'

I nodded and thanked her. I paid hundreds of dollars for my appointment, cringing at how little the rebate from Medicare was in relation to the amount paid, and made another one.

On the way home, I stopped to buy the medicine. I thought of the clichés I'd seen in documentaries: Big Pharma incentivising doctors to push various drugs onto their patients.

My feelings about Sandra – her pushiness and impatience with my slow progress with Radhika, which I was only able to process after the appointment – turned me off the idea of medication and psychiatry in general. The box of pills ended up at the back of my medicine cupboard, and I cancelled the next appointment. I told my GP things didn't work out. She didn't push me further.

By the start of the following year, I had mostly forgotten what my first placement had been like. When I went to buy an outfit for my thirtieth birthday, the owner of the clothing store chatted to me through the changing-room curtain as I tried on clothes. 'Just you wait. Your thirties are completely different to your twenties. You feel so good about yourself, in comparison.'

I listened with interest and looked at myself closely in the mirror. Maybe she had a point. I was wearing my hair down in public, rather than slicked with gel and tightly tied back, a style I'd developed in high school to hide my curls. I liked how I looked in the denim pinafore I was trying on, even though it wasn't my usual style. The shop owner had suggested it and paired it with a leather belt, and I was surprised to find I liked the result.

'What do you think?'

I left the change room and struck a pose. I felt a rush of adrenaline as the shop owner complimented me.

Maybe my thirties would bring about some big changes, I thought. I even felt positive about my decision to go into teaching, though it helped that the realities of the classroom were a distant memory: it was the summer break.

When the university semester started, a friend mentioned the list of placements for that year were up. I logged into my student email and scanned the list. I would be teaching at a Catholic boys' school. When I told the others the name of the school, my lecturer smiled.

'It's a footy school,' he said.

I wasn't nervous until I met up with my new mentor teacher, a severe-looking woman who ran many of the religious programs at the school. She arranged for us to meet on a pupil-free day, and when I arrived, she escorted me to the library and handed me a thick folder that said 'Year 12 English'.

'You'll be taking my Year 12s,' she said. Her tone implied this was a sacrifice on her behalf. I took the folder, hoping I looked grateful and that my fear wasn't too palpable.

I glanced at the timetable she'd printed for me, and my heart raced. I didn't feel ready to teach Senior English, which I believed required far more experience and skill than I had. But I wasn't going to admit that. 'I need to teach more classes than that,' I told her. 'We're expected to teach for a certain number of periods a week.'

'Okay, you can teach my Religious Education class, too.'

'Oh,' I said. 'I'm meant to be teaching English on this placement. Also, I'm Jewish.'

'That's fine,' she replied. 'You can cover the values side, not the Bible lessons.'

Things felt wrong from my first day, when one of the senior teachers made a transphobic joke in the teachers' lounge about Conchita, the drag performer who'd just won Eurovision. I realised immediately I didn't fit in.

The Year 12 students liked to test me, and usually I failed. I wasn't strict enough. During one lesson, one of the popular boys who liked to cause trouble called me over while I was checking on the students as they worked.

'Hey, Miss,' he said. 'Who's your favourite musician?'

I felt the pressure of getting the answer right. 'I don't know, I have lots of favourites.' It was a cop out, but he kept pushing.

'Nah, but you must have one favourite. Who did you last listen to?'

I thought back to the music I'd played on my drive in that morning. I'd had to pump the volume in an attempt to drown out my loudly beating chest. 'Florence and the Machine.'

He nodded, appraising me. 'Yeah, cool.'

I thought I'd made some progress with him, but later he asked to go to the bathroom and then disappeared for half an hour.

'You need to make the boys use hallway passes,' my mentor teacher said sternly after the bell rang. 'And make them take out both earbuds! These boys need rules!'

I felt pathetic, like a mix between a child and adult, but lacking the skills and privileges of either age group. All I had were responsibilities I couldn't seem to handle.

The other student-teachers seemed to be coping, even if they were stressed. One of them was from Australian Catholic University. She wore neat cardigans and pleated skirts to school, her long, brown hair tied up in a stylish messy bun. I couldn't imagine fitting in at the school the way she seemed to. On recess and lunch breaks, she made jokes I didn't find funny and started group conversations that I avoided participating in.

I experienced panic attacks in the bathrooms each morning and had to drag myself out from the relative safety offered by the toilet cubicle. When placement ended, I felt pride for having survived. But I also realised I needed help. I reached out to Radhika and was told my Mental Health Treatment Plan had expired. I needed a new referral.

My usual GP was away and I didn't feel comfortable booking in to see a new doctor for a referral. The thought of an unknown doctor asking very direct questions about my mental health was unbearable. I'd answered the questions with a cold, disinterested doctor once before, and I never wanted to do that again.

The university winter break helped, but my stress returned when the new semester started. As my next placement at the boys' school drew nearer, I went to see another GP at my usual clinic. It was beginning to dawn on me that I could see a different psychologist. Sandra's critique of my four years with Radhika had left me with niggling doubts about whether it was working, even though Radhika had told me she thought I'd made a lot of progress.

Mood

The GP, fortunately, had better bedside skills than I'd anticipated. She asked me what I liked and disliked about Radhika's therapeutic style.

'I like her sense of humour. And she's very empathetic.'

'Does she use cognitive behavioural therapy?' she asked.

I had heard of CBT but had no idea whether Radhika used it. The GP referred me to Karyn.

* * *

Karyn was based at a psychology clinic in the middle of the CBD, a block over from my workplace. I was still working at the same admin job, counting down the months before I could quit. I wanted to find a teaching job, despite being afraid of teaching.

I liked Karyn immediately. She looked like a talk-show host: well-groomed and with a disarming smile, but approachable and kind. Her consulting room was decorated in warm tones. There were pillows on the couches and boxes of tissues on both side tables. It seemed set up for maximum efficiency. I also liked the clinic. The turquoise décor, the long, silent hallways, and the chilled water machine in the waiting room made me feel calm and steady.

During our first appointment, I knew I wanted to see her regularly.

Karyn had been a psychiatric nurse and knew the limitations, assumptions and judgements inherent in the medical world. She avoided pathologising my feelings and nudged me away from diagnoses, gently. Instead, we explored the reasons behind my feelings.

'Are you aware you rarely cry during our appointments?' she commented after a few sessions.

'That doesn't surprise me,' I replied. 'I have practice keeping things on the inside.'

'You are very self-contained,' she said. 'You look so calm and even when you cry your emotions are tightly controlled.'

'That's bad, I know,' I said, sighing.

'Not always. It's a good thing for teaching, as you don't come across as vulnerable.'

'Teaching will be very good for helping me get over my issues. You know, if it doesn't swallow me whole,' I said. 'It forces me to deal with issues like bullying, aggression, wanting to be liked and worrying about what people think.'

'Oh absolutely,' she replied. 'It will be challenging for you. You'll have to work to see yourself differently and not assume the worst about yourself as a teacher. Some of your negative self-talk is based on the bullying you experienced at school. It will help when you realise most of the worst-case scenarios you're imagining don't usually happen.'

'How do I do that?'

'You can handle the anxiety through meditation and breathing. Use positive evidence and experiences to convince yourself to reframe your thoughts. Focus on the feelings, not what you conclude from them. Tell yourself you're feeling overwhelmed rather than doing a bad job.'

'I'll try.'

Sometimes, while Karyn talked, my mind wandered. I heard, over and over, the words, *You're such a fucking idiot*. I was embarrassed she needed to tell me information that seemed obvious.

Karyn used a form of treatment called schema therapy to identify and address maladaptive habits and behaviours developed early in life, based on negative core beliefs. It combines elements of cognitive behavioural therapy, psychoanalysis, attachment theory and emotion-focused therapy. I found it helpful for exploring the trauma I experienced in school settings.

'If you'd like, I can send you some readings about the two schemas we discussed,' she said. She had identified two early maladaptive schemas that she believed fitted me: unrelenting standards (believing you have to meet very high internalised standards of behaviour and performance, usually to avoid criticism) and self-subjugation (trouble setting boundaries, expressing feelings and dealing with conflict).

'That would be great!'

She smiled. 'I have a feeling you'll like schema therapy. It's intellectual, perfect for someone who wants to read a lot and really try to understand their behaviour.'

I trusted Karyn, so I was willing to learn about schema therapy and try it. I downloaded the chapters as soon as she sent them to me, knowing

Mood

I was being a perfectionist while learning about my perfectionism.

If there was a disconnect between the theoretical side of schema therapy and putting it into practice, and if I was grabbing hold of a new tool through which I could intellectualise my emotions, I wasn't aware of it then. That took a while to figure out.

After learning more about schema therapy, I told Rachel, 'You know, I'm kind of excited about trying a new type of therapy. I think the main thing will be managing my anxiety. I somehow have to reduce my avoidant behaviour and actually leave the house when I don't want to.'

'Ew.'

'I know.'

One of the things we had in common was a love of staying home. Neither of us ever particularly wanted to go out. Instead, it was something we did out of a sense of responsibility or obligation. We much preferred to cook the vegetarian spaghetti bolognaise we had perfected, then eat it while rugged up together on the couch in front of a crime show. Staying home was pleasurable but I knew it could be a bad thing, too. Sometimes, we would get stuck in individual anxiety cycles that would then fuse together.

***

Back at the Catholic boys' school, I realised how triggering school environments were for me. Seeing violence, even play-fighting, scared me. I was shaken by the sounds of yelling and even the smell of deodorant sprayed liberally around the locker blocks and intense body odour in my classrooms on hot days. It continuously brought back my experiences at primary school with my bully, and at high school, with boys who made it their mission to harass me. One of them used to throw items in his pencil case at the ceiling fan, which would then bounce off and hit people in the class. He would direct threatening comments at me under his breath, and I tried to avoid him when I could. Another boy pulled at my hair and told me my curls looked like pubes, or called me Roz the Pros to make others laugh. I felt unsafe in my classrooms and in the school hallways, so I hid out in the school library at lunchtimes.

As a teacher, I felt an acute sense of fear while I was on yard duty and had vivid flashbacks to being bullied. When students swore at each other, I froze before I recovered enough to tell them to stop using that language. There was something about the dynamics that formed and played out in the classroom that made me extremely nervous.

When I saw Karyn, she said, 'When you have those flashbacks to your past, try to think of little you at that time. What would you do for her? What would she need to hear?'

'I guess I'd protect her.' I looked at Karyn and saw she was waiting for me to say something else. I made myself say what I thought Karyn wanted to hear. I didn't believe it, though. 'I'd tell her she's beautiful and smart.'

'What else?' she asked.

'That the bullies are twisted and none of it is her fault.'

'Yes. And how would you protect her, as an adult?'

'I'd think of situations where she is triggered and then try to look after her.'

'Exactly. All that pain is too much for a young version of you to deal with.'

Sometimes I ran into the other student-teachers in the corridors. 'How are you going?' I'd ask, hoping one would confess to finding teaching as stressful as I was.

'I'm loving it! I hope I get a job here after I finish my Dip. Ed.,' one replied.

'That's great.' I couldn't imagine wanting to work there. 'It's such a nice school.' I felt I needed to say something positive, and, in terms of its grounds and facilities, the school was pretty impressive.

On my last day of placement at the boys' school, my mentor teacher, Cara, asked me to help out with a Year 8 Religious Education class in last period. The students were planning fundraising activities and I moved around the room to help different groups.

As I walked up to one group, a student laughed and said to his friend, 'I'm not going to go around and Jew people out of their money.'

'Oh, shit,' his friend replied, watching me closely. 'Bad timing.'

I walked to the front of the room and Cara touched my arm.

'What's wrong?' she asked.

'It's not a big deal,' I replied, but she insisted I tell her what happened. I told her what I'd overheard. Before I could finish the sentence, she started yelling at the boy to get out of her classroom.

'What did he do?' the other students started whispering.

'Quiet!' she replied. The students went quiet immediately. 'Keep working on your campaigns,' she said, and went outside to speak to the student.

As a student-teacher, I wasn't meant to be left unsupervised. I monitored the students' behaviour for the few minutes she was gone, hoping she would return soon. None of them played up for me: a good move on their part. I imagined they were scared of adding to her wrath.

When the bell rang at 3.15 pm, Cara dismissed the students and asked me to come with her. She nodded curtly at the boy waiting on the bench outside and led us into another classroom, where a teacher was waiting: the Year 8 coordinator. The boy looked very unhappy to see him there.

The coordinator told him off, then Cara talked about what had happened to Jewish people during the Holocaust. The boy started to cry. I felt for him.

'You know,' Cara said, rolling her eyes, 'as a punishment, I would demand that you go to the Holocaust Museum so that you can learn about the atrocities of World War II. But you've *already been there*,' she yelled. 'The fact you've already been there on an excursion and don't know better is even more disappointing!'

During some of my appointments with Karyn, I scribbled notes down while we talked. Over time, I tried to wean myself off the habit, worrying she was judging me. Instead, after each appointment, I went to the bathroom down the corridor. Once I was safely ensconced in a cubicle, I wrote notes about the session. One day, I told Karyn about it.

'What if you wrote down the general feelings after a session instead?' she suggested.

'I have so much to say, though,' I replied.

'Well, you could distil it into feelings and write down the top three things that come out of our session, rather than summarising every point we discuss.'

'Okay. I'll try that.'

But when I tried to distil each session into feelings, I found I was stuck. I tried to switch off the processing part of my brain, which ached to process the session into thoughts and dialogue. I couldn't force it to perceive the murky shapes of the feelings behind those tangible things.

I also wrote about my dreams, which were spiralling into dark places. My dreams forced me back into the school setting and left me feeling lost. I didn't feel safe there.

On better nights, I felt like I was floating out of my body, all-knowing like a god or mythical being. I enjoyed the break from reality. Some dreams involved solving complicated mysteries. Others were erotic. I'd wake horny, but too stressed to do anything about it.

When I had nightmares, though, I woke up feeling fearful but also wanting more, needing some resolution to the dreams. I fooled myself into thinking this was possible when, of course, they would not be resolved. Even if I slept forever, I would never find out the ending to my dreams.

* * *

At many moments during Term 2, I think back to Karyn's early advice in therapy. It was only two years earlier, but it feels like a decade has passed. I try to implement the suggestions she provided when I was a student-teacher. I feel like I haven't grown in confidence or gained skills, though she assures me I must have.

There's a group of students in my Business and Economics classes who refuse to follow my instructions. During one of my dreaded double periods, on either side of the lunch break, a student leans back far enough in his chair that it topples to the ground, leaving him laughing and shouting as other boys jump on top of him. I write their names on the whiteboard, following the school's system of behaviour management, but feel helpless. If I followed the policy stringently, at least five students would have to be kicked out of every class.

When the bell rings, I move chairs back into position, wipe the whiteboard, tidy papers, turn off the lights and collect rubbish. I want to cry, or to drag something sharp along my arm, but instead I sit on my chair in the dark classroom. I stay there throughout my lunch break, not wanting to eat. I've stopped eating lunch at school. I wonder if I'll lose weight. I alternate between disliking my appearance and not caring about it at all.

As the bell rings again, and students fill the hallways for their next classes, I look down at my school ID card, hanging from the lanyard around my neck. I stare at the photo on the card, judging the moles on my face and my unfashionably slicked-back hair, and think, *No wonder the students don't respect me.*

Mum flies in for Mother's Day. We meet at Federation Square on a cold autumn day that feels more like winter. The persistent rain seems to have put people off, and the area is mostly deserted.

We decide to go for yum cha. Throughout lunch, I press my fingernails into my palms and try to talk and occasionally smile. I'm exhausted afterwards and don't know if putting on an act achieved anything. I wonder if my parents saw through it.

Dad is still living in Melbourne. After Mum's trip, we meet up for a library day. He recently started a PhD and is eager to do some reading while I try to make sense of my lesson plans.

In the afternoon, as our attention is waning and we're ready to leave, he asks, 'How are things going at school?' He'd asked earlier, but his tone had been light and surface-level. Now it's serious.

'Not great,' I reply. 'A part of me thinks I should quit.' My inner voice is scornful. *You shouldn't just quit your job; you should give up on everything. Just kill yourself.*

'I think you should stick it out,' he replies. 'You're such a good teacher; a natural. It's bound to get easier.'

I nod, but feel my stomach contract.

We don't communicate well verbally. Our emails and text messages to each other are delightfully constructed, but we still can't deal with emotional subjects. Instead, he shows his love through food. He invites me back to the house and cooks a vegan curry and rice for us while I continue planning for class. As he toasts a packet of pappadums, I feel sad in a way I can't explain to myself. Maybe because I know he isn't going to stay, and this isn't forever. Maybe it's wishing I knew how to express what I feel.

As Melbourne shudders into another winter, with torrential rain and a foul mood among public transport users, Dad begins to pack. He will be joining Mum in New South Wales. He asks if Jess and I can help pack up the house in Northcote.

We work our way through items that haven't sat in the house long enough to gather dust or have a set place. Jess and I go through our old school papers and drawings again, remembering we'd gone through them when our parents were preparing to move to Melbourne. This time, we're less sentimental.

It doesn't help that my depression feels unmanageable. It's so hard to motivate myself to get out of bed each day, no matter what time it is. But there's so much going on in the world that it feels wrong to focus on my feelings and exhaustion.

On 10 June, I read about the shooting death of twenty-two-year-old Christina Grimmie, an American YouTuber and singer. I listen to her songs on repeat, especially her cover of David Guetta's song 'Titanium'. The lyrics, about shooting her down but her not falling (because she is titanium), cycle around my mind whenever I try to fall asleep.

On 12 June, we follow the news live as a gunman kills forty-nine people and wounds fifty-three others in a mass shooting at Pulse nightclub in Orlando, Florida. I can't stop thinking about the people and communities affected.

Eleven days later, the Brexit referendum returns with a 52 per cent 'leave' vote, stunning many around the world. I listen to colleagues' discussions and analyses of both events. They're very passionate, arguing that the world is in trouble, but I don't say anything.

I'm aware I'm not fully able to process these events.

When I return to therapy, Karyn's psychology clinic has moved to a different building in the city. My appointment is on a Saturday, since that's the only day that works for me now, and Karyn has sent me instructions for how to get into the building. As I walk through the empty corridors, I'm relieved no one is around. Maybe my feelings can take up more room than usual.

I sit in the waiting room, pressing my nails into my palms and trying to slow my breath.

'Roz?'

I don't understand why, inside Karyn's room, everything I share sounds so much easier than the reality. As I tell her about the antisemitic incidents at school, I feel like I'm blowing things out of proportion. She speaks soothingly, but I'm embarrassed. I try to let myself take in her words, her comfort, but I'm mostly too focused on what I should tell her. I don't know what she needs to know, to help me with my mental health, and what is extraneous.

'Honestly, the only thing that helps at the moment is avoidance. Watching terrible TV. Otherwise, my panic is so high, it's impossible to plan for my classes. It's not even procrastination, which I've dealt with before. It's an actual inability to bring myself to do it.'

'You know, if you need to, you can quit.'

I know she's right. I've been told this by Rachel, Mum and my mother-in-law. But I'm ashamed to quit. The idea of telling the school I'm leaving so soon into my contract seems ridiculous. None of the possible reasons I could give seem adequate or understandable.

After therapy, I exit the elevator. It's pouring and windy outside: one of those Melbourne winter days that would depress me even if I were feeling good. While I wait in the lobby to see if the rain stops, I notice that the ground floor of the building connects to a cupcake bakery. I've been teaching my Business students about complementary businesses, and the proximity of the psychology clinic and bakery strikes me as an amazing example.

I stare at the bright cupcakes on display. I don't especially want a cupcake but there's a childish quality to them, especially the mini ones with the Tiny Teddies on top, and I need something that will bring even short-lived comfort right now.

Chapter 6

I can't quite work out how I want my students to see me. Do I want to be the hip teacher I saw who went viral online for using rap in some revolutionary way in the classroom? Do I want to be my students' friend and equal? Have I returned to school as a teacher to try to do over my traumatic school experiences?

Honestly, I think my role with my 120 students is mostly parental. Sometimes, students call me 'Mum' accidentally. I don't mind being called Mum. I find it sweet, and feel sorry for them when they're mortified. I fuss over them – even when they're being awful – and make sure they're okay, that they know what they are meant to be doing and feel supported.

'Miss, my mum has that top,' one of the popular Year 10 girls says one period, chuckling. I look down at my top – a white and gold striped T-shirt, which I'd thought trendy when I tried it on – and see it through her eyes.

Another day, a Year 7 student asks, confirming my fears, 'Miss, do you like the song "Bitter Sweet Symphony"? My mum said it was popular when she went to school!'

'Yes, I do. I was your age when it came out,' I reply. I mentally compare what I remember of myself at my students' age to them now. I listened to the nightly Hot 30 on the radio as I recorded my favourite songs on cassette tapes. My students are similarly obsessed with music, but it seems to be in a different way to how I was in the nineties. We didn't have the internet; music was our main escape. They jump between music and video apps on their smartphones when they think I'm not looking.

Mood

I might want to be the cool, relatable teacher, but I'd be better off accepting my role as quirky mum. When I return to the staff room after teaching, I try to take care of my own needs, like I do theirs, but I usually fail.

In therapy, I talk about my students often. Sometimes, Karyn follows this up by asking questions about my childhood, teenage years and my relationship with my parents now. When I'm vague, she asks her questions again, phrasing them differently.

'How are you finding not living in the same city as your parents again?' she asks.

'I miss them,' I say.

We talk about that for a bit and then Karyn says, 'Maybe having that physical distance will be a good thing.'

I look at her and don't say anything.

'We've talked, before, about you playing a particular role within your family. Perhaps now you will be able to take control, in a sense, of your life.'

I nod. I don't know what to say. I'm still trying to adjust to their move and don't feel ready to take control of anything – not my classes and definitely not my relationships with family. I've told her I see my role in the family as being the peacekeeper, the mediator, and perhaps the people pleaser.

'Yeah, I've particularly felt the need to play that role since coming out.'

Karyn seems to recognise my discomfort in talking about my role within my family and shifts the conversation. 'When did you work out you're gay?'

I tell myself to ignore the word 'gay'. It's not worth saying that I am bisexual; I don't want to pay to educate her during my appointment on the nuances of queer identity.

'I guess it was never really "a thing" for me,' I say. 'I was always different from those around me. As I moved through high school, I didn't think about what it meant that my sexual attraction wasn't limited to one sex or gender.'

* * *

Reading helped me figure out everything I wasn't learning at school. I picked up *Annie on My Mind* by Nancy Garden, a young adult novel I found in my local library, and as usual, read it sprawled on a beanbag. It seemed like any other book until the protagonist, Annie, and her friend, Liza, fell in love and eventually had their first kiss. I continued to read it wide-eyed, with disbelief and a growing sense of longing. I didn't even know what 'gay' looked like, apart from a few outdated stereotypes on TV shows like *Will and Grace*, but the book helped me work it out. At home, I came across Armistead Maupin's *Tales of the City* on my parents' bookshelves, and wanted to live with the characters at Barbary Lane. Later, I found *Rubyfruit Jungle* by Rita Mae Brown. When the characters had sex, I could have screamed hallelujah in the suburban library. I fantasised about the worlds and characters depicted in these books for years to come.

It wasn't only books about queerness that I read in secret; I hid myself away in the library shelves to learn other things my parents weren't yet ready or willing to tell me. Local library branches were where I first discovered some of the intricacies of sex, violence, illness and death. Later, I continued this habit at university libraries and state libraries.

I was furtive among the books, as though their spines would give me away. My giant tortoiseshell glasses, curls tied back in a navy scrunchie and school uniform were so visible; I was sure they would signal to the librarians that I wasn't supposed to be reading these books.

Once, a librarian spotted me crouched by a shelf and approached me. 'What are you reading?'

I wanted to hide the book and make myself invisible, but I answered. School had taught me how to be polite and friendly with adults, to put them at ease. Luckily, I had some young adult books with me in my reading pile. 'It's a Melina Marchetta book,' I told her. And it wasn't a lie – I loved Melina Marchetta. But that wasn't all I was reading.

Occasionally, I found a book that explored several taboo topics, like Danielle Steele's memoir about her son's struggles with bipolar disorder, and his suicide. Reading it was eye-opening and taught me a lot about symptoms of mental illness. Almost all I had known about mental illness before was when people joked about someone being 'crazy' at school.

I had figured out certain behaviours were seen as red flags. My dad's mother, Nana, occasionally bounced between highs and lows, ranging from excitedly offering presents and art activities to us children to sometimes becoming very terse and flat. I loved it when Nana was happy. When I was a child, we had made bunnies out of cottonwool balls by tying thread to make a little head and ears and drawing on faces. When she was sad, I took it upon myself to try to cheer her up.

I knew there was mental illness in my family, but didn't know the details apart from a relative being confined to bed for vague 'health reasons'. In the Soviet Union, most forms of mental illness were referred to as neurasthenia, or 'nervous disease'.

I'd also heard something about Dad's mother, Nana, being sent off for 'screaming therapy'. I had a lot of questions, but sensed that asking them might make my parents uncomfortable.

My family avoided confrontation. This rendered me unable to express conflict for many years. Intense emotions expressed in other ways, like sobbing, were also seen as something to hide and to be ashamed of.

Whenever I recognised these behaviours in myself, I was careful to hide them from others. There was a distinct lack of societal awareness of depression and anxiety in the nineties, so when I repeatedly refused to leave my room, avoided contact with my friends, or stayed up most of the night, it seemed like nobody thought much of it. It was only years later I found out my parents had noticed these behaviours at the time and had worried about them. I'd always thought I saw school psychologists, as a child and teenager, because of the bullying I experienced, but I now think there was more to it.

I've read my GP's referral letters to Karyn. They mention I've been dealing with generalised anxiety disorder for many years. I know symptoms of depression and anxiety in my teenage years are relevant to my treatment, but I hesitate to talk about them. I still blame myself for the bullying I experienced at primary school and high school, and see my younger self at school as a pushover.

Karyn doesn't ask me whether I think I had anxiety and depression when I was younger. She's much more interested in discussing my sexuality. 'Did you feel you had to keep your sexuality a secret?'

'Yes. I didn't think of it as a big thing. I just liked people. But I knew I needed to keep quiet about sexual and romantic feelings that weren't heterosexual.'

'At school?' Karyn asks.

'Yes. And at home.'

'How did you think your family would react?'

'I didn't think I had much reason to worry. My parents and sister are warm and caring, and open-minded, which made me believe they might be accepting. But I kept it a secret.'

'Why did you keep it secret, do you think?'

I pause. The question makes me uncomfortable, even if I can't pinpoint why. Perhaps it's because I remember how it felt to be furtive about my sexuality – enlivened and excited, but also fearful. Or maybe it's because I don't want to talk about when I came out.

'I don't know. I remember wanting to keep that part of myself private, away from prying eyes. I had the sense that keeping it to myself was the safest option and that it would give me time to become comfortable and confident about my identity.'

'What do you mean by "safest"?' she asks.

'I didn't want to be rejected. Even if that was unlikely, I wanted to avoid any possible rejection for as long as possible.'

I told Karyn about watching the free public broadcast of the Sydney Gay and Lesbian Mardi Gras parade each year. My parents had put their old, tiny television in my room, and I was able to watch it alone. I loved the proud and fierce Dykes on Bikes, the spectacular drag queens, and the roar of the supportive crowd. I watched it on the lowest volume level, terrified I would be caught. Not that my parents seemed to have an issue with the parade, but being caught watching it alone seemed like it would reveal something. It was the nineties, before TV featured any queer characters I related to and before the internet was available as a private agony aunt. I'd been on my own.

'What about your community?'

I don't know which community she means. 'Apart from a man in my congregation who wore a rainbow tallit – I later heard he was in a relationship with a man – I didn't have a community that embraced being Jewish and gay.'

We had lived in the eastern suburbs, on the land of the Gadigal and Birrabirragal peoples of the Eora Nation. Bellevue Hill was one of the most expensive and exclusive suburbs in Sydney. In their youth, my parents were bohemians who prided themselves on not following the rules. They put off having children for seven years because they weren't ready, much to the shock of their extended families, and they worked, travelled and socialised. They wanted to learn about and experience the world as much as possible. Dad focused on history and philosophy; Mum studied art and fashion design.

Eventually, they had a choice to make. There was pressure from their families to have children. Once I was born, they moved out of their quirky art-deco flat in Kings Cross.

Bellevue Hill was beautiful but claustrophobic, a life lived among extreme wealth.

I felt alienated and anxious at school. Fortunately, my parents provided a witty, intellectual and occasionally cynical commentary on 'life in the suburbs' as I grew up, and I began to develop my own version of this. Twice during my schooling, Mum and Dad took us on trips to Byron Bay where we walked along the beach, watched drummers play as the sun set over Main Beach, ate vegetarian food, shopped at the hippy markets, had our auras read at Crystal Castle and relaxed. I felt like I could breathe properly there, away from stress.

Back home, in between school, my casual retail job and the Jewish youth movement I joined in Year 10, I started to keep an eye out for alternative ways of living. There was a mural my family often drove past called The Lady of Edgecliff – depicting a woman with constantly-changing outfits – that was incredibly camp. I took buses to Oxford Street with my friends to see films at the arthouse cinema, and absorbed as much as I could of the gay scene while I was there.

Mum took us to galleries, musicals and arthouse films. To my pleasure, queer images and storylines were often featured. We saw *Velvet*

Goldmine, Todd Haynes' 1998 film about a glam-rock bisexual star. I did not understand it, but liked what I didn't understand.

Around my fifteenth birthday, Mum and Dad took me and Jess to see the musical *RENT* at Theatre Royal, Sydney. The musical was a revelation to me, particularly as my school didn't provide us with any depictions of female sexuality or queer identity. Seeing Christine Anu dance as Mimi Marquez at the Cat Scratch Club was breathtaking. She had beautiful curly hair, and she was sexy and talented. I sat back in my seat, shocked to notice I was attracted to most of the cast.

I was particularly drawn to the confident and feisty bisexual character, Maureen. I didn't know the word bisexual yet, apart from hearing the word 'bi' among the gossip at school. As Maureen sang to Joanne that since puberty, everybody has stared at her – both boys and girls – my heartbeat quickened. Not because boys and girls noticed me, but because I noticed them.

1999 was a particularly good year for queer content. *Cruel Intentions* includes an unforgettable scene in which Sarah Michelle Gellar, as Kathryn, teaches Selma Blair's Cecile how to tongue kiss. I couldn't look away and later borrowed the VHS so I could rewind and watch it again and again.

I listened to the *Cruel Intentions* soundtrack, which included 'Bitter Sweet Symphony', whenever I could. Later, when my Year 7 student mentions the song, it's funny to think that while they associate it with their parents, it meant existential dread for my generation – the soundtrack to our nascent sexuality.

In Year 11, we had to do a certain number of community service hours and we were then rewarded with a ball. My best friend, Phoebe, and I decided not to attend the ball. We explained to anybody who would listen that we didn't think we should get a ball in return for doing good in the community. We decided to do the community service without attending. That was our official stance. My personal reasons were more complex. I didn't date. I was too confused and shy, and I felt ugly and undesirable.

One of my close male friends, Ari, called me in the lead-up.

'Um, hey,' he said, 'I was wondering if you want to go to the ball together.'

It was the first time I had been asked out on a date. I imagined trying to navigate working out how to dress and act at the dance. I pictured the other girls in my year, so confident and fearless about dating. There was no way I could go through that. After an awkward pause, I remembered my official stance.

'Oh, I'm not going to the dance,' I said. 'Phoebe and I are going to stay home and watch *Buffy*. We disagree with the idea of rewarding people for doing community service.'

'Ah, right. Okay,' he said, sounding embarrassed. 'No problem.'

I later found out Ari was struggling with his own sexuality at the time. He wanted me there as his beard, a term which didn't exist in my world at the time. He didn't tell me any of this when he asked me. Later, when I found out his reasoning, I wished I had agreed. How cool would that have been: two questioning teens being each other's beards at a Jewish community dance? I stayed home, as planned, but wondered if I should have gone.

In Year 12, I was meant to be preoccupied with studying for the Higher School Certificate exams but I was in love with both my goth-looking English teacher and the smartest boy in my English class. This led me to spend English classes thinking about sex as well as exams. I fantasised about the teacher and the boy constantly, creating vivid sexual scenarios in my mind that made it hard for me to talk normally to either of them.

I had first come out to myself after sticking both the Mulder and Scully stickers from *TV Hits* in my diary. I found both actors incredibly sexy. I censored myself in my diary, sticking in pictures of celebrities I found hot, regardless of gender, but writing about my crushes using code words and initials. I painstakingly crossed out any identifying words and initials, as a safeguard in case someone found and read my diary. I never wrote about what having crushes on girls might mean. When I wrote lists of my crushes, the 'boys' list was always longer than the 'girls' list, so I figured that meant I was okay.

Now, I started seeking more queer content, both for fantasising purposes and to learn more about diverse sexualities. There were very few lesbian or bisexual characters on TV. There was the lesbian couple on *Queer as Folk*, which I watched late at night on SBS, but they had a weird, confusing relationship. There were plenty of funny, camp gay men to watch, but hardly any women. When there was a lesbian storyline in a movie or TV show, one of the women usually turned out to be evil and the relationship ended in misery or death.

I started watching *Buffy the Vampire Slayer*. Willow's love story with Tara stirred up something potent in me. The show's producers made it clear that Willow was, in her words, 'gay now', which annoyed viewers who had been fans of her relationships with male characters Oz and Xander. I didn't care, though. Willow being a lesbian was good enough. I didn't know enough to demand bisexual representation.

I found it fascinating, thrilling, terrifying and joyous to see their relationship on the screen, particularly when the show moved to another network and was able to depict the sexual relationship between the two women. Willow was Jewish and had previously been in love with a male character. I related to her and wanted to find my own Tara.

The following year, I had my nose pierced, dyed my hair a vivid red and started dressing in fisherman pants and ripped shirts. I felt very edgy and countercultural, but I was really just adopting the uniform of the left-wing Jewish youth movement I belonged to.

I started university and enrolled in the same program as Ari. He had since come out to me as gay, and I recognised, respected and envied his courage. His coming out may have been a great opportunity to bring up my own sexuality, but I felt I needed a compelling reason to come out. While I knew I was attracted to multiple genders, I believed I needed to choose between identifying as a lesbian or as straight. Bisexuality wasn't a valid option. At the time, it only made sense to me to come out if I was in a same-sex relationship. If I ended up in a relationship with a man, I believed I wouldn't need to tell anyone about my sexuality. Later, a straight friend told me she thought I had been 'duplicitous' by not reciprocating and telling Ari my own secret, and I worried she was right.

University offered some anonymity and freedom, but I felt unable to do much more than walk past the queer student room or admire a woman in my class from afar. Sometimes, I left campus and walked to Glebe or Newtown, where I was enthralled by Sappho Books and Gould's Book Arcade. I perused books on sexuality, gender, politics, religion, sociology and history, feeling so much more comfortable than I did at university.

I had a crush on two female Norwegian exchange students, as well as an Australian guy in my class. I thought about them all the time, at the expense of my grades. I related to some of the stigma around bisexuality – that bisexual people are greedy or indecisive – because I felt this way about myself, even though I didn't yet identify as bisexual and wasn't hooking up with anyone.

My sexuality felt like a naughty secret. It filled me with adrenaline. I found so many people attractive. I didn't need to talk to friends about it or label it.

As I became more introverted, I found the Kitten Board, the *Buffy the Vampire Slayer* online forum I often used in place of a social life – where I would, of course, meet Rachel. Too shy to talk to people in my classes, I headed to the communal computers and logged onto the forum in my breaks.

I made online friends and even checked out the dating threads on the board. I emailed back and forth with some women from the dating threads but didn't feel anything. I had never dated, kissed or slept with anyone, so I didn't know what I was looking for, but I assumed there was meant to be some chemistry.

Sometimes, in 'real life', I watched a couple of *Buffy* episodes with friends. I had to keep my squeals internal as we watched, since I wasn't comfortable telling them that I thought I might be gay myself. I pretended I was viewing the characters and storyline the same way they were. When one friend called Tara 'annoying' and 'weird', I wanted to disagree, the way I would about any other character, but I was too scared to defend her – or talk about her at all. When another *Buffy*-loving friend made a comment about the 'carpet munchers' in his apartment block making gross sexual noises, I kept quiet. I felt like a coward, but didn't know how to speak up.

In May 2002, the *Buffy* episode 'Seeing Red' aired in the US. The episode begins with Willow and Tara in bed together, after they reunited in the previous episode after their break-up. It ends with Tara dying in Willow's arms after being shot. I hadn't seen the episode when I found out about it on the Kitten Board. The board's moderators were horrified and tried to warn fans. They worried about how it would affect queer and questioning people.

It was a violent and graphic ending to the relationship that had helped me work out part of my identity. Even if I wasn't any closer to telling people in my life about it.

Separate to my internal debate over whether I was gay, I was trying to find ways to feel desirable. Attractiveness at my high school meant girls with white skin and pin-straight blond or brunette hair, while I had olive skin and frizzy hair.

Hollywood films like *Clueless*, *She's All That*, *10 Things I Hate About You*, *Never Been Kissed* and *The Princess Diaries* reinforced my belief that I was unattractive. The plot was always the same: beauty was achieved after hair was tamed and eyebrows shaped. Only then could a female character be considered attractive – and therefore desirable.

Like the protagonists in these films, I experienced my first kiss when my hair was blow-dried straight. In between semesters of my first year of university, I went to my Jewish youth movement's winter camp as a leader. I felt more confident than usual. For the first time, I met someone who was obviously interested in me.

One night, when we were on night duty together, he leaned over and kissed me. Flushed, feeling guilty for kissing someone while I was on duty, I suggested we go and check on all the dormitories. He held my hand as we went from room to room. Once our duty was over, we made sure our replacements were awake, then he led me to a grassy area away from the camp. We kissed, and he slid his hands under my shirt and bra. It didn't feel amazing, like I hoped it would, but I was glad it happened.

We saw each other for a short time after camp. At the camp reunion, I sat outside with him and an attractive guy he'd brought with him. He pulled me onto his lap and we passed apricot-flavoured *nargila* back and forth. It was our first time kissing in front of others, and I let him lead the way. Afterwards, I turned to the guy with him and saw he was looking at me. My heart raced.

Later, I went back to my date's house. His friend turned out to be a European exchange student staying with the family. As my date went upstairs, the exchange student whispered, 'Are you sure you want to go up there with *him*?' He winked at me. I smiled at him and shrugged. Honestly, I wasn't sure, but I followed anyway. When I got home that night, I fantasised about what it would have been like to go off with the cute exchange student instead.

That night started a string of everything-but-sex hook-ups where I would go to his house and we would make out in his bedroom while his parents, siblings and the sexy exchange student slept in adjacent rooms. We had to be quiet, which I liked at first but it soon added to my general anxiety during our encounters. One time, after we kissed, he told me I used my tongue too slowly.

Another night, he picked me up on Oxford Street. I liked going to gay clubs and bars on Oxford Street with Ari and an extended circle of our friends, absorbing everything that went on with a sense of wonder. I figured my friends assumed I was there for fun, like some of the straight women in our group who put on dresses and high heels and joined them for an evening free of being pursued by aggressive straight men.

I danced, nodded appreciatively when they pointed out various men they were pursuing and drank, but kept any other feelings inside. I could easily discuss attractive men, avoiding any mention of the few butch and androgynous women and gender-diverse people with short hair, piercings and tattoos who caught my eye. They moved around the room with a boldness and confidence I could not imagine possessing. Sometimes we made eye contact from afar – mine tentative, theirs bold – but I was too afraid to approach. I felt like I had to explore my attraction to women in private, not at the clubs with my friends.

At least I received compliments at the club. 'You're dancing in such high heels,' a drag queen said. 'Bless your heart!'

I was wearing the sexiest clothing I had – a glittery, mesh, body-hugging skirt and a tank top – when the guy I was seeing texted me. 'Come on,' he said. 'Leave the gays and come and see me.' I rolled my eyes at his comment but hurried to meet him.

He pulled over to the curb in his expensive family car and I got in. We kissed. He drove off and parked somewhere discreet near Rushcutters Bay. We climbed into the back seat and pulled off all our clothes except our underwear. We didn't speak. I found the riskiness of getting it on in a public space appealing and was more excited than usual.

While I was seeing him, some friends treated me quite differently. Dating a guy, albeit one who mainly wanted to get me into bed once his family had gone to sleep, gained me respect. But I couldn't tell if it was that straightforward, or if I felt desirable for once and was acting differently as a result.

Later, at a leadership camp with leaders from all the youth movements – progressive and Orthodox – I overheard him talking about me to a group of guys I didn't know. He was thoroughly reviewing a blow job. I was horrified but also not that surprised. We stopped seeing each other.

* * *

I realise our appointment time is almost up. I notice Karyn looking at her clock as I finish speaking.

Once I walk out of the building and turn up onto Little Collins Street, I question, as I often do, how honest I have been with Karyn. I think about the things I shared and wonder if I should have corrected her about my bisexuality.

After I came out, people believed I was a lesbian. I struggled with that label, partly because of internalised homophobia and partly because I wasn't sure it was the right one for me. But I figured if being with Rachel meant I was gay in society's eyes, so be it.

It took years for me to realise that I didn't identify with the binary categories of gay or straight. If I had to be one or the other, it was gay, but that wasn't completely suitable either. I had always felt attraction to people of all genders, including men, but when I came out, I disregarded this. Plenty of lesbians had had crushes on, or dated, men. I thought of my attraction to men as formative but no longer relevant.

Mood

I began to understand that bisexuality is a valid identity and that I could claim it for myself. I figured this out as more people came out publicly about being bisexual, and after reading articles and books that helped me understand myself. I read articles by Lisa Diamond about sexual fluidity in women and felt certain things click for me. I read Lidia Yuknavitch's memoir, *The Chronology of Water*, and was enticed by her descriptions of her sexuality. I bought Shiri Eisner's *Bi: Notes for a Bisexual Revolution* and encouraged a friend to borrow it after he made assumptions about my sexuality.

When Evan Rachel Wood and then Anna Paquin from *True Blood* – it was always the vampire shows that helped me work out my sexuality – came out as bisexual, both also defended their right to identify as bisexual and be in relationships with men. It helped me every time someone who was in a committed relationship came out as bisexual, knowing the social pressures at the time to 'choose a side'.

Once I became more confident about my sexuality, I felt I should say something every time someone called me a lesbian, even if I had let them think that for years – and though I still identified as one at times. People would discuss attractive men in my company and then look over at me awkwardly, the same way they did when they offered me a bite of meat, forgetting for a second that I don't eat it. I wanted to correct them, but was scared of how people would react.

I wrote an article about bisexuality and was asked to appear on a community TV show to discuss it. I found myself connecting with Melbourne's bisexual community, particularly the Melbourne Bisexual Network. The more I engaged with the community, the less willing I was to let biphobic and bi-erasing comments slip past me. But here I was, not even bothering to correct my therapist.

As I walk along Little Collins Street, I spot Princess Highway, a quirky clothing chain, and decide to distract myself. The mannequin in the window looks the way I think I ought to be dressing as a teacher: she's wearing a thick cardigan over a dress with a fun print on it. I walk in and I'm glad when no one talks to me beyond the initial greeting; I'm not feeling up to chit chat.

Depression makes me question the point of therapy. Teaching is already a form of exposure therapy: a way of forcing myself to cope with my traumas and triggers. By going to therapy, as well as being a high school teacher, I'm making myself reckon with the past in two very different but equally painful ways.

I take two dresses into the change room and try them on. I have some image, in my mind, of what 'teacher Roz' is meant to look like. I seem to be drawing on the teachers I liked the most when I was a student. Many of my teacher crushes dressed in a traditionally feminine way. Even the athletic teacher I'd been shocked to have a crush on, considering my fear of PE teachers, had dressed in a feminine blazer and fitted skirt when she wasn't taking PE practical classes.

I stare at my reflection. I'm wearing a black A-line dress – fitted at the top and widening out from under the bust – with little colourful foxes on it. The other dress has apples on it, which feels like a playful outfit for a teacher.

You look cute, I tell myself. But I don't believe it. I'm not sure whether I look the part I am trying to play. For one thing, my smile should be natural; I imagine the teacher version of Snow White bouncing into a classroom with birds hovering by her shoulders. I buy the dresses and some hair clips, and hope that a costume will make me more convincing.

Chapter 7

By the middle of my first teaching year, I'm surprised to notice that I feel a little better. I am no longer thinking about suicide, though I'm still highly anxious. At night, I turn onto my stomach and press my chest and face into the mattress to block out the feeling of heart palpitations.

When school returns for Term 3, I'm excited to teach History and Civics for the second half of the year to my Year 7, 9 and 10 classes. While I will be teaching Business again, to a new group of Year 10 students, I know what I'm doing this time.

But then there are the antisemitic incidents in my history class. *Hitler tried to kill the Jews. He should have killed all of them.* The swastikas on the desks. Stereotypes about Jews and money.

I struggle after these incidents. I can't fall asleep, and when I finally do, I have terrifying dreams. I have experienced antisemitism before, but usually it has been a random act of cruelty, not part of the school day, normalised.

One Yom Kippur, the holiest day of the year for Jewish people, I was on the way to the synagogue with my family when a group of white men screamed antisemitic obscenities at us from their car window. Later, I thought about the men and wondered who they were. I wished I had looked more closely at them to see if they were skinheads or just average Australians; some days, I wondered if there was even a difference.

I've seen antisemitic phrases, swastikas and sentiments spray-painted or scribbled on walls, street signs and playground equipment. When I encounter antisemitism, I think of my mother's stories about life in Odesa, Ukraine, in the late sixties. When her teacher would leave the classroom, the non-Jewish students would turn off the lights, pull down the blinds and scream, "The programs are coming!"

Later, I read a similar story in Maria Tumarkin's book *Otherland,* about her schooling in Ukraine in the late eighties, where her classmates would grab the class journal whenever their teacher left the room and read out the names of those listed as Jews. Maria writes:

> The outing was accompanied by name-calling and the joyous recitation, in a voice filled with triumphant, slimy disdain, of obscene little ditties that held the Jews' legendary greed and cunning responsible for all the world's ills ... They were simply repeating what they had heard at home, on the street, in the school.

My mother had sat there quietly, afraid but unsure what else to do. She knew from her parents that sometimes you couldn't stand up to antisemitism. Her grandmother – and namesake – had been pushed out of a window in her wheelchair in the apartment she'd lived in, when the Nazis occupied Odesa and went door to door looking for Jews. Most of their family had already fled Odesa at that point, except for my mother's grandmother and a few other family members who believed the Nazis wouldn't harm them.

By the time my mother was thirteen, her family left the Soviet Union to move to Australia. Her parents were happy and proud to live in Australia, where they could freely and safely be Jewish. Then again, Australia wasn't as free and safe as they had imagined. My mother told me that many of her classmates at Randwick Girls' High School bullied her for her accent, appearance, religion and background. One of her teachers told her class, 'Jews killed Jesus.'

Deda found a job where he worked hard and kept to himself. One of his co-workers made regular antisemitic comments, which bothered him deeply. Eventually, he had enough and went to see his boss. 'I'm used to that kind of talk. I experienced it all of my life, living in the Soviet Union, but here? I don't think I should have to put up with it.' His boss spoke to the co-worker, but not much changed.

At the Jewish school I attended, we were taught the Modern Orthodox version of Judaism, which was very religious and didn't appeal to me. I preferred Jewish Studies, where we learnt about the Holocaust and the many other tragedies that make up Jewish history. The world outside our community was depicted as untrustworthy and threatening. The school had security guards on-site, pacing and watching cars, due to threats.

Assimilation was a hot topic. Many of our grandparents had been forced to hide their identities for safety during World War II. There was a sense that assimilation provided safety and protection, but it also presented a threat: the loss of culture and community. The religious teachers at our school tried their hardest to ensure we would practise Judaism in the future.

One teacher, particularly obsessed with us marrying within the faith, quoted *Fiddler on the Roof*. She said sternly, 'A bird may marry a fish, but where would they live?' This was a segue into the dangers of marrying outside our faith.

My family's stories and my teachers' messages about antisemitism indicated I was only safe in the Jewish community. But after I came out, I didn't feel safe there, either.

After the incidents at school, I realise I haven't really belonged to a community in years. I've assimilated into mainstream Australian culture, keeping my distance from both Jewish and queer communities, as though being out there on my own will keep me safe. But now I keep hearing that student's words and seeing the swastika on the desk, and it dawns on me that I'm afraid.

On the weekend, Rachel and I drive to a kosher restaurant in North Caulfield. We have dinner plans with Rachel's school friend and her husband. Once we have covered all the usual topics, they have questions about what it is like to teach on the other side of the city.

'Do you ever hear any antisemitic comments?' our friend's husband asks, reaching for a slice of pizza.

'Oh yeah, often,' I reply.

'Like what?'

I sigh and share a basic summary of recent events in my history classroom.

His jaw tightens. 'Are you serious?'

I nod.

'And what do you do when that happens?'

'The usual. I report the student to the year-level coordinator. Sometimes we have meetings with their parents, but often the ones who most need to hear what we have to say don't show up.'

'I would have hit him,' he says.

I look at Rachel: she's a teacher too. She looks shocked by his response. Not that you need to be a teacher to oppose violence towards children. 'Yeah, well . . .' I trail off. 'That's not something I would do.'

'You must be a very patient person,' he says, wiping his hands on a tissue.

'Patient or masochistic?' I reply.

I regularly hear and see things at school that leave me reeling. Along with antisemitic remarks, there's racism, Islamophobia, homophobia, transphobia, sexism and ableism, which the students have likely picked up from home. I wonder how teachers who are First Nations, people of colour, from diverse religious backgrounds, and those who are disabled manage the prejudice, the unsubtle comments and behaviours, in their classrooms: at this school and in schools throughout the country.

Many of my students are experiencing challenges too. Their issues tend to be systemic and go beyond what I have the capacity to solve. But I expect myself to solve their issues and blame myself when I can't, which exacerbates my mental health struggles.

At our next appointment, Karyn listens to my description of the recent events at school and says, 'Try to remember they're teenagers, trying to shock or provoke adults. Don't take it on.'

'I don't feel capable of not taking it on,' I tell her.

'Being back at school seems to be bringing up shame and fear,' she says. 'It's important to know your triggers; what all of this brings up for you.'

'At the moment, everything is a trigger! I might have to quit my job. It can't be worth what it's doing to me mentally,' I say.

'That's completely understandable. It's up to you, of course. I do want to say that part of having meaningful, important, interesting work involves challenges and hard work.'

This prompts me to confess – ashamed and blushing – that I have no control in my classrooms. 'I don't have the confidence to manage their behaviour,' I admit. 'I feel pathetic.'

She nods. 'That must be really hard for you. It might be useful to figure out what would help you step into your authority. Look at role models of leadership at the school and emulate them for now.'

'I have some role models and I see how they work with the kids, but I don't feel able to emulate them at all. They seem so at ease, in a way I rarely am when I'm teaching.'

'What happens for you in the classroom?' she asks.

'I literally feel unable to manage my students' behaviours, especially when I'm in a bad place.' I look away.

'What if we spend some time delving deeper into your past?' she asks. 'It would be helpful to explore what your fears stem from.'

'Okay,' I say.

'I want to share an anecdote with you about my daughter's primary school teacher. He was a graduate teacher, too, and according to my daughter he was "too nice" at times.'

'I can relate to that,' I say, thinking about the time one of my students stayed back after the bell rang to empathise with me and make a suggestion about managing the class.

'During a parent-teacher conference, I asked if I could give him some advice and he said yes. I told him not to let the monkeys run the zoo.' She looks at me closely. 'You know what I mean, don't you?'

I know – and he would have known – exactly what she means. You need to be strict; you can't be too nice or you will fail. I feel bad for her daughter's teacher. I know Karyn means well but I'm aware I am doing it all wrong, and I'm sure her daughter's teacher knew that too. We're aware we should fix it, but may not know how. Or worse, we know how to fix it, but feel utterly incapable of doing so.

I have some successes at school. I teach the Year 10 History students about the Holocaust in Ukraine, playing a powerful video about the Babi Yar massacre and then telling them that the Nazis came to my family's home town. I share some personal stories, and they listen in horror.

Later, I meet with the student who said all Jews should have been killed. After substantial amounts of time spent in the assistant principal's office, he is deemed ready to return.

'He's begging to return to your class,' the assistant principal tells me.

'Oh, okay,' I reply. 'That's good.' I smile at her but feel very nervous.

We meet up with the student in her office, where he has been working during my classes. His textbooks take up all the room on the table. His nervousness and my own mingle in the stale air.

'Now, you wanted to say something to Ms Bellamy, didn't you?'

'Yes,' he says quietly. 'Sorry, Miss. I shouldn't have said that.'

'Thank you,' I say. 'I appreciate that. I need to know that you are ready to come back to my class, and that you understand what was wrong with what you said.'

'I know it was wrong,' he says, unable to meet my eyes.

'You weren't there when I told the class I'm Jewish. It's important you realise the impact of saying something like that about a whole group of people.'

'I heard from some of the boys,' he says. 'I'm sorry, Miss. I don't think that.'

By the end of our meeting, we decide to start again. As human beings, not as representatives of particular religions or cultures. We reach across the crowded table and shake hands. When I walk out of the meeting, feeling moved by our conversation, I think I should go on *60 Minutes* to talk about my amazing teaching moment.

I feel good at school for a few days. On the train home after work, I listen to music. Usually all I can do is flick through social media apps, desperate to distract myself from how bad I feel.

One evening, my mentor teacher, Sonya, comes to speak to me about the incident with the student. 'I'm sorry you went through that, Roz,' she says. 'I hope he's learnt from the experience.'

'Thanks. He has, I think, but it makes me wonder what else we could do to address this.' I reply. 'At Jewish schools, we learn about the Holocaust from a young age. It's a bit shocking to me that at other schools, it isn't taught until Year 10, if at all.'

Sonya doesn't say anything at first. Then she replies, 'I think Jewish schools teach students about the Holocaust when they're too young. Learning about it at that age can create a victim mentality.' Her words shock me, but I don't respond. Conflict avoidance, fear and passivity take over.

What she thinks of as a 'victim mentality' is more likely to be trauma, even in second or third generations who did not experience certain traumas personally. There are triggers, often stemming from memories that have been passed down through the family storytellers and the documents we hold onto, like my great-grandfather's pardon from the Soviet Union after he finally left Stalin's gulags. His diary renders his own capture, the people he left behind.

'Just be careful,' Sonya adds, as though responding to my silence. 'I wouldn't tell all your students that you're Jewish.' Awkwardly, she alludes to some of them having dangerous families.

Great. Not only do I feel like shit, but I'm also worried.

Rachel and I start talking about moving 'northside', to Melbourne's inner north. We're sick of our commutes to work and it makes sense to live closer.

Jess has been encouraging us to move closer to where she lives in Northcote. Her urging echoes that of my friend, Cameron, who has been telling us to move to the inner north. Cameron has become close friends with my sister Jess, and I've heard them talk about how to get Rachel and me to move near them.

After years of living on the south side, where the majority of Melbourne's Jewish community lives, Rachel and I have been looking at rental properties in the inner north. The final straw was when Cameron and his new boyfriend came over for dinner. His boyfriend looked around at our colourful and eclectic decor and said, 'You two don't belong in Armadale! You should be living in Brunswick or Fitzroy!'

Funnily enough, the inner-city, alternative suburbs he mentioned had been part of my decision to move to Melbourne. Between the vegetarian restaurants, visibly queer couples and indie bookshops and record shops, I had been smitten.

We narrow down the search to rental properties that will allow us to have a dog. I visit one after work, and it doesn't feel right. But the agent says, 'If you're looking for a place that allows dogs, I have the perfect place in mind and it's nearby.'

I like the other property immediately, even from the outside. It's a small house with a courtyard, which feels so different to the series of apartments Rachel and I have rented since 2004. We like the light and the space. During the inspection, we see other couples shaking their heads at the small kitchen, but we don't care. We sign the lease in August and give ourselves a month to move, even though it means paying rent twice.

Before we even pick up the keys, we start looking at rescue dogs. After thirteen years together and countless animals over those years, including doves, canaries, rats, mice and fish, we're ready to adopt a dog together.

We became interested in adopting a greyhound after spotting a greyhound adoption stall and sitting down to pet two of the rescue dogs. While we easily could have left with one that day, we couldn't have a dog in our apartment at that time. We decided when we moved, we would upgrade our rental to a place that allowed a dog and had room for one.

A quick search online leads us to Dexter, a fawn greyhound cross. The description makes us want him immediately: he's shy but eager and he loves cuddles.

The rescue organisation is a twenty-minute tram ride from school. I contact the organisation and make an appointment to meet him, knowing that if we adopt him, we're going to have to sneak him into our apartment until we move.

I can barely concentrate that day. At lunchtime, I see a missed call from Cameron. We've been trying to find a time to speak but we're both busy. When I reach him, I tell him about Dexter excitedly. 'He's so gorgeous!'

His tone is thoughtful, cautious. 'I wouldn't go running into it,' he says. 'A lot of rescue dogs are broken, and you'll need the time and space to work with them.'

'I'm not actually looking for advice,' I reply, trying to keep my tone from getting too defensive. 'Of course we would do that work with him.'

Mood

Cameron is a social worker and he seems to forget, sometimes, that we are friends: not counsellor and patient.

'I know you're busy and stressed, and it might not be the right time to rush into this.'

'Well, I'm going to see him today.' My tone is cool, but tears form in my eyes. Even if he has a point, I don't appreciate him sharing it.

I call Rachel afterwards and she is shocked when I repeat his comment. 'Broken?' She's able to access anger in a way I struggle to.

I head to the rescue organisation, determined for us to make the decision regardless of Cameron's opinion. I am led to Dexter's cage, where I coo at him through the bars. The attendant unlocks the door. 'He cries a lot,' she tells me. 'But he'll adjust well.'

I stroke his fur and the attendant attaches his collar to a lead.

'Would you like to walk him?'

'I'd love that.'

As we walk across the small yard, I get to see Dexter's character. He's not broken. He's beautiful, luminous and joyful. He prances around the grass, sniffing bushes and breaking into a trot occasionally. He leans against me as I pat him, and his fawn fur is even softer than it looks.

When I leave, I tell Rachel about him as I walk to the train station. Along the way, my phone runs out of battery, ending my call and my GPS directions. I realise I am lost when I reach the M2 Freeway. I'm next to a creek, under a bridge, and it looks like the scene of a crime in *Law and Order*. I make it home and before we can discuss Dexter any further, another couple adopts him. It's too late: the decision has been made for us.

By the middle of Term 3, we start packing up our apartment. I'm thrilled by the prospect of our new life on the north side of the Yarra River. We'll be much closer to work. The new property is located in a safe Labor seat, which is a relief after living in safe Liberal seats since we moved in together. The couple next door are academics with a greyhound, while two doors down there is a woman who has a folk music show on the queer radio station. We make friends with them immediately. I walk along the Merri Creek Trail. Golden wattle lights up the pathway.

But there are complications. We keep stopping to look at the items we find in the back of our cupboards, meaning it takes twice the time to pack. I find a box of old diaries from my teenage years. It hurts to read them. I sound more depressed, and suicidal at times, than I remembered. They lead me down a path I'm not ready to go down.

Rachel's parents, who live south-side, treat the move as though it is to another universe. It's challenging for Rachel, and tensions with our parents often translate to conflict between the two of us. Some of our fights are terrible.

Rachel reminds me, 'They are supportive. They're lending us their car whenever we need it for the move.'

But I don't want to hear it. I'm angrier than I can remember getting, which is surprising, since I used to try to end our arguments before they spun out of control. Sometimes, I want to hurt her. I critique her word choices and her interactions with people. I roll my eyes when she cries and mouth 'pathetic' when she isn't looking.

During one fight, I tell her she doesn't know the real me at all. 'I have these dark thoughts that you know nothing about. You'd leave me if you knew.'

I shake my head when she asks what I mean. Mentioning my 'dark thoughts' makes me embarrassed, the way I was about so many topics as a child. There's no way I can tell her what I mean. For some reason, I'm thinking about the erotica I read as an adolescent. It was about erotic dreams – and by erotic, I mean people fucking aliens and animals. I knew I wasn't meant to be reading it, and my sexual response to the content made me feel dirty. It started a thought process in my mind – *you're sick, you're perverted* – that only heightened when I thought to look up erotic stories and pornography as a teenager.

'When you say "dark thoughts", do you mean you want to hurt someone?' Rachel asks.

I'm shocked by her question, but only because she's asking it. I've wondered it before. I've questioned what I'm capable of. I don't know the answers.

'No,' I rush to reassure her. 'I mean, sometimes when I'm driving, I feel a level of rage at other drivers that scares me.'

She nods. She's seen my road rage. And then we start talking about something else and kiss each other good night. I lie awake thinking I'm disgusting.

On some mornings, I struggle to wake up. I rush into my classroom ten minutes before the school bell. I don't feel panicked about my classes or work the way I used to but I feel like I've sped up all of a sudden. It's hard to focus on each task before me.

In my Year 9 first period classes, I marvel at the difference in myself compared with how I was during the first two terms. I used to head to class almost thirty minutes early, turn on the lights, set up all the chairs, write on the whiteboard, and then, once I had completed everything I needed to do, I would stand there feeling excruciating panic flooding my body. I couldn't stay in the staff room, where the other teachers chatted normally while I felt like I was headed to my own execution. At least in my own empty classroom, I could try to soothe myself – aloud, if needed – before the students arrived.

But now it's different. I turn up right before the bell rings and feel comfortable writing on the whiteboard while my students chat. When I start the class, I get discussions flowing quickly. I teach the students about colonisation, First Nations peoples, the White Australia Policy, anti-immigration sentiments and racism in Australia.

Often, the students' contributions teach me as much as I teach them. Many of the students' families are migrants and they share thoughtful commentaries and observations about their communities.

I walk around the room when my students are working and talk to each of them in detail. Two of the highest-achieving students in the class chat animatedly to me about their work, and I'm surprised to remember how intimidated I used to feel around them, certain they saw right through me for the shitty teacher I was.

'Ms Bellamy, what do you think Trump's chances are of becoming president?'

'That's a good question. I don't think he'll win, but you never know. Are you going to watch the presidential debates during the school holidays?'

'Of course!'

I chat to them for a bit longer about Hillary Clinton and Bernie Sanders, and then walk around to check on other students.

'Jamie? How are you going?' I ask regularly, prompting one of the distracted boys to participate. I remember how I ignored his behaviour in the past, afraid to create conflict.

While I love my newfound confidence as a teacher and finally have a sense of what it is like to teach without being frozen with fear, I know I'm often not as organised as I could be. Sometimes I'm unprepared for my classes. I continue to take my laptop home every day, along with piles of student work I meant to mark and return to students over a month ago. But I can't bring myself to take any of it out of my bag when I get home each night. Instead, I watch TV with Rachel and try to push thoughts of the next day out of my mind.

On my worse days, I rush to figure out what I will teach next period while I'm running around the staff room, or even on my way to the classroom, which reminds me of a comment one of my lecturers made when I was studying teaching: 'You always need to have a lesson plan,' she had said. 'Don't let yourself do the old three-step lesson planning: where you take three steps from the staff room to the classroom and quickly make something up. Your students deserve better than that.'

I think about this often and berate myself for not giving my students my best.

Rachel and I start sleeping at the new house, but most of our belongings are still at our apartment in Armadale, south of the Yarra. We still have access to our old apartment for a few more weeks while we try to find time to pack. I like the feel of the new house: the high ceilings, the pane of stained glass above our bedroom window, the small courtyard with a tidy herb bed and potted clementine tree, and even the lush green of the weeds growing quickly between the pebbles on the ground.

I start taking days off from teaching when I don't feel I can do it justice. I'm embarrassed to use up my sick leave: I'm no longer depressed, but I'm struggling in other ways.

Mood

One of the days, I take an unpaid sick day and wake up at dawn so I can leave decent lesson plans and materials for the replacement teacher. Unlike the sick days I've taken so far, where I lie in bed thinking about unpacking boxes but not making any progress, today I would like to go out. I suggest we go to Carlton and wander the shops on Lygon Street. It's a novelty to be so close to suburbs we used to reach by a train and a tram.

Like many of our outings lately, we take an Uber. My current levels of stress make public transport feel unnervingly slow. I try not to look at the credit card statements as the Uber rides start appearing, adding up to large amounts on the monthly bills.

I notice a shoe shop that's been in the same spot, run by the same family, since 1895. From the stark print lettering on the old-fashioned sign to the proud rows of sturdy leather shoes, it looks like the kind of place I would have shopped at with Mum and Baba during my childhood. Mum's side of my family took shoes very seriously. 'Ooh, I'd love to find good shoes for teaching.'

We walk in and look around. The shoes cost more than I would usually pay but they suddenly seem critical to my success as a teacher. I wonder if bad footwear has contributed to my struggles so far this year. Mum took me shoe shopping while she still lived in Melbourne but I was so depressed at the time, I shook my head sadly at every pair she suggested until eventually we gave up and went to her place for tea.

'What are you looking for?' Rachel asks.

'I need something better than my current options. My boots are falling apart and my ballet flats seem to work like car crushers and keep compressing my feet until they're swollen.' I wave down at my feet, exposed in the Birkenstocks I'm wearing. 'See? They look like shit!'

I accept a sales assistant's help, while Rachel sits in a chair. We leave half an hour later with high-quality shoes, with sensible straps and low heels.

We treat ourselves to lunch at an old-school Italian restaurant on Lygon Street. My phone vibrates. I prop it against the parmesan cheese shaker on the red-and-white tablecloth. It's a message from the greyhound rescue group we've been in touch with.

My eyes widen and I summarise the message for Rachel. 'OMG. The greyhound rescue has a dog match for us! *Rosie is two years old and is ready for a home.* Okay, you need to see these photos.'

We pass my phone back and forth to stare at Rosie's profile. She is an affectionate girl who loves to play with a squeaky toy and cuddle with humans. The photos show a white and black greyhound curled up in a bed, playing with a toy and wearing a high-vis raincoat. 'She's beautiful,' Rachel says, and I nod, wanting to cry.

After lunch, we walk along Lygon Street. I keep pointing out shops, wanting to go in and spend money. I suggest we go into a new age shop a block up from the restaurant. 'Shall we?'

In the store, I fixate on a glorious rainbow necklace of small crystals. I flit between incense and smudge sticks, jewellery, household objects and books about improving one's life, and end up spending ninety-five dollars on an assortment of books and crystals. Rachel tells me she'll buy the necklace for my birthday. I'm excited and thankful, but as we walk out of the shop, I lose interest, already focused on the next thing.

At my next appointment, I tell Karyn what has happened since the last appointment, enjoying her reactions to my positive updates about school, our new house and Rosie.

'So you're feeling good about things at the moment?'

'Yes, it's a relief.' I'm speaking fast. 'I love our new house. It's so cute. I'm so glad we have finally moved northside. Things have been good between Rachel and me. We're having a lot of fun together. It reminds me what I love about our relationship.'

'Tell me more about that. The things you love about your relationship.'

I pause. I'm sure it's obvious to therapists that I don't want to talk about any issues in my relationship. I think about the main things I've told Karyn about Rachel, including the story of us falling in love. It is a well-formed narrative by now – a 'meet cute' story – but more painful to re-live than my carefully curated version would suggest.

'We have a similar eccentric sense of humour. We're quirky and laugh at the strangest things. We like to go on impromptu adventures. We experiment with new vegetarian recipes and try out new restaurants. And I think adopting a dog together will be great for us, too.'

'I'm glad to hear you're doing so well.' Karyn smiles.

'I hope it stays that way. Also, weirdly, sometimes I enjoy teaching now. It challenges me to be my best, most creative and empathetic self. But it also causes me to have mental breakdowns. I'm glad I stuck with it, though.' I don't mention all the sick days I've taken to reach this great breakthrough with teaching. I just keep talking about how well I'm doing.

'I'm so glad to hear that,' she says.

Chapter 8

It's close to the end of Term 3, and almost the start of spring. Rachel and I have been fighting regularly: often about our families, if not our relationship and our differing expectations. When we're not fighting, we get along so well, but I've noticed my anger simmering in the background, like the lowest flame on our gas stove.

I attend a workshop with Ivan Coyote, a Canadian nonfiction writer I really admire. I've been looking forward to this workshop for months but on the day, I'm struggling. I find myself oversharing in the middle of one of our tasks.

'What do you recommend,' I ask, 'if you're angry all the time? Can you make that work for your writing? Or should I try to wait for it to subside? I'm *so angry*. At everyone. Everything. The world.'

The other students look at me curiously.

Ivan seems to recognise that my question comes from a place of pain. Their reply is validating and reassuring, but I feel embarrassed immediately after asking the question.

One night, Rachel and I have a fight before going to sleep. In the middle of the fight, I start drifting off to sleep. I keep jolting awake, partly because I feel guilty and think I should try to stay up and finish our fight, but also because Rachel is crying.

Eventually, realising we're not going to resolve our fight, I ask her to leave the bedroom, telling her that her crying is keeping me awake and she's being abusive by preventing me from sleeping. 'Sleep deprivation is a form of torture,' I tell her.

But even when she leaves, I can't sleep. I can hear her crying from the other side of the house. I go into our lounge room and tell her to cry more quietly.

She stares at me, narrowing her eyes. 'I'm sorry my sadness is stopping you from sleeping,' she says.

On the morning of the parent-teacher conferences, I dress in pants, a nice shirt and a blazer and put makeup on. I feel more 'teacherly' than usual, whatever that means. I'm a bit worried parents will ambush me during the meeting, that their children have told them stories about my classes and my feeble attempts at regaining control. Compared with the Term 1 conferences, though, I am ready for combat if needed.

When the meetings start, I'm surprised to find I enjoy talking to the parents this time. The meetings go quickly, unlike the ones in March that dragged on for me in my depressive haze. This time, I tell the truth. For those who've brought their children with them, I ask my student, 'How do you think things are going?' and then build on top of whatever they say.

As the sun starts setting behind the classroom window, I grow bolder, talking intimately as though I'm chatting with old friends over glasses of wine.

'Has your son told you about the situation in our History class?' I ask.

'No.'

'We have had some issues with antisemitism in the class.'

The parent reacts with a look of horror. 'What? No, he hasn't said anything.'

'Yes, I've been addressing it, along with other staff and management, but I wanted to let you know.'

The next parent starts by telling me I am her daughter's favourite teacher. I'm so accustomed to my inner depressive and pessimistic voice, even though I've been feeling better lately, that I immediately think, *Probably because she doesn't do any work in my class.*

When I tell her what happened during the unit on the Holocaust, she asks, 'How are *you* doing?'

I am so shocked by the question – one teachers aren't asked often, if at all – that I feel myself becoming emotional.

'It has been challenging, but I'm okay. They are a great class, and History is so important. I'm glad I can teach them about World War II and the Holocaust. I'm Jewish, actually, and have a family connection to this topic and so I'm able to bring in a personal side to the curriculum.'

My student's mother starts to tear up when I mention I'm Jewish. 'I'm so sorry. I didn't know that, either. It must be incredibly tough for you. Thank you for your work.'

I smile and thank her, wishing I could tell her what her words mean to me.

I chat to a Year 9 student, Jamie, and his father, mentioning I'd like to help build his writing skills.

'Maybe you could get a little notebook,' I suggest, 'and write occasionally, like when you're on the train. It doesn't have to be anything too deep or profound; it can be little observations. It's really helped students I've tutored in the past.'

'That's a great idea, Jamie,' my student's father replies. 'And there's a bonus: you can give other people the impression that you're smart.'

'He *is* smart,' I reply, quickly, but see Jamie's crushed expression.

Later, as I walk back from the bathroom in my short break, I see Jamie crying by the lockers. I experience an intense feeling of tenderness for him and fury over his father's casual cruelty. It's a side of Jamie I haven't seen at all this year, as he usually ignores my instructions, refuses to do any work and laughs with his friends. I want to say something to him, but it's time to go back for my next meeting.

At the end of the conferences, the teachers mill around, eating leftovers from the catering and swapping stories from the long day. I turn down an invitation to go to the pub and cram a piece of chocolate cake into my mouth.

Rachel texts me. *Congratulations! You did it! Please take an Uber home.*

I follow her suggestion and order an Uber, feeling triumphant. I lean against the school fence as I wait for the car. Jasmine and gardenia scent the air.

Once the driver pulls away from the curb, I stare out at the dark street, thinking back to the parent-teacher conferences in March. I had been exhausted, my throat aching from all the talking, but I'd taken public transport home to save money – saving money becomes a top priority when I'm depressed.

I wince at the memories – of crying as I walked from the tram stop back to our old apartment, my feet sinking into wet, crushed autumn leaves in the gutter when I misjudged my step – and try to focus on how much better I feel now.

A week later, Cameron and I have plans to go out for dinner in Chinatown. I watch as his tram arrives on Bourke Street and wait for him to step off. I spot him quickly: he's wearing double denim. We hug tightly and then walk along Little Bourke Street, trying to choose a restaurant for dinner. Somehow, we end up choosing a seafood restaurant even though I'm vegetarian. I assure him there are at least a couple of tofu and vegetable dishes.

Once we're seated, he speaks with his usual intensity, looking into my eyes.

'I've found this winter particularly long and difficult. I can't wait for spring. How are you going?'

'I'm okay,' I reply, not sure whether to bother explaining that any problems I have aren't related to winter. I know why he thinks I'd be struggling; for a while, I was certain my depression was linked to the seasons.

'Are you? That's good.' Again, he stares at me. I feel uncomfortable under his steady gaze.

Hoping he'll give me objective advice about my mental health, I talk about some of my recent stressors and symptoms.

'My depression seems to be under control,' I tell him, 'but my anxiety keeps bubbling up and interfering in my life.'

'In what way?' he asks.

'I'm angry. Constantly. Especially when there's anything remotely stressful at work or home. Recently, Rachel's family was dealing with some conflict and I found myself trying to mediate for them. Then Rachel and I headed home and I started picking fights with her because I felt enraged and frustrated about being involved in it. It's not her fault, and it's not like she wants me to do it, but I can't help myself and then I blame her. I find myself looking for the most hurtful thing to say, regardless of whether I mean it or not, and I'm not satisfied until I manage to hurt her.'

Cameron nods. 'I wonder if you would consider going to see a psychiatrist.'

'I've tried one before. She wasn't great. And I'm happy with my psychologist,' I say. I feel defensive about Karyn, all of a sudden.

'I'm sure your psychologist is helpful, but a psychiatrist might be more effective.'

I shrug.

'Actually, I just thought of a GP I've seen before. You might find her helpful, Roz. She's very direct, but I think you'll appreciate her personality.'

When I get home, I tell Rachel about my conversation with Cameron. She isn't happy when I mention I told him about her family and our recent fights. Again, our arguing escalates and I find myself shouting, quickly losing control. Our fight ends with an uncomfortable apology from each of us. The next day, I call the GP Cameron mentioned.

The doctor's clinic is located among the thrum of Lygon Street. I make my way into the clinic, tentative and nervous.

'Now I want to check you're okay with me having two medical students sit in on our appointment,' the GP says after briskly shaking my hand.

'Uh, okay, sure,' I reply.

The medical students are from the University of Melbourne. They are well-dressed and look sharp, ready for anything. I don't know exactly what I want to talk about until I open my mouth. I describe my recent surging anger and inability to stay calm in a fight, and the constant state of anxiety I find myself in. I mention how much this all stresses me out, especially since my depression subsided recently and I was starting to appreciate feeling good again. The doctor nods, interrupting me every so often to clarify something or to offer her opinion.

'Is there anything that happened recently that may have exacerbated your anxiety? And your anger?'

'Uh, yes, I guess so,' I say. I tell her that conflict or tension at my in-laws' house leads to heated arguments between me and Rachel, and that I end up feeling very resentful.

The doctor looks at me thoughtfully. She starts to speak before stopping abruptly and spinning her chair around to face the medical students. 'Jon and Belinda, can I please get you to go out into the waiting room? I think we need a one-on-one session.'

They nod, ever professional if not a little disappointed to be missing what's coming next. Once they leave, she leans forward.

'Okay, Roz, I'm going to say it like it is. It sounds like you're dealing with baggage that isn't yours. My suggestion is to think about whether your current relationship is working. Because if it isn't, then it doesn't make sense to drag all of this out for both of you.'

I've been avoiding her eyes but look up at her when she suggests this, shocked by her response. 'Sorry?'

'I see it often. If the relationship isn't working, you don't have to put up with this.'

I don't know how to react. I wonder if Cameron said something to her.

When I get home, I tell Rachel the GP was a bit strange and that I felt very uncomfortable. I don't go into details and feel myself closing off from her, being evasive.

After she asks more questions, I say, 'The doctor said we need to break up.'

Rachel tells me later that I shared this information like I was sharing a judge's deliberation, that I seemed to think I had to break up with her regardless of whether I wanted to or not.

Following the appointment, I continue to apply the GP's words to our relationship. The next time Rachel and I fight, I go harder than I ever have. I tell her I hate her.

Later, after we have made up, I'm so sorry, so loving, so forlorn. We make love and it is so tender, so intimate; I try to make up for my wrongs through touch and pleasure.

She takes me back, over and over, both when it's deserved and – truly – undeserved.

I book an appointment with my usual doctor. She works at a clinic near our old apartment, far from where we live now, but I decide it's worth the travel, especially after what happened. When I tell her about my recent appointment with the new GP, she looks sympathetic.

'I'm sorry you experienced that. How have you been going?'

I try to tell her and end up sitting back with tears prickling, so ashamed I feel the need to cover my eyes. I manage to say, 'I think I might have something wrong with me. Possibly a mood disorder, or maybe something else.'

She asks me some questions, gently, and then refers me to a psychiatrist named Susan.

* * *

I have wondered whether I have a mood disorder before. I mentioned the possibility to Karyn not long after I started seeing her.

Back when I was studying teaching, before my second placement at the Catholic boys' school, my university lecturer told us about an overseas teaching placement opportunity that would involve teaching English at an international private school in Tianjin in November. It was a pilot program, he said.

'You would be part of the first group of student-teachers at a brand new school. This is not for the faint-hearted.'

I was interested and not only because it sounded like an adventure. Rachel had been asked to teach at a university in Wuhan, China, around the same time as the overseas placement. I had never been to China.

'Imagine getting to teach overseas for my final placement,' I said to Rachel.

'You'd love that,' she said.

'It's three weeks long and I'll only have two weeks left to complete after this next placement. So I would be doing an extra week voluntarily, but it's worth it. Plus I could see you in Wuhan beforehand and we could travel together.'

There were lots of reasons I wanted to go to China, apart from wanting to travel with Rachel. The overseas placement meant avoiding a third placement at the Catholic boys' school, which was very tempting.

I also felt a strong aversion to teaching in Australia generally. After encountering racism, antisemitism, sexism, homophobia and transphobia on placements, I believed Australian schools were culturally unsafe for teachers from marginalised backgrounds. The only reason I could see to continue teaching in them was to provide support to students from marginalised backgrounds.

I decided to apply and was asked to come into my university for an interview. When I arrived, another student was leaving the office.

'This is Lisa,' the academic overseeing the program said. 'She's going to be teaching science in China.' They seemed chummy. I felt nervous and competitive even though Lisa had already been selected.

When Lisa left, the academic said, 'So, Roz, I've heard very positive things about you from the English lecturers. Whatever you did, you impressed them.'

I felt deceptive. The English lecturers knew me as a university student, not as a teacher. I probably seemed confident and creative in my uni tutorials, but none of them knew how tongue-tied, shy and inept I was when I was the one teaching, or how I froze under the spotlight.

A week later, I received an email telling me I had been selected for the program. The email included an invitation to attend a meeting at the school's Melbourne campus to prepare for the trip.

The school was out in the south-eastern suburbs of Melbourne. I parked and walked past fountains to the reception area. As I waited for my classmates, I looked around the foyer area and saw a framed photo of a right-wing politician visiting the school.

On a guided tour of the school grounds, a teacher took us to the cafeteria. There was a sign advertising fair-trade coffee next to a huge Italian espresso machine. 'You've *got* to try the espresso,' the teacher said.

We were led up to a board room where we met with someone from the school executive team as well as one of the teachers who had taught at the school in China. The teacher told us about the cultural context at the school. 'Make sure you are very sensitive to the political climate there,' he said. 'Don't talk about China from a Western perspective. Don't mention the Tiananmen Square Massacre.' We nodded, scribbling down notes.

The following week, our group met at university to discuss logistics.

During the meeting, I kept talking. I was joking around with the others, even though I barely knew them. I wondered if this was happiness, or just excitement about the trip. I felt as though I'd come into myself and found a confidence I'd been lacking.

Sometimes, when I tried to process that I was going to China, I felt my pulse whirring. My hands shook occasionally, but I didn't worry about that. Nana used to tell me I had inherited her shaky hands.

When I told Karyn I would be away for a month, she made some suggestions for strategies to manage my mental health while I was away.

'Just remember,' she said at the end of an appointment. 'Try not to strive for perfection when you are teaching. I'm certain that you're more than capable and will do a great job.'

Days later, I flew out of Melbourne, which was already sweltering, to Wuhan to meet Rachel. She had organised a taxi to meet me at the airport. It was a very old car with no seatbelts and as the driver sped down the freeways, alongside enormous city buildings with words in Mandarin above them, then past an enormous lake, I felt scared and exhilarated.

By the time the driver dropped me at the hotel, Rachel had finished teaching for the day and met me with green tea, stir-fries and cakes. We waited until we were inside the hotel room before we kissed.

When Rachel had breaks in her teaching schedule, we took the metro to various temples, museums, galleries and the East Lake, ignoring the heavy rain and wind. We found Baotong Temple Vegetarian, a Buddhist restaurant that made the tastiest buns and dumplings we had ever eaten. I found an area called Tan Hua Lin, which sounded alternative. We headed out there and noticed rainbow flag stickers on buildings as we approached. As soon as we went into the first shop, we discovered cat imagery everywhere. We decided the area was our new favourite.

After Wuhan, we visited Shanghai and Xi'an and Beijing, then Rachel returned to Australia. I met up with the other student-teachers and our supervisor from our university at a hotel in Beijing.

I felt nervous. I didn't know the other three student-teachers very well. I barely spoke any Mandarin. I had never lived in a school boarding house as a student, let alone as a teacher.

Mood

That afternoon, we were driven from Beijing towards Tianjin. The industrial streets turned to highways and then to farmland as the sun set. When we got out of the van, I tucked my hands into my coat sleeves, trying to protect them from the cold. We couldn't see much in the dark, but could tell the school buildings were newly built and the grounds looked expensive. Inside wasn't much warmer, and we kept our coats on. We found out the Chinese government wouldn't turn on the heating for our region until a particular date, so we would have to wear winter clothing indoors.

That night, I tried to set up my single room in the children's dormitories to be as comfortable as possible. If teaching in China was anything like my past experiences, I would need all the comfort I could get.

On my first day of teaching, I met with each of my Year 10 students individually. I realised that they misunderstood the nature of the meeting.

'Hi Sam, it's nice to meet you,' I said. The students used English names at the school, which was meant to prepare them for future studies at Western universities.

Sam looked nervous and gripped his hands together under the table. 'Nice to meet you,' he answered in a singsong voice, like he'd been practising.

'Where did you study before coming to this school?' I asked.

'Xi'an Gaoxin No. 1 High School, in Shaanxi Province.'

'What was it like?' I smiled.

'It is a very good school. It has very good results in the Gaokao.'

Halfway through the chat, I decided to clarify. 'You can relax, Sam. This is just an informal conversation.'

'It isn't an oral test?'

'No!'

'Oh.'

Once the students realised the student-teachers were there to learn, just as they were, they relaxed with us. Soon, they went from staring at us to treating us like low-grade celebrities. 'Miss! Miss! Come and sit with us.' They often brought us sweets and stationery.

I went into perfectionist teacher mode, despite having read the chapter Karyn had sent me on the unrelenting standards schema. The bit that said, *My health suffers because I put myself under so much pressure*, had particularly resonated with me. But I hadn't yet put strategies in place to combat my perfectionism, and I knew being a perfectionist yielded some wonderful results.

I bonded with my students in a way I hadn't yet managed back home. The many cultural differences between us were helpful for me, as someone who always worried about fitting in. There didn't seem to be any expectations we would bond, which was so different to Australian teachers and students making connections over topics like the footy or what they got up to on the weekends. Also, respect for teachers had been ingrained into these students – and enforced – from a very young age, so there was little need for classroom management and I could focus on their learning.

The students' school day went from 7 am until 10 pm, which was shocking to me and the other student-teachers. The students were keen for us to be part of their co-curricular activities. I found that I loved participating in these activities, where my students corrected my badminton technique and, another night, interviewed me for the school newsletter. We went swimming on an icy night, attended inter-school basketball games and cheered for our students, and spent weekend bus rides into Beijing chatting to the students.

I became close friends with Lisa and Shelly, the two student-teachers I was sharing a dormitory floor with. The fourth student-teacher was living by himself in separate accommodation and seemed uninterested when we tried to include him.

At night, we would dress up, dance to Taylor Swift, make and eat peanut-butter sandwiches, and laugh until we cried. I realised I hadn't had this much fun with friends in a long time.

One morning, Lisa woke me up earlier than usual to tell me it was snowing. On our way to the staff room, we squealed as we ran along the pathways, grabbing each other's arms along the way and taking photos of the snow-covered trees and school grounds.

When we were asked to speak at the whole-school assembly, my friends hesitated, so I volunteered to do it. I wrote the speech and then read it to a full gymnasium, as an interpreter stood beside me translating my words into Mandarin during my pauses. I felt like I had to have every possible experience and learn everything I could.

We were still teaching when a Missouri grand jury – consisting of nine white and three black jury members – declined to indict a white police officer, Darren Wilson, for killing Michael Brown in Ferguson. I was able to view international news through a VPN, and saw Ferguson in flames.

My mentor teacher encouraged me to talk to the students about it. I repeated the instruction from the school's Australian campus about avoiding politically sensitive topics, but he waved off any concerns I brought up. So I delved right in: I used images of the riot police, protestors and a burning police car, and ran activities about race in America and different forms of political activism. The students were fascinated. I had been so afraid to talk about certain topics, especially the Tiananmen Square Massacre, but my students told me they knew all about it from using a VPN on their phones. As wealthy students at an international school, they appeared to have protections other Chinese people wouldn't have. Later, I wondered if I would have taken such a risk if it weren't for my elevated mood and my associated impulsive, reckless behaviours.

On our final day of the placement, one of the Australian teachers took us out for dinner in Sanlitun, an area of Beijing filled with shops and nightlife. We ate burgers, moaning in pleasure after three weeks of boarding school food, and drank too many cocktails. The restaurant was playing Western music and video clips, including a parody of Alicia Keys' song 'Girl on Fire', called 'Boy is a Bottom'. In the clip, a group of drag queens sang and acted out very explicit lyrics, to our amusement.

We went dancing on another level of the building. I flirted with the Australian teacher. The male student-teacher jumped up and pole danced, which seemed very out of character. We were given roses by a stranger. In the middle of the street, we tried to buy a huge children's balloon. It was filled with bright lights. I was hiccupping from all the breathless chatter and giggling.

My friend opened her wallet in the middle of the street and started flipping through piles of cash. 'Oh my God,' the rest of us exclaimed. 'You don't do that!'

Once we got back to our hotel, I lay on the bed, thoughts and sensations whirring around my mind and body. I remembered, all of a sudden, that I was staying in the room the Australian teacher had slept in the week before. I started fantasising about him. When I tried to drift off to sleep, I realised I felt out of control. I had never experienced a feeling like it and I knew it wasn't just the alcohol.

Back home, I started thinking about my fluctuating moods more seriously. Since moving to Melbourne in my twenties, I had noticed some changes in my mood that occurred in autumn and lingered until spring. As summer faded, my energy followed and seemingly disappeared. At first, the changes were subtle, like losing interest in projects I had been working on prior to the change in seasons. I found myself becoming more withdrawn and depressed. I stopped being excited about things and stopped writing.

I blamed these changes on external factors, like stress over study and work. After several months of this, I began to feel this was who I was: a depressive, reclusive person without much energy or direction. Then spring rolled around. I started leaving my apartment voluntarily again, instead of having to force myself. I chose to contact friends, instead of remembering them in a haze of guilt. I resumed exercising, socialising and writing.

By summer, I was overflowing with energy and truly delighted by life. I couldn't believe all that time I had wasted in bed, now that I was bursting awake each morning to start tackling all the wonderful things I had planned. Sometimes I had too much energy; after hibernating all winter I was buzzing at a frequency some people found startling. Family and friends commented that it was sometimes hard to keep up with me: not just what I was doing, but even what I was saying. It was too fast.

I did not make the link to the seasons at first. On one visit to my parents up in Byron Bay, it had dawned on me I might have a mood disorder. 'I wonder if I could possibly have bipolar disorder,' I said to my dad and sister.

We were in the front garden, waiting for Mum to get ready. I breathed in the sweet smell of the blooming jasmine. Dad and Jess looked at me curiously. Mental health wasn't usually our topic of choice. 'I go between bad depression and hyperactivity that could be mania,' I explained.

'I suppose it could be,' Dad replied. It seemed like he had more to say but wasn't willing to say it.

Some internet searching suggested what I had wasn't serious – or dangerous – enough to be bipolar disorder. Instead, I figured I must have seasonal affective disorder (S.A.D.), a type of depression linked to the change in seasons and specifically the lack of light exposure in winter. I liked the idea of my problems being seasonal, rather than bouts of recurring depression. Having a name for it helped me understand what I was going through and legitimised what I was feeling and experiencing. But I found it a bit strange that my symptoms were based on my body's reaction to the seasons.

It was hard to explain to the people in my life that the change of seasons filled me with dread and meant things were about to turn ugly or get better. No matter how medically savvy or jargon-filled my explanations were, there was an element that struck me as mythological, like a human transforming into a werewolf during the full moon. If I didn't truly understand it, how could I expect anyone else to?

My fluctuating mental states throughout the year made it hard to plan for the future. If I organised an event while I was feeling happy and excited, I knew I might have to suffer through it when I was depressed later in the year. If I turned down opportunities when I was depressed, or said no to my friends enough times that they stopped asking, I might regret it when I was feeling better.

I didn't find a magical fix, despite having a better idea of what was going on. I still spent months fearing the arrival of a depressive state, which I unscientifically pinpointed to the day daylight savings ended. I felt bleak, always anticipating the return of the depression. Each year when the summer solstice, the longest day of the year, came around, I obsessed that the days would soon be getting shorter, instead of enjoying summer.

One year, sitting at a cheery vegan cafe during summer, I had compiled a list of ways to avoid experiencing depression during winter. Surrounded by books about gratitude and blessings, my list contained reminders to exercise, meditate, socialise, talk about my feelings, volunteer or help others in some way, and have a healthy daily routine. I emailed it to myself with the heading, 'How to survive winter and S.A.D.'.

But the next winter, when I became depressed, I found the list unhelpful. I judged my 'summer self' for being naïve. I didn't follow my instructions and instead huddled up under blankets at home, feeling lethargic. I checked social media, never posting anything myself. I eyed photos from friends in the northern hemisphere with unrestrained envy. I wanted to believe if it were summer, I would be okay again. But I also doubted this, despite previous experience that strongly suggested this would all change again soon.

I started to suspect this was the 'real me' and the summer version of me was fake, however much I wanted to believe it was real. I thought of my 'winter self' as an introvert while my 'summer self' was a hyperactive extrovert. I avoided any form of social interaction that took place in person, because I felt I had nothing to say. If I was asked about my life, I cried. I judged myself harshly, irritated by my limitations. If I cried, I found myself horrified by my sadness and scornful of my emotions.

Rachel found some treatments for S.A.D. online, including psychotherapy, light therapy lamps (which help by providing artificial light) and antidepressants. Concerned about my flat mood, she ordered me a pair of light-therapy glasses. When they arrived, we laughed at how they looked like something out of *The X-Files*. I set my alarm for earlier than usual and sat at my desk wearing the glasses before work. I couldn't tell if they helped.

After China, I found myself wondering whether S.A.D. explained everything that was going on. While I definitely preferred the spring and summer months, and my mood dipped in autumn and winter, it had been strange, startling and concerning to have been 'up' during winter while I was away. Not only had I felt good at odd times, I had sometimes felt *too* good. I'd assumed that was the excitement of going on an overseas placement and the fact that it was summer back home.

But I worried that wasn't it. The idea of having something else going on inside freaked me out; I could no longer trust that my mental health would follow what had become a familiar and formulaic seasonal pattern. I wanted some sense of permanence again, rather than one mood state swallowed by another.

Mood

'What do you think is wrong with me?' I asked Rachel. 'Do you think I have a mood disorder? I spend months severely depressed and then end up in an over-enthusiastic and manic state.'

'I don't know,' she replied. 'But you've mentioned the possibility of bipolar disorder to me a few times now. You should talk to Karyn about it.'

I went to see Karyn before the next university semester started. I felt very anxious about raising the possibility of a mood disorder. I dug my nails into my hand while we talked.

'It went so well,' I told her. 'It's so lucky that I went to China as my "summer self".'

'You know,' she said, 'I think it would help if you tried to stop viewing yourself as two separate versions – a winter and summer version – and to start accepting that these are both you with different energy levels.'

'I'll try,' I said, looking at her doubtfully. 'But when it's summer, I honestly feel like myself again.' When I was depressed, I judged myself for not getting things done. I was impatient with myself if I didn't work on my writing but incredibly critical of anything I managed to write. I judged myself constantly.

'When you're feeling low, it's okay to rest. Think of it as recuperating from higher energy times.'

I nodded. Maybe it was okay if the words didn't come, and okay if I lay in bed and watched TV on my phone for hours. It was okay if I felt like I wasn't good enough. I waited until the end of our appointment to mention I thought I might have something beyond S.A.D.

'I've been noticing I have these distinct periods of being very depressed and then when I stop being depressed, I go too far the other way, almost manic,' I said. 'I have wondered, in the past, whether I have bipolar disorder, and now I'm starting to think that again. It's like the mania is a self-protective mechanism after severe depression – a way for me to push away everything the depression brought up for me.'

Karyn considered this. 'Okay. As you know, I used to be a psychiatric nurse. I can tell you that lithium is awful. Let's not go down the bipolar road unless we have to.'

* * *

After seeing my GP, I call the psychiatrist's consulting room and book in a first consultation. Then I text Cameron. 'I just made an appointment with a psychiatrist. I wonder if you know her.'

He calls me immediately. 'Tell me everything. Who are you going to see?'

When I say the psychiatrist's name, I can tell he has something bad to say about her. His long pause is very revealing.

'Look, I don't think she'll be a good match, to be honest.'

'Why not?' I feel my heart speed up, along with rising stress and annoyance. Cameron's doubts make me second-guess myself. I'm not sure I should trust his judgement, since he had been the one to suggest seeing the awful GP. When I had told him about her, he said in hindsight, she probably wasn't the right match: she tends to be very blunt. But what I experienced went far beyond bluntness. I couldn't see it at the time, but it veered into projection.

'She's a good psychiatrist but I don't think she will offer the type of psychotherapy you need, which is someone who can push you to really understand where your issues are coming from.'

The way he describes Susan stops me from wanting to see her. I call the psychiatrist's office and cancel my appointment.

As well as conflict with Rachel, and my irritation with Cameron, I can't stop thinking about an event looming on my calendar. Before the end of term, I'm meant to be taking my Year 10 History students to the Jewish Holocaust Centre, along with another teacher's class. Between the two classes, we have students who display some of the most challenging behaviours in the year level.

In the lead-up to the excursion, I tell the other teacher that I'm very worried about taking some of my students to the museum. We're meant to split into small groups at some point during the excursion, giving students the chance to ask questions. 'I wouldn't feel comfortable introducing them to the Holocaust survivors,' I explain. 'I'm honestly worried about what they might say.'

'It'll be fine,' she says. 'There'll be the two of us and we can bring along a student-teacher to make sure we have the right ratios.'

Some of the anxiety symptoms I've had in the past decide to rear their ugly heads again. I start experiencing heart palpitations, chest pain and breathing difficulties.

I talk to Mum about it and she tells me not to go on the excursion.

'I don't have a choice,' I reply.

The night before the excursion, I suggest Rachel and I go out for a drive, trying to forget my worries. We've been using a car-sharing service to help us move items from our old apartment to our house. The idea was to save money when it came to hiring a removalist, but we've been racking up large bills, largely because we keep deciding to keep the car for another night rather than return it.

I love driving at the moment. There's something about pushing my foot against the accelerator, riding a little over the speed limit – not enough to get fined – as I pump music and drown everything out. We drive along the Eastern Freeway with no destination in mind and I watch trees and streetlights spin past. I bring up my fears about the excursion, and Rachel says, 'You can do this.'

When we get home and go to bed, Rachel falls asleep, but the more I try to sleep, the more I think about a couple of students in particular. I've heard them say so many things about Jews. I'm certain they're going to swear at a Holocaust survivor, maybe even deny the Holocaust ever happened. Lately, I've spoken to school management when I think there's a point, but increasingly there doesn't seem to be one. Nothing happens.

I manage to fall asleep and have stressful dreams about teaching. I wake at 1 am, my heart racing, chest hurting and body covered in sweat. I try to calm myself down. Eventually I wake Rachel up. I try to explain what is happening. I talk about losing Deda and my friend Jenny in the same week, back in 2015, then move on to telling her about planning my lessons and all the marking I need to do.

'Honey, slow down,' she says. I don't think I am speaking quickly.

I try explaining things again. Rachel thinks we should call a nurse or organise an ambulance. I laugh the idea off, but she is adamant I call the NURSE-ON-CALL hotline and explain my symptoms. As soon as I mention my chest pain and the sweats, the nurse puts me through to an operator to organise an ambulance. Rachel speaks to the operator, who tells her to turn on lights at the front of the house and leave the front door open.

When Rachel leads the two paramedics into our bedroom, I start obsessing about what our neighbours must think. We've lived here for under a month and here I am, creating a spectacle. The paramedics are nice and ask me questions about my symptoms while they check my blood pressure and apply electrodes so they can do an ECG. They quickly ascertain it's not a heart attack. I'm concerned about what else could be wrong with me. I tell them I've had a chronic thyroid condition and that this could be a thyroid storm, an evocative name for a condition also known as thyrotoxic crisis, which is life-threatening.

I end up at the nearest hospital's emergency department. While we wait, I contact my sister. Jess replies to my message quickly, considering it's the middle of the night, and asks if she can do anything. I say no. She tells me she'll keep her phone on loud in case I change my mind.

At 5 am, after hours in the emergency department, now in a cubicle, I ask Rachel to contact Mum.

'Maybe it was brought on by the excursion?' Mum asks, after her initial shock. 'She was stressing about it.'

Rachel tells her this has been building for weeks, but agrees the excursion is a factor. 'She's very stressed about it,' she adds.

Nurses and doctors come in and out, taking blood, doing another ECG and asking numerous questions. I'm told my thyroid tests came back normal. I'm given a Valium and the nurse turns off the light in the cubicle so I can get some sleep while I wait.

By the time I speak to Mum next, we've seen the doctor. My symptoms were a severe panic attack. I'll be discharged from hospital soon. I'm mortified, thinking about the doctors, nurses and paramedics involved, the wasted resources, and the awful, stressful night Rachel has had.

I'm also a bit disappointed.

'At least I get to miss the excursion,' I say. 'But I feel bad about missing it. And I'm embarrassed that this is anxiety related.'

Mood

'They'll find someone else to go in your place, and that person might learn something,' Mum replies.

I admit the awful thing I've been thinking. 'I wished for a medical reason, even though I'm relieved.' The words, *You wanted to be sick*, keep echoing in my mind.

'Okay, now,' she says, 'Dochenka, you must stop beating yourself up. Don't go there. Just be grateful it wasn't a thyroid storm!' Dochenka is the diminutive and affectionate form of the word 'daughter' in Russian. I feel touched by her worry.

On our way out of emergency, I tell Rachel I'd like to go into the hospital chapel. I feel magnetised by it: desperate for a sense of calm, even in a Christian place of worship. I stare up at the stained-glass windows, relieved my symptoms weren't related to my thyroid and heart. A few minutes later, she joins me and hands me a toy lion in a little bag. I hug it and thank her, then tell her I want to stay a moment longer.

I feel a sense of profound gratitude towards my anxiety – even if I'm embarrassed and ashamed *that's all it is* – for offering me a way out of a situation that didn't feel survivable.

Chapter 9

The spring school holidays start early for me. I use a letter from the hospital as my medical certificate. I have used up all my sick leave and have to take unpaid leave. By now, I've called the school receptionist so many times to let her know I'm not coming in that I don't even sound apologetic, but I do feel ashamed.

I go to see Karyn and tell her about my visit to the emergency department.

'What do you think caused your anxiety to become so severe?' she asks.

'I don't know. I guess all my marking, the parent-teacher conferences and an excursion I was meant to go on . . .'

'So your anxiety is mainly about teaching?'

'No, not just teaching.'

She looks at me and waits until I'm ready to answer. I think about how I felt after hearing the GP's opinion about my marriage. I don't mention it, though, because it might lead to talking about Cameron. Karyn reacts, I think unconsciously, when I mention him.

'Rachel and I have been fighting a lot lately.'

'What about?'

'All sorts of things.' I'm deliberately vague. 'Also, our friend Sharon is coming to visit from the US. She wants to help us move from the apartment to the new house.'

When Sharon offered, we thought she was joking, but then she started looking at flights and booked a two-week trip to coincide with the upcoming school holidays. It's unsurprising, in hindsight; she has always been generous to us.

'Do you think that will be helpful during this time?' Karyn asks. She looks dubious.

'Yes.' I frown, wondering what I'm missing. 'That's why she's coming to visit us.'

'No, I don't mean in terms of packing your apartment. I mean in relation to your relationship with Rachel, especially since you've been fighting a lot recently.'

'Oh.' The question surprises me. I haven't thought about our move, Sharon's visit, or even picking up our dog, Rosie, in terms of our relationship. Usually, I would have considered it. 'It should be okay.'

When I first told Karyn about Sharon's role in my relationship with Rachel, she seemed suspicious, especially when I mentioned we were eighteen when we met, and Sharon was thirty-four.

'She has the best intentions,' I told her. 'I'm sure it seems strange she helped people she hadn't met, who lived on the other side of the world. A family friend took care of her when she was a teenager going through some rough times. Also, internet friendships can be stronger than 'real life' friendships; we've become family. It's kind of like that in the queer community, where we try to take care of each other regardless of our own mental health.'

'Oh, is Sharon gay?'

I laughed. 'She would say she's straight. But Rachel and I have always been convinced otherwise. She loves Angelina Jolie and has a *lot* of lesbian fiction for a straight woman.'

'Can you tell me about your relationship with her?' Karyn asks.

This is hard to answer without going back to 2003, when I felt like a child in many ways but had very adult emotions. I sigh and tell her an abbreviated version of the story.

* * *

My stay with Rachel and her family ended on Valentine's Day. I had booked the train for my return to Sydney. When I got to Spencer Street (now Southern Cross) Station, I saw couples kissing and giving each other roses or balloons.

I stood at the platform until the last possible moment, dreaming of a reunion scene from the movies. Rachel would rush over to me, having taken the train to meet me for a romantic farewell. We would kiss for the first time and then head off into the sunset together.

Instead, I boarded and took the train to Sydney.

Even if Rachel felt the same way I did, it was beginning to occur to me that for her, loving me might involve risking everything else she had.

When I arrived at Central Station in Sydney, my parents were waiting to pick me up. They took one look at me and knew something was up.

I made them wait until we got home. 'I have something to tell you,' I said.

'Okay.' Dad stopped in the kitchen instead of joining me on the couch. 'I think this calls for a Scotch,' he said. There was subtext in that, since he barely drank. We mainly kept Scotch for Shabbat or Jewish festivals, which we celebrated with my grandparents.

He returned with his Scotch and took a seat on the couch opposite me. 'What happened to you in Melbourne?' he asked.

I could tell I wouldn't be able to get away with evasive, one-word answers. My gaze moved from Dad to Mum, who was sitting next to me. They looked worried.

I was silent, angry at myself for not managing to hide my feelings the way I usually did. I had hidden my growing love for Rachel in the months before I went travelling. And in the few days I had been back home before I went to Melbourne, it was easy to act like the old me. I was genuinely happy to see my family and return to the warmth of a Sydney summer. I kept my feelings private, only to be examined alone in my room.

Now, I felt like everything about me had changed. Since meeting Rachel online, before my trip, my feelings and hormones had been explosive. An internal battle was swallowing me up, distracting me from my studies, consuming all my attention and thoughts. I'd remained present and attentive to those I loved, listening to other people's struggles, giving advice and spending quality time with people. But I wasn't being honest.

I was afraid of losing my family. We were close and I knew they loved me, but up until now, nothing had threatened that love. My parents encouraged me and told me I was beautiful and smart and could do anything I put my mind to. They were quirky, like me. They'd both been the weird ones – the black sheep – in their families. Dad, an animal rights activist in a meat-and-three-veg family, had started a club to save lobsters from being boiled at restaurants. My arty, creative mum had gone into fashion design; her parents had worked in business and accounting.

Mum and Dad were alternative and supportive, and I didn't think they would have a problem with me being a lesbian, but I couldn't be certain. While my sister had always been a source of support, I could feel myself pulling away from her, from all of them.

They knew me as the person they had all had a part in shaping, the person they loved and supported, but I had discovered an important part of my identity online, with the help of people who were strangers to them. My new identity could be seen as threatening to divide our close unit of four, to take me away from them.

I had only recently started to appreciate how lucky I was to have a loving, supportive family. Being close to my family and actually liking them as people turned out to be rare, unusual. It was something to hold on to and protect. I believed we loved each other unconditionally, but I also knew that, eventually, I would be expected to marry a Jewish man and start a family. I dreamed of a loving, romantic relationship, but was unsure about marriage and children.

While my family was not particularly religious, our Jewish heritage shaped our lives. Our community emphasised the sacrifices of our relatives and ancestors. My grandparents had lost relatives in the war, and Baba and Deda had had to flee their home town. This contributed to a sense of obligation as well as guilt. I knew exactly who I was supposed to be, early on, and I also knew that I didn't fit the description.

I had often thought if I ever came out, Jess would be the most accepting, my grandparents the least accepting, and my parents somewhere in the middle. There seemed no point in coming out and facing the consequences if I wasn't in a relationship.

After developing feelings for Rachel, I worried that coming out would change my life. I liked my life the way it was, apart from the loneliness.

I wished I could be with Rachel without changing the way people perceived me.

'You're not yourself. Are you okay?' Mum asked.

'Yes, I'm fine.' Physically, I *was* fine. Telling them about Rachel would involve admitting I had lied about my trip to Melbourne. I didn't think they would be surprised, though; now that I thought about it, I was sure my explanation hadn't sounded remotely convincing. I wondered, briefly, why they hadn't asked more questions about my mysterious one-way trip.

We sat there on the couch for what felt like an unbearable length of time. Normally, I could have kept my feelings hidden and continued answering vaguely until they gave up. But I couldn't stop thinking about Rachel, and my vulnerability led me to share.

'Tell us what's wrong,' Mum said.

I shut my eyes and told myself I had to be honest with my parents. Perhaps they would offer much-needed comfort and support.

'I'm infatuated with a woman,' I said, my voice quiet but steady. I summarised my trip to Melbourne.

There was a long pause.

Mum said, 'I had a feeling you were going to say something like that. You know, lots of people go through this at your age. It's normal to have crushes on both girls and boys.' This surprised me. She hadn't said anything like this before. She continued, talking about phases and curiosity in a way that suggested my feelings would disappear eventually.

'Why didn't you say anything earlier?' Dad asked.

'I thought I wouldn't be your Rozy anymore.'

'You will always be our Rozy,' he said. 'There's nothing you could do that would ever change that.'

I looked from Dad to Mum, who nodded.

At the time, I was mostly happy with their reaction. I had convinced myself it would be much worse, having read some terrible coming-out stories. Later, I realised it wasn't great – it was basically the *being gay is a phase* trope.

The word 'infatuated' played around in my mind afterwards. As a language lover, my own word choice bothered me greatly. Infatuation implied impermanence; a silly obsession. It didn't describe lasting, romantic love. While I'm sure they were more focused on the 'woman' part of my admission, it was easier to fixate on my bad choice of verb. Maybe if I'd worded it more eloquently, they would have taken me more seriously.

After my trip to Melbourne, my conversations with Rachel became more intense. We spoke as often as we could. I could finally sense that my feelings for her were reciprocated.

Sharon was my one source of emotional support during this time. I was a bit intimidated by her, and had been since Rachel first introduced us over chat, but was getting to know her. She was in her mid-thirties and married. She and her husband had two young children and lived in a rural part of the American Midwest. When she and I chatted online, I found myself wondering what had brought her to the Kitten Board – not that I had the courage to ask her.

During one chat, Sharon went from asking pleasantries to being very direct. 'Are you in love with Rach?' she asked, her voice sombre. 'You have to work out your feelings because if she wants to be with you, her whole world is going to change.'

I was stunned by her question. I thought about my email correspondence with Rachel and our phone conversations, the strength of my feelings for her, the way everything felt lighter when I was around her or talking to her, and my willingness to do anything to be with her. I imagined us having a life together where we could be open about loving each other.

'Yes, I am,' I said. And it was true, but also terrifying to admit. It wasn't just Rachel's world at risk. I had not prepared myself for my own life changing.

Sharon and Rachel had been close since my time in Europe: before Rachel and I met. Now, Sharon said since I'd left Rachel's house, things had been tense there. Rachel was struggling and Sharon was considering offering her a place to stay. It would take twenty-four hours to travel to her home in the US – and an expensive overseas airfare. There was more to Rachel's struggles than our not-quite-relationship, but I can't write about it all. It took some time for me to realise that not all of what happened to me and Rachel in our love story, including the trauma, is our story. Some of it is hers alone.

Four days after I returned to Sydney, Rachel and I had the chance to catch up properly on a late-night call.

'We have to talk,' she said. 'I think we both know there are things we've been avoiding talking about.'

I was too afraid to help her along. 'Yes,' I said. 'I think I know what you mean.' I paused, unsure how to say what was needed. 'Would you like to go first?' I was being a coward, but she didn't seem irritated by my inability to talk about my feelings.

'Well, I love you and you love me, right?' she said.

And with that, I knew if her feelings for me were anything like mine for her, we would make it work. She was braver than I'd realised.

Things changed quickly after that phone call. Rachel was still experiencing conflict at home. She made the decision to leave.

Rachel and I didn't know anything about moving out of home. She'd only just graduated from high school. I lived at home and was a full-time university student with a casual job. Sharon could offer Rachel somewhere to live – all the way across the world. She would pay for her flights to the US and Rachel would pay her back once she'd saved enough money. Rachel had both US and Australian citizenship, which made things easier. This extreme plan suddenly became the only real option we had.

We had less than twenty-four hours together in Sydney before Rachel's flight. That night, we stayed up talking in my bedroom. Mum was away and Dad kept his distance. I hadn't come out to Jess yet and she was nonplussed by Rachel's presence in our home. I'd said she was a friend from summer camp, using the same lie I told my parents before my trip to Melbourne.

In my bedroom, on a warm and sticky summer night, I wanted to kiss her, but I couldn't do it. Each time I tried to lean forward and kiss or touch her, I froze. We had become a couple over the phone and internet. Translating my feelings into something physical felt much further than what I was capable of. My previous sexual relationship had been entirely initiated by the guy I was seeing, never by me, and I didn't have much confidence in myself as a sexual or romantic person.

Instead, I sat on the floor in front of her, not even facing her directly. I glanced around my room, occasionally peeking her way. She was sitting on the edge of my bed, and even seeing her against my turquoise bedding, where I had fantasised about her so many times, made me blush. She started stroking my neck, which was both tender and erotically charged. I was turned on immediately, but was far too shy to make a move. It wasn't even just shyness; a part of me was still scared that she would reject me. I wasn't sure I would kiss or touch her properly, given it was my first time with a woman: let alone someone I had such strong feelings for. Maybe the chemistry wouldn't be there for her and she would realise that our relationship – and maybe even thinking she was a lesbian – was all a big mistake. I didn't want to do anything that might risk our relationship, even though I wanted her badly.

Later, she told me she had wanted to touch me, beyond stroking my neck, but felt shy, and my obvious nerves and hesitance gave her pause. It would have been her first kiss, and she didn't want to screw it up.

When I tried to fall asleep, I thought about how differently the night could have gone: what it would have been like to have had sex with her before she departed, whether that would have helped us with the months of separation ahead, and how much closer we would have felt afterwards. I felt bitterly disappointed and frustrated with myself.

The next day, I took her to the airport and helped her check in. The person at the airline desk asked, 'Do you have any bags to check in?' and Rachel shook her head.

'I just have my backpack.'

The woman looked at her strangely. I worried about her, with her few possessions. I hoped Sharon would make sure she had everything she needed once she moved there.

We walked to the departure gate and held each other tightly. 'I love you so much.'

'I love you, too.'

'I'll miss you.'

She walked away from me, and when she turned back, she looked sad and scared.

After she left, I sat in a toilet cubicle and cried. I wanted to run after her. Every part of my body ached with the idea of her leaving, but I couldn't see any other way than what we had planned.

While I waited to hear from Rachel, I found myself thinking of worst-case scenarios about her flight and her new life. I hoped she wasn't walking into some kind of trap. I teared up, wondering when I would see her again. That night, I didn't say much to my family. I went to bed early and lay awake, wondering how she was going.

When I woke up, I saw she'd sent me a message from Sharon's phone. 'Hi baby! I'm here. I love you so much.'

Rachel called me on video chat and I was relieved to see the familiarity and comfort between her and Sharon. She told me that after we went through departures at Sydney airport, she was taken off into a room with a customs agent. It turned out she had used her US passport rather than departing on her Australian one.

'I miss you too. This is going to be so hard. I wish you were here with me.'

Another friend from the Kitten Board, Mickie, built Rachel a computer for her birthday. Sharon recorded me saying messages to Rachel over chat and sent them to Mickie, who set them up as the alert sounds on Rachel's computer.

Considering we had met through computers, it felt reassuring to know she had one in her room. I was using the family computer in the living room, which meant a lack of privacy.

We chatted online and spoke over the phone whenever we could, often about what we would do when we saw each other, in between working hard and saving up to see each other. Our messages ranged from very sweet to very sexual, or both. We kept saying how much we 'craved' each other.

Finally, by winter, I had saved up enough money and bought the cheapest flight to Chicago available. I had an overnight layover at an airport hotel in Tokyo, which was included in my airfare. I was too nervous to eat properly. I had a bath so I could shave my legs. In my determination to remove every hair, I managed to cut my leg. I chastised myself – if I wasn't careful, I'd bleed out in a bathtub in Japan before I could reunite with Rachel – and then chuckled aloud.

I couldn't wait to see her, but was scared. What if, after all we had gone through, we didn't have chemistry? What if she wasn't attracted to me anymore? What if she liked her life there so much she wouldn't ever want to leave?

On the flight to Chicago, I binge-watched films, trying not to think about all the things I was nervous about. About an hour before landing, I went to the bathroom to put in contact lenses, apply eyeliner and fuss over my hair. I stressed about meeting Sharon and her husband, David, and wondered what they would think of me.

After landing, I lined up to go through the arrival process. I couldn't wipe the smile off my face and hoped the officer wouldn't get suspicious. I practised what I would say when they asked what I was doing there. I wouldn't say I was going to visit my girlfriend in case they thought I'd try to stay in the US permanently; I'd been warned by other couples from the Kitten Board that you had to be careful during the arrivals process. But when the officer called me forward, he was disinterested in my situation. He waved me through after asking a few questions about why I was there.

I walked through the exit to the international arrivals hall, and there she was, in a Disney jumper and jeans. The jumper was oversized and fluffy. It was geeky – and she looked gorgeous in it. She was leaning against a railing and had clearly found the closest possible spot to the front so I'd see her as soon as I entered the hall. I stared into her hazel eyes, which had found and focused on me, as I walked down the arrivals ramp towards her. We grinned at each other and hugged for a long time. I felt like something that had been taken from me had finally been returned.

Sharon and David were standing over to one side, giving us space, but I reached out and hugged them. We'd had so many video calls that I felt like I knew them well, rather than that I was just meeting them.

In the car, leaving the airport, I kept thinking I should touch Rachel. But just like that night in my bedroom in Sydney, I couldn't do it. I told myself off for being so cowardly. Then Rachel reached for my hand. She stroked my fingers and traced my palm lightly, before holding my hand in hers. Not for the first time, I reprimanded myself for being so shy and awkward. I gripped her hand back and stared out at the expansive farmland as we drove from Chicago to nearby Wisconsin, my heart beating wildly.

I'd never been to the US. I marvelled at everything, even though Sharon kept saying they didn't live anywhere exciting. We went to IHOP for pancakes and I ordered a Mickey Mouse pancake off the children's menu: I'd been warned about American portion sizes. We drove around parts of Wisconsin, and they showed me places Rachel had told me about during the three months she'd been living there.

Finally, we arrived at Sharon and David's house. It was set back from the road down a long driveway, and had acres of land surrounding it. Everything was green and lush. I was given a tour of the house. Love, family and individuality seemed to be defining features. There was a room Sharon used to store objects related to Ancient Egypt, one of her long-term interests, and a dining room and living room packed with family photos and mementoes. I hadn't met their young children yet, but their personalities were on display everywhere.

Sharon and David helped me with my bags and then left me and Rachel alone in her room. They had set up a spare bed right next to her bed, but we chose to lie together on her bed while a fan spun gently above us. We gazed out the window, which faced the sprawling greenery of the garden, a pond surrounded by reeds and powder-blue sky. We held hands, breathlessly talking.

It took three days to build up to our first kiss because we kept waiting for the other person to make the first move. On the first two nights, we lay together in her bed and snuggled but didn't kiss. We wore pyjamas but could feel each other's bodies in excruciating detail – I could feel every curve, the warmth coming from her body, and smelled the mint of her toothpaste. Her hands were silky smooth, and I ran my fingers around both sides of them. The bed was small and cramped, but neither of us seemed to care. We fit perfectly.

On the third night, we had gone to bed but hadn't turned out the lights. We lay there, talking and laughing and touching each other's hands, when I realised I felt ready. The fear had gone. I leaned towards her and took her face in my hands, lifting her lips to mine so I could kiss her. It turned out that was all I needed to do. She kissed me back, and then we couldn't stop kissing. We threw our clothes onto the floor and revelled in getting to know every part of each other's bodies.

Afterwards, we couldn't stop laughing that we had our first kiss on the night we first had sex. We also laughed at the way we had talked to each other online, with such bravado and incredibly direct sexual comments, compared with the build-up to our first kiss. Any shyness, awkwardness and hesitation between us was gone, and I realised I was living out the fantasies I'd been having back in Australia for months.

Later, we went on a road trip to Disney World with Sharon and David. Rachel and I were unable to keep our hands off each other, including when we travelled though the red states. I'd never had much interest in Disney World, but enjoyed making out with Rachel on the more private rides.

Our friends were fun to travel with and had a great sense of humour. Sharon loved to make sexual jokes in front of her conservative extended family, who blanched every time, particularly when she tried out some lesbian humour. Rachel and I teased Sharon about being bisexual or a lesbian, which she shrugged off or laughed at.

When it came time to go back to Australia for university, I thought about dropping out and staying with Rachel. But we were practical and had a vague plan for our life together. It involved continuing our long-distance relationship while Rachel worked and I finished university, then eventually moving in together in Australia.

We spent the last night of the trip listening to a song we loved, 'Crystal' by Stevie Nicks, on repeat. I was meant to be packing but we were on Rachel's bed, holding hands, kissing and crying like a lesbian stereotype from a movie. On the road trip, Sharon had been playing the *Practical Magic* soundtrack and it had inadvertently become the soundtrack of our time together. When 'Crystal' made us too sad, we swapped it for another of Stevie Nicks' songs from the soundtrack, this one called 'If You Ever Did Believe'. As it played over and over, the words about wanting to hold someone for just one more night made us grab on tighter to each other.

Before I left, Rachel gave me a Claddagh ring: a traditional Irish ring that features two hands holding a crowned heart. The hands represent friendship, the heart symbolises love, and the crown stands for loyalty. In *Buffy*, Angel gave Buffy the ring on her seventeenth birthday, telling her, 'Wear it with the heart pointing towards you. It means you belong to somebody.'

In Australia, Rachel had told me that when I left for Europe the previous year, she had started wearing a Claddagh ring with the heart pointing towards her. Hearing how she'd felt about me before we'd even met allowed me to think maybe we would make it.

I returned home, sad and distracted. Months passed, and even though I crammed all my Semester 2 university classes into two days so I could work as much as possible, I wasn't close to saving up enough money to visit Rachel again.

Towards the end of the year, Nana and Popsi told me a distant cousin would soon be celebrating his bar mitzvah in Canada. Nana loved the idea of me visiting family in other parts of the world and getting to know them. She and Popsi offered to help financially with the airline tickets. My mind buzzed, thinking about the proximity of Wisconsin to Canada. All I cared about was seeing Rachel again.

I planned a trip to North America for the long Christmas break. Once it was booked, I could barely sleep at night. I was so excited to see Rachel. She was all I could think about, and eventually I decided to cancel my plans to go to Canada. I asked my grandparents if I could use the tickets to stay with my friends in Wisconsin. They said that was okay, but I felt guilty. It wasn't the sort of thing I would normally do, but I would do it again in the same circumstances. All I cared about was my relationship with Rachel.

Late one night, in the lead-up to the trip, Mum walked into the lounge room while I was chatting with Rachel. I minimised the chat window and looked up.

'I don't want you to go on this trip,' she said.

I was shocked that she couldn't understand what it meant to me. We had always been close, but ever since I had come out, she continued to talk about me and Rachel as though we were friends, and seemed to be hoping it would all go away.

I stared at her. 'Of course I'm going. My flights are booked,' I said.

'I'm not going to argue about it,' she said. 'I decided I should tell you how I feel. I don't know these people, and I don't want you to go.'

I frowned. If this was my first trip to Wisconsin, I would have understood her reservations about me going to stay with total strangers. In fact, I was surprised she hadn't said anything earlier. But I had travelled there safely once and reassured her that my friends were good people. There was no reason I could think of for her to object, apart from her having issues with my relationship.

'I need to see Rachel again. I miss her so much.'

'How do you even know you're gay?' she asked. 'You haven't been with a boy. How can you know for sure?'

'You have no idea who I've been with.'

She shook her head. 'That's more than I need to know about my daughter.'

I sighed. 'I'm sorry, but I'm going.'

'I can't stop you, but you don't have my blessing to go.' She walked out of the room.

She had never said anything like that before. I stared at the door for a while after she left. While part of me felt like I probably shouldn't go, I was determined to see Rachel. If I didn't go on this trip, it could be a year or more before I saw her again. The only way to ignore what Mum had said was to view it as unfair and melodramatic. I fumed at her trying to stop me. And I went on the trip.

Much later, I can see these events the way they may have come across to her at the time. I'd returned from Europe a year ago, on their dime, claiming to be homesick. I had fallen in love with a stranger I met online and spent all my waking hours trying to get to the US. Mum wanted to protect me – which, at least partly, may have involved keeping me from getting into a serious same-sex relationship.

***

Karyn has a thoughtful expression on her face when I tell her about my second trip.

'So, how was that trip, Roz?' she asks.

'Amazing. We felt so free.' I tell her about the time Sharon took us to a lake that had frozen over, near her parents' house. The ice had been thick enough to skate on, but we had stepped on it hesitantly, tentatively – neither of us had ever stood on a frozen lake before. Footage of people falling through broken ice ran through my head. Rachel and I moved further out onto the ice, until we felt steady enough to stand still and hold onto each other. It was completely silent around us. All we could see was the snow falling onto our bodies and the maple trees surrounding the lake. Opening my mouth so snow would fall directly onto my tongue, my body had thrummed with excitement. I had marvelled at being lucky enough to be reunited.

'Did you get much time to yourselves, away from Sharon and her husband?'

'Yes. We spent a lot of time with them and their children, but they also left us alone. We went on our first date, which was amazing, and our first trip away together.'

I smile as I remember our date at a Chinese restaurant on Christmas Eve. Sharon and David dropped us at a Chinese restaurant. Rachel and I had spent the afternoon getting ready, dressing up and putting on jewellery and perfume. At the restaurant, we giggled and joked, holding hands whenever we weren't eating.

We had been given fortune cookies when we paid the bill, and I remembered some of our friends from the Kitten Board had taught us to add the words 'in bed' to the end of our fortunes. My fortune read: 'It is quality not quantity that matters. Do a good job tomorrow.'

'In bed!' we had exclaimed in unison, collapsing into laughter.

We had spent New Year's Eve in a cabin, complete with a log fire, overlooking a snow-covered forest. The ranch was run by two gay cowboys, and we had talked to the couple at length about queer identity.

Mood

'Did you resolve things with your mother about the trip?' Karyn asks.

'Yes, eventually. It took a while.'

'And how are things now?'

'We have a good relationship, thankfully.'

Working on relationships with both of our families is an ongoing process that has taken time, work and patience, and years of difficult conversations. These don't always lead where we want them to, but nearly two decades later, we're in a pretty good place with both families.

'Sharon was very generous towards you and Rachel,' Karyn says. 'She hadn't met Rachel before, but she invited her to live with her. And Rachel felt comfortable enough to fly across the world to stay with her. Can you tell me more about the relationship between you three?'

'There isn't a romantic or sexual side to our relationship, if that's what you mean,' I say, feeling the need to clarify.

'Not for her, either?' she asks.

'No! Honestly, she sees us as her children. Her kids call us their sisters. We joke to ourselves that we're their sisters who get it on with each other.'

Karyn chuckles. I feel my heart racing as I try to explain Sharon's motivations. It takes me back to being nineteen, trying to justify the situation to my parents.

'I'm wondering if she was projecting onto you and Rachel in some way,' she says.

I feel a ball of anger forming in my chest. *So what if she was projecting? If by caring for us she got to work on pain in herself, then I'm glad for her.*

'Sharon experienced a lot of criticism and suspicion for inviting Rachel to stay with her,' I explain, trying not to sound too defensive. 'She has been judged by family and friends for it. She lost friendships over it. She shrugs it off but I know it must have hurt her. Our relationship might seem strange, but there's nothing bad there. We really are family.'

'I see,' she says. 'I just want to make sure you're prepared for someone else to be coming into your home, even if she is a close friend. You've had a tough time, lately, and I want you to be ready.'

'Things might get tense,' I say, 'but we have been through a lot worse.'

* * *

On the day Sharon is due to arrive in Melbourne, I wake up hours before her flight lands. Lately, I've been sleeping less and less each night. My depression seems to have given way to something else.

It's a clear, bright spring day and I feel optimistic. On the way to the airport, Rachel and I park outside my school. It's the last day of term and I want to pick up some of my things before the holidays. Nobody is in the staff room, which is a relief. I don't know what I would say if I ran into someone.

We end up stuck in peak-hour traffic. By the time we arrive at the airport, Sharon has already gone through customs and is waiting for us in arrivals. We give her a long hug and thank her for caring about us enough to fly all the way here.

'Guess what, Shaz?' I say on the way home from the airport.

'Oh dear. What?' As we don't speak to each other that often, by the time we remember to update her on our lives, our decisions often come across as impulsive. She teases us about it.

'We're getting a dog while you're here!'

'What?' she says again. I don't know if her nervous response is because she's a bit scared of dogs, or if she thinks we're a bit mad, since we're in the middle of a move and dealing with a lot of stress. Maybe we are, but I can't wait to pick Rosie up.

After breakfast, and a lot of coffee, Sharon, Rachel and I head into the city and meet Jess at the Wheeler Centre, a literary organisation. We've booked tickets for an event called Diverse Women Writers. It's for Aboriginal and Torres Strait Islander writers, writers of colour, queer and trans writers, writers with disabilities, and writers from diverse cultural backgrounds. It's so different to writer talks I have been to where the Q&A is dominated by white, straight, cisgender and able-bodied audience members.

Usually, I walk into the Wheeler Centre feeling quite anxious. I'm very focused on who I might run into, and whether I'll have to make small talk. But I walk in confidently, take a seat without worrying about our proximity to people I recognise, and wait impatiently for the event to begin.

On the panels, there are writers, publishers and literary agents I follow online, and I listen with avid interest. Even though Sharon was eager to attend the event, her jet lag starts to hit. I'm at the opposite end of the energy spectrum; I can barely stop taking notes and putting my hand up to make comments.

In the breaks between the panels, I chat to the people sitting around me, including Maxine Beneba Clarke, an award-winning Australian writer of Afro-Caribbean descent, and her publisher. I'm in awe of Maxine's writing, after reading her short-story collection *Foreign Soil*, but I'm not shy at all talking to her, which is unusual for me with writers I admire. There's no need for pleasantries; we delve into talking animatedly about politics and social issues.

In the afternoon, Rachel decides to head home with Sharon, who is wilting and needs to nap. I'm in my element and am content to stay.

At the end of the event, I check in with Rachel and she tells me Sharon is still sleeping. I send her a message. 'Why don't you come back and join me?'

She replies, 'Really? Sharon has come all this way to see us. I don't think I should leave her at home.'

'Why? She's sleeping.' I'm annoyed. I'm having fun and want her to join me.

'I don't think that's right. Just go out. It's fine.'

I sit and talk with my sister Jess and a few writers I befriended during the day, and we decide to move to The Moat, the bar downstairs, for drinks and snacks. It's buzzing with people from the event, the food smells wonderful, and I settle in for a fun night. The wallpaper is printed with shelves and shelves of books. Surrounded by books, with candles on the tables, I feel like I'm in a secondhand bookshop or library, which happen to be the places I'm most comfortable.

We order drinks, and I remember school is over for another term. The endorphins hit hard, along with the alcohol. As we drink, we start talking about sex. One of the writers rues the fact that she is single.

'Maybe I should set you up with my friend who lives in Manhattan,' I say. 'She's a writer, she's rich and she's bi. You could live a delightful New York lifestyle with a sugar mama.'

'What about me?' one of the writers asks. She's attractive and I blush when she asks the question. 'Who would you match me with?'

I fumble a response by asking what her type is.

'I'm very attracted to butch women,' she says. I wonder if she thinks I am butch.

'Hmm. I think I have someone in mind for you.' I look at Facebook and find the friend who comes to mind. 'What about her?'

'Yes! She's one hundred per cent my type.'

As I continue to joke with the table about matchmaking, I wonder what makes me do this. 'It's my Jewish roots,' I explain, later. 'I'm a yenta, and a total busybody.' But I wonder if there's more to it. Perhaps it's because Rachel and I became a couple when I was young, and fiddling in other people's love lives and sex lives is a way to live vicariously through them.

Jess and I order more glasses of wine and some food for the table to share. When I get back, I say, 'You know, I think I'm going to get a tattoo after this.'

'Tonight?' one of the writers asks. 'I want to get one but don't have any tattoos so I'm too scared to get one just yet.'

'This will be my first, actually,' I reply. 'I'm ready.'

Jess looks thoughtful. 'I want to get one. If you can hold off, we can go together.'

'I really want to get it tonight,' I say.

'What are you going to get?'

'A quote by Audre Lorde. *Your silence will not protect you.*'

The group approves. I feel a burst of excitement. But when I look up local tattoo parlours, they've already closed. I haven't looked at my phone in a while and it's late. Rachel has sent numerous messages asking when I'll be home. I'm not quite ready to go home yet. I have so much energy.

'I have to get home to my boys,' another writer says.

'Do you have children?'

'No, I mean my husband and my boyfriend.' To our surprised faces, she says, 'We're ethically non-monogamous.'

'Oh, right!'

'I should get home to Rach and our friend who just arrived from overseas,' I reply.

One of the writers says, 'I'm the only person here who doesn't have someone to go home to.'

'You're welcome to come to our place,' I impulsively offer, though we haven't really spoken much.

We take the train back to my place, chatting away, but I start to wonder if I should have invited them. The conversation doesn't flow as easily as it did in the bar with the others. I'd hoped bringing them back with me might extend the fun I was having.

When we get home, I find Rachel and Sharon looking quizzical. They've been waiting for me and haven't had dinner. It's 9 pm. We're all usually introverted, verging on antisocial, so they're surprised to have someone else in our midst.

The four of us attempt to make conversation and it grows more and more uncomfortable. Rachel and I go into the kitchen to get drinks for everyone.

'It's Shaz's first night here,' Rachel whispers to me. 'Who is this person?'

I shrug off her questions and suggest we go out for a late dinner at an Italian restaurant near our house. At the restaurant, the writer talks animatedly while I watch Sharon try to stay awake. Occasionally, Rachel and I make eye contact. I have used most of my energy during the day and don't have much to offer in the way of conversation.

I hear Sharon ask Rachel, later that night, 'Is it normal for Roz to bring someone home like this?'

I don't listen to the response. She's a homebody who lives in a rural area. What does she know about socialising and making new friends? I start reading about tattoo artists.

Two days later, it's finally time to adopt Rosie. I've been staying up late and waking up very early, and the excitement of Rosie's impending arrival makes it even harder to get more than four hours of sleep per night.

We drive to a large pet shop forty-five minutes from our house. Rosie's foster carer, who lives in Gippsland, had offered to meet us in Cranbourne, where he was helping out with a greyhound rescue fundraiser outside the pet shop. When we get out of the car, we can see a white and black dog hiding behind the kindly-looking older man who has been looking after her for a few months. She's wearing a muzzle and it's obvious she's very nervous. He's gentle with her. He is working at a sausage sizzle as part of the fundraiser, but instead of begging for some sausage, Rosie leans against his legs.

After we shake hands with her foster carer, we hold our hands out for Rosie to smell. She's timid, but curious. Her foster carer tells us to take our time walking around with her; he'll wait as long as we need.

Rachel and I take Rosie's leash and try not to bombard her with our enthusiasm. We lead her inside the pet shop and walk up and down the aisles, watching her reactions to the various sights and smells. She seems fascinated by the fish tanks, then gets very excited as we near a hutch full of bunnies behind a glass display. She lifts her big, wet nose in the air and we give her time to take in all the smells before leading her away. We see the whites of her eyes as she tries to take it all in.

We buy Rosie a soft, fleece coat, with colourful polka dots all over it, and head back out to the fundraising table. Rachel says to Rosie's foster carer, 'I heard it can be soothing for a rescue animal to get the smell of a person they're familiar with on a blanket or item of clothing.' He agrees readily and puts Rosie's new coat over his shoulders. I can see the love between him and Rosie; he has cared for her so well.

On the way back to our place, we let Rosie out and walk her along some grass. She's nervous, and each new sound seems to add to her anxiety. We get her home and settle her in her new bed. We try to introduce her to her food, toys and environment slowly, knowing it's a lot to take in for an ex-racing dog.

Jess comes over to meet Rosie and sits next to her quietly, stroking her.

While we're sitting there, I say I want to get a tattoo. 'Like, right now,' I say. 'I'm happy to go and get it by myself.'

Sharon decides to get her first tattoo too: something small. She has wanted to get a tattoo for years, but her sudden decision still strikes me as unusual. I'm too focused on myself to think about why she has agreed. Later, I wonder if she was worried about me.

Jess comes with us, too intrigued to miss out, and Rachel stays home with Rosie. We take an Uber to a tattoo parlour in Thornbury. One of Jess's friends has recommended it, and they take walk-ins. They're getting ready to close for the night when we arrive.

'Oh, damn, we were hoping to get tattoos tonight,' I say. 'We've built up our courage.'

'What are you ladies planning to get?'

We describe what we're after and the tattoo artists take pity on us. 'We can do that.'

I text Rachel photos of my tattoo in different fonts. She calls me. 'I'll come and join you,' she says.

'What about Rosie?' I ask.

'She should be okay for an hour or two. She's had dinner and she's sleeping. She seems settled.'

I wonder why she decided to join me. Maybe she didn't think I would go through with it and changed her mind when I did. Sharon and Jess don't seem surprised when Rachel arrives; they probably both expected her to join me. We do most things together, but I know she's had to wrestle with her conscience by leaving Rosie home alone.

I'm relieved to have Rachel there. Maybe I didn't think I'd go through with it, either. It's comforting to get her opinion on the font for my tattoo, and to have her hold my hand as the artist tattoos my thigh.

Afterwards, I'm on a high. I expected the tattoo to be painful, but all I really felt were the vibrations of the tattoo gun. This makes me want more tattoos. Sharon is excited about her semi-colon tattoo, but I'm beyond excitement. My adrenaline keeps growing. I want to go out. Then it hits me I'm being selfish: Rosie is home by herself, in a completely new house and life.

When we get home and open the front door, I see little pieces of dried white paint on the floor. 'What the hell?'

Rosie runs to us and leans into our legs. I inspect the house and realise she urinated on the floor while we were out and left long scratches along one of the doors in the house. We scrub the carpet and try to figure out what to do about the wood. Sharon is very handy with home repairs and has some ideas.

Once we clean up what we can, Sharon goes to bed, followed by

Rachel. I can't sleep, which has become normal for me lately, but tonight it's for different reasons. Rosie settles on her bed in our room and I feel a rush of love towards her. I think about how fearful she is and how she must have felt when we all went out. I'm furious at myself for being so selfish.

Now that I have my tattoo, all neatly covered up with plastic wrap and starting to ooze blood, my sense of urgency is gone. I can't remember why I thought I needed to get it at that exact minute, and why I overlooked Rosie's needs in favour of what I thought were my own. She's had a difficult past, we were told, and has marks on the insides of her teeth from biting the bars of her cage during her time as a racing dog.

As I lie awake for hours, I think about the massive life shift she has experienced, what that must be like for a dog who has gone through tough times. I realise that just because we rescued her it doesn't mean she is now 'saved', or that her traumas are now healed.

I've been craving love, attention and care lately, and Rosie certainly needs and deserves some too. I get up and sit by her bed. I wait until she realises I'm there before I pat her. She settles into sleep. I go back to bed. Eventually, I fall asleep, too.

Chapter 10

I struggle with the move. I'm sleeping for about four hours a night and my attention span has become uneven. I jump from task to task, without completing any of them. Despite buzzing with adrenaline, I can't focus on anything for more than a few minutes before I lose interest and become absorbed in something else. Every time I find an interesting album, or piece of jewellery, or some old documents, I try to show Rachel or Sharon.

Sharon seems intrigued – and confused – by my energy. She compares me to a toddler and I'm not offended: it's how I feel. Everything piques my curiosity and fascinates me. After months spent in a depressive slump, I enjoy these bumpy, excitable and jittery feelings.

One day, Sharon and I are setting up lights at the front of the house when one of our new neighbours stops for a chat. Sharon answers her questions and then heads back inside. A while later, she comes back out, sees that I am still talking to the neighbour, and goes back in again.

That afternoon, she mentions our neighbours. 'Is that normal?'

'What?'

'That your neighbours are so friendly and chatty. Is that an Australian thing?'

I explain this is the first time I've had a conversation with a neighbour since I first started renting. 'I guess people are extra friendly in this area.'

And I love the friendliness. Rachel and Sharon can't always keep up with me. I talk to all the neighbours surrounding our house and make early-morning phone calls to Cameron and Ari, who are early risers. When Rachel wakes up each morning, she asks, 'Who were you talking to today?'

The pace is fun and exciting for about a week. Then, without warning, I start getting angry with Sharon. It's the same anger and irritation I've been directing at Rachel, though I hold it back more with Sharon. She points out a billboard that features Beyoncé looking powerful and sexy, her hair in large curls, while I'm driving to our old apartment. She questions how empowering the billboard is, considering the skimpy outfit Beyoncé is wearing. I lecture her about everything I find wrong with her statement.

'I don't remember you being so combative,' she says.

'It's not combative; I'm just not afraid of speaking my mind anymore,' I retort.

During Sharon's visit, Rachel and I fight more than we have in our thirteen years together. I think about how Karyn expressed concern over Sharon's visit, and wonder if her presence has added tension. But I don't think it's her. When Rachel and I fight, Sharon works solidly on packing a section of our apartment or setting up something in our new house. She flits past us and never adds her opinion when things are already contentious.

I'm angriest early in the morning, if I haven't had enough sleep, and late at night. Sharon still hasn't adjusted to her jet lag, so goes to bed hours before we do. I collect a litany of irritations, frustrations and judgements throughout the day and then try to provoke a fight with Rachel by offering them up to her at night.

It would be nice to enjoy this time alone together but I seem unable to keep my complaints to myself, and unable to speak diplomatically, kindly or thoughtfully. I have the strangest sensation as I do this: I'm enjoying behaving without limits or care for those around me, though I've always taken such pride in the kindness and respect in my relationship with Rachel. I like seeing the knife go in. I like waiting to see how she will react. I like waiting to see where she will draw the line.

When Rachel cries, especially if it follows something I have said or done, I have to hide my irritation. I whisper, 'You need to be quieter; Shaz will wake up and hear us.'

Rachel says, 'So you care if Shaz hears us but not about saying those things to me in the first place?'

'I guess.'

In the heat of the moment, I say things I've never said to her before. I tell her I hate her and don't want to be with her anymore.

Later, I feel remorseful, regretful and ashamed. I blame my mental health and tell her I don't mean those things. I tell her I won't do it again, but even as I say it, I know it will happen again. When I'm calm, later, I realise how much this pattern is a cycle of abuse.

The next day, when Rachel is heading off to her own therapy session, I say, feeling desperate, 'If you tell your therapist everything, she's going to tell you to leave me.'

Rachel replies, 'Maybe she will. But I can make up my own mind. I don't make decisions about our relationship based on what other people tell me.'

It's a bit of a burn, since I constantly bring home the views of Cameron, Karyn and various GPs and take them on as my own. I deserve it. I think maybe her therapist should tell her to leave me.

Another day, we are driving to Jess's place for dinner. Cameron has also been invited. Sharon offers to stay home with Rosie; she tells us she is not feeling social and is happy to continue unpacking. It's likely, I realise later, that she's giving us space, having noticed my behaviour and our fights.

On the way up High Street in Northcote and Thornbury, we pass couples walking to trendy restaurants and bars. We get into a fight over something minor. Lately, whenever I'm stressed, I end up becoming enraged with Rachel. It doesn't matter what we're fighting about. I see her as an obstacle to my freedom. I feel childish but find myself searching inside for the most cutting, hurtful things to say to her about her family or about her as a person. I forget what I've said almost immediately after the fight, but Rachel remembers it all.

Whatever I say on this occasion, I wince afterwards. I might not have a huge amount of self-awareness when I'm manic and angry, but I can tell when I've gone too far. She is quick to reply, but I see the impact of the words before she opens her mouth. She is usually a cheerful and playful person, but the first word that comes to my mind is *broken* when I look at her tight shoulders and the pain and confusion on her face.

'I don't even want to go with you anymore!' she yells.

I feel a strange combination of shame and righteousness, the latter making me resolute.

'Fine. I'm happy to drop you off somewhere. But can you lower your voice? I'm driving. This is unsafe.'

'You are such a jerk.'

'No, seriously. Can you please calm down? I'm at least talking quietly.'

'No! Speaking quietly while you say nasty things doesn't make you better than me,' she argues.

'Fine, then. Get out of the car,' I say. 'I don't feel safe with you yelling like this.'

She refuses to get out. I pull over near Jess's apartment and tell her to get out of the car again. I feel rage pushing upwards and outwards, originating near my stomach. In the past, Rachel raising her voice has led me to shut down. I become scared and avoidant when people raise their voices or display negative emotions, even when they aren't directed at me. I've learned it comes from my fear of abandonment or being hurt. But now I'm angry, too.

'If you don't get out of the car, we're done.'

She undoes her seatbelt. 'Fine.' She storms away from the car.

I text Jess. All I say is, 'Rach and I just broke up. I don't know what to do.'

'I'm so sorry! Please come over anyway, if you still want to.'

I start crying as I walk along the quiet, residential street.

Arriving at my sister's apartment, I pause and take some deep breaths outside. I wipe my feet on the mat outside her front door and peer in through the kitchen window. I see the usual pot plants, and my sister and her boyfriend working in the kitchen. It smells like garlic and herbs, but I've lost my appetite.

'Can we do anything?' Jess's boyfriend asks as I come in, after they both hug me.

I shrug. They offer me a few different drinks: wine, beer, spirits.

'Do you have any weed?' I ask. All I want, suddenly, is any form of drugs. Rachel is very uncomfortable about drugs, so I stay away from them. I feel rebellious. 'Rach is so against me smoking.'

Cameron arrives and is brought up to speed. 'I'm so sorry,' he says.

I don't mention weed again, worried Cameron will judge me for it.

We all move to the dinner table and Jess brings over some of the dishes. I keep looking at my phone on the table. No texts arrive. I text an old friend, Michael, to tell him Rachel and I have broken up. He replies immediately, shocked. He asks if he can message Rachel about it and I tell him he can.

As we eat, I start feeling guilty about the fight. I text Rachel and ask her where she is. She doesn't reply. I text Sharon and tell her Rachel and I have broken up and that I haven't heard from her. I start freaking out about where she is and what she might be doing. I start imagining terrible scenarios. Then, I hear back from Sharon. She has heard from Rachel. She doesn't tell me anything else.

A bit later, Sharon messages. *I really don't want to get in the middle of things. But I think you should come home and deal with this.*

Cameron tries to engage me in conversation, and I respond but I'm distracted. I look at my phone and see a message from Rachel.

It says, *What the fuck? Apparently we've broken up, but I'm the last to know that.*

I ask her if she'd like to talk. When I mention to the others that I'm going to go outside to talk to Rachel, Jess says okay, and Cameron asks if that is a good idea. I ignore him.

Rachel wants to know where I got the impression we broke up. I try to respond but have nothing coherent to say. I don't want our relationship to be over. I'm relieved to hear it isn't, but I have no words to explain why I thought it was. We decide to meet at home.

Cameron walks me out to my car. 'I hope everything is okay,' he says. 'You know, this is the first time you've ever said anything negative about your relationship. Conflict is healthy. It isn't possible to have a relationship without it.'

Even though I have been asking him for advice a lot lately, I don't appreciate his comment. I don't say anything. Rachel and I keep our issues private because we don't want people to judge our relationship. Rachel doesn't think it's anyone else's business. I used to think that, too.

* * *

Rachel returned to Australia less than a year after moving to the US, and we'd moved into an apartment in Sydney together. Our main companions were our pet rats and birds; Rachel had grown up with pet rats, lizards and hermit crabs. Watching her care for rescued animals – handling them with such gentleness – made me fall for her even harder. I knew, and loved, that a lesbian couple tending to a menagerie of animals was a stereotype.

We fit lots of the stereotypes about queer women couples, but we weren't connected to the queer community. We didn't feel comfortable tagging along to bars and clubs with my gay male friends, and the only lesbians we knew were our online friends from the Kitten Board, who all lived in the US. When we went to pride events, like the Mardi Gras or Fair Day, we mostly kept to ourselves, having a great time together but also conscious of the way everyone else was partying with their friends. We were both socially anxious.

I wanted to feel involved in the community and kept reading the events and nightlife section of the local lesbian magazine. It wasn't as important to Rachel. She doesn't drink alcohol, and many queer events are centred around drinking and clubbing. We tried out a bar in Darlinghurst with a night for queer women. As soon as we entered, we felt out of place; everyone seemed to know each other. Their clothing, like the bar's décor, was very trendy – all black, with silver adornments. We felt relieved when we left.

I kept an eye out for a very different type of event and eventually found it: a regional pride festival in the Blue Mountains. We booked two nights at a motel in Katoomba. We drank hot chocolates with marshmallows by the motel's fireplace, sneaking kisses. We were shy around the largely straight guests.

One night, we dressed up for the pride festival's lesbian bush dance. Rachel wore a plaid dress and I wore jeans and a flannel shirt. The crowd was much older than us, and we felt comfortable in their company. There wasn't a 'type', the way we had noticed in Sydney – there were butches and femmes, but also people who didn't seem to fit into any obvious category. It was reassuring, as we still didn't know where we fit into the community. The country music started and we took each other's hands. We tried to follow the steps for certain dances, but mainly held each other and twirled around the dance floor, laughing. It was our first time dancing together in public. On the way back to our motel, we saw people we'd met at the dance walking in the streets and waiting at the train station, and it felt like we'd found our way into a lesbian utopia; for one night, we were in the majority.

We returned to Sydney, buoyed by the experience in the mountains and ready to try the lesbian scene again. Not long after our return, there was an event called Dykes on Mics in Enmore, an alternative and queer-friendly area. We spent the night dancing, listening to a singing competition and managing our social awkwardness quite well.

When Rachel went to the bathroom, an older woman approached me. 'You're straight, aren't you?'

'Excuse me?' I replied.

'I can tell you're not into it, not the way she's into it.' She stretched her back and leaned forward. 'Get out of it while you can.'

I stood there, stunned. I had no idea what she was talking about. Rachel returned soon after and joined us. She smiled at us and shook hands with the woman. By then, the woman's partner had joined us. The three of them made small talk while I stood there trying to process her words. On our way home, I told Rachel what the woman had said to me.

'What the hell?' Rachel was furious. 'What the fuck is wrong with her? Is she projecting onto us from her own unhappy relationship?' She looked at me. 'You don't feel that way, do you?'

'God no!' I was equally furious. Since coming out, I had become more private and protective of our relationship and didn't want anyone else's opinions – whether they were family, friends or strangers.

After that, we stayed away from lesbian nights. We joked that the queer women we wanted to know were probably at home snuggled up on the couch, not out in the bars. We felt lonely and isolated, but took comfort in each other.

By the time we moved to Melbourne, ready for a change, we were convinced we didn't need queer community. We didn't feel that different from our straight friends. But each year, at the few queer events we attended, I looked around at the groups of friends and wished we could find where we fit in.

It took us years to realise how much work we needed to do if we wanted to be out and proud as a couple and as individuals. Rachel wasn't out at her first few teaching jobs in Melbourne. While I was out at work, I had intense anxiety, which led to other issues, like preferring to hide rather than have lunch or walk to the train station with a colleague.

I still have to stop myself from pulling away when Rachel reaches for my hand in public. I feel guilty: holding hands is significant to us. It was our first form of intimacy when we were shy teenagers. It's romantic, but also a way to communicate fear or insecurity, or to express a need for comfort or protection.

But instead of reaching for her, I let go of Rachel's hand if I feel unsafe. Even if there is no obvious danger, I find an excuse to let go after less than a minute. If she tries to kiss me in public, I make sure it's quick. After the rejection we experienced from certain family members in the early stages of our relationship, it can be hard for us to trust people. And now, with ongoing challenges around my mental health, I have managed to hurt Rachel, over and over, and made her unable to trust me.

* * *

I feel awkward when I park outside my house. I don't know what to expect. Thankfully, Sharon has gone to bed, leaving me and Rachel to talk.

We hug and talk quietly in our bedroom. Both of us cry. Rachel tells me how hurt she is that I told people we had broken up. I can see how fearful she is over the prospect of our relationship ending. I feel terrible – disgusted with myself – knowing that part of me wanted her to react like this. I want her to need me, to stay with me regardless of what I do.

'It wasn't your place to tell anyone, especially when we hadn't actually broken up,' she says. 'I'm still confused why you thought we had. None of your responses have explained that.'

'I don't know.' I remember telling her if she didn't get out of the car, our relationship was over. But my threat feels ridiculous now. I can't even remember what our fight had been about – let alone how it escalated. 'I just got so angry, so quickly.'

'Well, I wish you had talked to me rather than telling other people something that wasn't even true.'

I nod. 'I'm sorry. I'll message everyone I told.'

I send Michael a message first. He was devastated by the news earlier. *Just letting you know that we are not breaking up. We are working things out. I'm sorry for involving you by telling you. I should have talked to Rach first.*

I kind of figured that based on Rachel's reply when I messaged her, he replies.

Rachel and I talk for hours. The next morning, we kiss and hold each other.

'Poor Shaz,' Rachel says. 'It was bad for her, since she was kind of in the middle of it.'

'Yes, it would have been really bad and stressful for her,' I say. *And what about you?*, I want to say, *I'm sure it was worse for you*, but I don't have the guts to ask.

Sharon returns to the States. The mood at home is still tense. Despite Rachel's urging, I don't go to see Karyn. I feel misunderstood, like Karyn judged me, Rachel and Sharon during our last appointment. Perhaps she doesn't understand the idea of found family: that the three of us built our own family structure to support and protect ourselves.

Also, it's clear to me that I have some sort of mood disorder, even if Karyn and the psychiatrists I have seen don't think so. Whether my current energy and excitement is mania, hypomania, an 'elevated' mood – as one psychiatrist called it – or all in my head, I intend to enjoy it. I don't want therapy to interfere.

I continue to do things that are out of character for me, like signing up to read at a queer erotica literary event at Hares & Hyenas, the queer bookshop in Fitzroy. I delay writing my piece until the day of the event, and only start writing when Rachel reminds me we have to leave soon. She's stressed about how late it is, knowing I tend to be late to everything even at the best of times. I have a bath and scribble my piece in a notebook. It comes out of me, onto the page, with barely any effort.

I feel beyond energised, as though I could write thousands of words in my current state if left to my own devices. I jump out with just enough time to type out the piece, email it to myself, throw on clothing and leave.

We arrive late and I ask the bookshop owners to print my piece for me. I apologise, realising all of a sudden how disorganised I must seem, but they don't seem bothered.

I order a glass of white wine and drink it as they print my piece. It's hot and I'm flushed, the wine only warming me further, but I don't care. Usually, the set-up at Hares & Hyenas makes me nervous and exacerbates my social anxiety. It gets so crowded at events, which take place in one long room without any private nooks; you can see people wherever you look. But tonight, I enjoy being on display. I wipe sweat off my brow, grin and chat to everyone I know, and introduce myself to a few strangers.

My piece is about sex, masturbation and grief, and I share stories that I generally keep private. I know how nervous I would usually feel when reading a piece on stage, let alone a piece about my sex life and masturbation habits, which I would never thought I'd be prepared to share, but I am oddly confident, fuelled by adrenaline.

After the event, Rachel and I talk to some of the performers. It's nice to speak to them after sharing intimate stories on stage together. Not sure what to talk about first, I focus on the terrible fear of spiders one writer shared in his piece. I seize on it and start babbling about everything that comes to mind.

'I recently read Alison Bechdel's *Are You My Mother?* and there's amazing stuff about arachnophobia and mothers in it. She—' I pause, noticing Rachel and our friends staring at me. 'What?' I ask, confused.

They look at each other and don't say anything, so I continue.

'It was so funny to realise that spiders are meant to represent mothers, because the other night I went to put on a dressing gown that Rach's mother gave her and a spider jumped out. Like, my mother-in-law was *right there* in our bedroom with us!'

Nobody responds and I look at the writer. His face is bright red.

Afterwards, Rachel tells me it was quite obvious that he wasn't comfortable right from the start of the conversation, but I hadn't picked up on any of his cues.

Mood

I try to take something away from the experience, that just because a writer shares something on a stage or page, it doesn't mean they necessarily want to talk about it. Especially if it's about their deepest fear.

* * *

Back at school for Term 4, I'm as energetic as I was in the school holidays. I'd thought that my energy during Sharon's visit was because I didn't have to teach, but now I'm up at 4 am every day and filled with ideas. I write and speak to friends and often end up late to school despite having woken up four hours before I need to be there.

At first, I'm thrilled to be feeling good. I drink more coffee than usual. I follow it up with cups of tea and stop counting how many I have at school. I buy chocolates from our staff fridge and eat them between classes. My students love my energy and excitement.

My Year 7 class, who are now nearly Year 8s and have become confident and challenging, joke with me constantly.

'Miss, what music do you like listening to?' one asks me.

'I like Beyoncé,' I reply. 'I'm obsessed with *Lemonade* and listen to it every day on my way to school.'

'Can we listen to *Lemonade* while we work?' he asks. 'Please?'

'The lyrics aren't appropriate for the classroom,' I say, running two of my favourites through my head.

'That's fine!' he says. 'We're mature!'

I agree to playing some songs, at low volume, and they cheer. 'You're the best, Miss!'

Another student tells me one of their teachers looks like a monster when she's angry.

'Don't talk badly about your teachers,' I say to them, then turn to face the whiteboard so that I can laugh without them seeing.

When I meet up with my friend Lisa for coffees or quick chats between classes, I no longer have to press my lips together to hold off the tears when she asks how teaching is going. 'It's going well,' I tell her with surprise.

Rachel and I have a lot of fun together when we're not fighting. I start buying items in a kind of frenzy, including a never-ending series of reusable coffee cups, birthday cards and sparkly gift bags. Rachel is surprised by my shopping choices, but isn't concerned until I start buying costly items with abandon, like a completely unnecessary chest of drawers with a painting of a deer on it.

It's exciting to feel energetic again after so many depressive periods. I enjoy being flirtatious and am convinced of sexual innuendo in many conversations with friends and colleagues. But I am often confused, vague or foggy. Sometimes I go out by myself and can't completely account for my time away from the house. The only evidence I've been out is on my clothing – which smells of cigarette smoke, alcohol or marijuana – and I buy Glen 20 and a heavy-scented sports spray-on deodorant to keep in the car. My behaviour changes quickly and steeply. I do things that I can't write about, because I hurt Rachel enough when I did them. I don't want to do further harm by recreating those betrayals on the page. I'm also aware that in trying to be respectful now, I am also being evasive. I force the truth down, tucking the secrets away in my heart and feeling them occasionally in my gut.

* * *

Despite some great weeks at school, I am starting to struggle again. I'm fixated on some of the issues I notice, from the school's behaviour management policy to the school counsellor's unavailability to students in need. Sometimes I feel more like an undercover journalist gathering evidence of systemic issues in the public education system than an educator. Once I collect the evidence, I don't know what to do with it.

I put so much energy into worrying about these issues that I don't have much left for everything else. I find it difficult to manage writing lesson plans and teaching, let alone all the administrative aspects of the job – remembering to turn up for yard duty, organising school excursions, preparing for parent-teacher meetings, filling in report cards, getting my marking done on time – and fitting all of this in alongside excessive staff meetings.

I call Susan, the psychiatrist my GP referred me to. I ignore Cameron's concerns about her suitability. It's not hard to disregard them, as I've started feeling strange about my friendship with Cameron and the dynamic between us. I've noticed how I keep seeking validation from him, as though he is my therapist. I keep oversharing with him, desperate to hear words of comfort and support. I can't work out – and to this day, am still not sure – whether he was just trying to help me and didn't see our boundaries becoming murky. Or did it give him a sense of power and authority? Maybe it was both.

The receptionist sounds terse when I give him my name. 'Yes, I remember,' he says. 'You cancelled your first consultation with Susan. Can I ask why you want to book it now?'

I provide a very simple explanation of what happened with Cameron. 'I see,' he says, sounding bemused.

A few weeks later, I take the train to Richmond to see the psychiatrist. I'm nervous about how the appointment will go, and keep thinking about the classes I'm missing in order to attend. Her consultation room is in a historic terrace house. It looks appealing from the outside.

Susan seems to dislike me from the start. She asks a series of rapid-fire questions, and eventually can't hold back from asking, 'Can you please tell me what happened with your appointment? My assistant summarised the situation but I'd like to hear it in your own words.'

'Oh okay, sure.' I tell her about the conversation with Cameron, leaving his name out. I see fire in her eyes.

Susan is not The One. She runs through what feels like a checklist of questions, barely making eye contact. I share some revealing things about my recent behaviour, which she doesn't engage with apart from asking me which of the behaviours are unusual for me.

At the end of the appointment she tells me two things. The first is that she has diagnosed me with having a personality disorder.

I start to cry. 'Which one?' *Oh please, please don't be borderline.*

'Borderline personality disorder.'

I cry harder, unable to hold back my emotions. I haven't considered that I might have borderline personality disorder, but as soon as she mentioned a personality disorder, I could only think of that one. One of Rachel's family members has borderline personality disorder, and I have only ever heard harrowing, devastating information about the symptoms, treatment and outcomes. Susan doesn't tell me what I want to hear most: that I'm going to be okay.

The second thing is that she is not going to be able to continue seeing me as a patient. Due to what happened with Cameron, she does not feel comfortable. 'I will not be able to separate you from what I believe was a transgression of boundaries.'

Unlike what I've been doing with my loved ones, I'm not able to vent any of my anger, frustration or sadness to Susan. I feel like she has ripped open my wounds and left me on the operating table.

I pay the ridiculously high initial consultation fee and walk out in a daze. I call Rachel and sob while she tries to ask me questions.

'She diagnosed me with borderline,' I say.

'Okay.' Rachel sounds calm. Her voice is soothing. 'Come home, sweetie.'

'I don't know what to do,' I say. 'I have class in an hour. My phone has only got three per cent battery left. I can't book an Uber.'

'Let me—'

My phone runs out of battery and switches off. I walk the streets of Richmond in disbelief. It takes me a while to remember I can take a taxi and that Rachel can pay when I get home. Once I'm in a taxi, I think about Susan. I wonder why she even bothered to see me once she found out about the situation with Cameron and made the decision not to take me on as a patient. Her diagnosis was presented quickly and brutally, like a punishment. I question her professionalism. Her duty of care. I think about the way she left me on my own after I received a diagnosis that terrified me. She did not hold space for me: just dumped me, like I used to find myself dumped by the waves at Bondi Beach as a child.

Chapter 11

I give up on psychiatry for a while. Instead, I decide to investigate my mental illness like I am solving a mystery: go back to the beginning and locate fragments, then figure out what they mean and how they fit together. I have to become an anthropologist working on a dig where something terrible happened, a forensic scientist looking at DNA from the scene of a crime, or an engineer trying to understand why a bridge collapsed. I know I'm not okay, but *why?*

Occasionally, I wonder if there is some truth to Susan's diagnosis. When I look up borderline personality disorder online, it is characterised by an unstable sense of self, inappropriate anger and an intense fear of abandonment. The words 'inappropriate anger' make me feel angry in a way I believe is entirely appropriate; I've read that far more women are diagnosed with borderline personality disorder than men. Women's anger is often considered less appropriate than men's, even when it stems from larger societal oppressions. I find 'abandonment' surprising – I wasn't aware I had abandonment issues before the diagnosis. It starts to make sense to me, though, and I wonder if a diagnosis is self-producing. Maybe I've inherited a whole new collection of symptoms.

Rachel does some research, too, and discovers some support groups online for partners and spouses of people with the disorder. It is helpful for both of us to have a wider understanding of the diagnosis, even though we thought we knew a lot about it. In one of the groups, people talk about having relatively stable relationships apart for a sudden, unexpected shift in their partner that they refer to as 'the fuckening'. The first time I hear the word, I cringe, but I relate to the burst of intense rage it refers to.

I make an appointment to see Karyn. I respect her opinion and want to know what she thinks of my diagnosis. I'm not scared of psychologists; they don't have the power psychiatrists have to enforce compulsory treatment in a hospital under a legal Treatment Order.

When it is time to leave for my appointment, I tell Rachel I don't think I can go. I'm scared of what Karyn will say when I tell her about Susan's diagnosis, and worry she has been thinking I have the disorder for years.

'Even if I do go, there's no way I can deal with public transport right now,' I say, feeling a lump in my throat and starting to tear up. Lately, I've been finding it hard to deal with trains and trams – the proximity to strangers, the intimacy of knees pressing up against each other, the quizzical looks on people's faces if you do anything out of the norm.

'What if you drive there?' Rachel suggests. 'We still have Jess's car.'

'I don't want to be away from you and Rosie. Can you come with me?' I feel pathetic asking this, but it strikes me, suddenly, as the only option if I want to go through with my appointment.

'Would you be allowed to bring Rosie in with you?'

'I don't know.'

I call the clinic and the receptionist hesitates when I ask if I can bring my dog to my appointment. She puts me on hold, then comes back to tell me that Karyn said it was fine, but Rosie would have to stay out in the waiting room.

Once I'm in Karyn's room, I feel silly when I think about Rachel and Rosie in the plush waiting room outside. Karyn doesn't say anything about it, which I appreciate.

'What's going on for you, Roz?'

'I've been particularly distressed since I went to see a psychiatrist recently.' I tell her about the ill-fated session with Susan. 'She diagnosed me with borderline personality disorder and I've been furious ever since. But sometimes, when I do something vengeful, in anger, I think *Oh, that's why I got diagnosed.*'

Karyn scrunches up her face as she listens.

'Roz, you know I'm not a psychiatrist, and I'm not able to make a diagnosis, but I worked with many patients with BPD when I was a psychiatric nurse and I am really struggling to understand why she thought you have it. I've worked with you for over two years now and I haven't seen any signs of it whatsoever.'

Rather than feeling comforted by her words, I'm more confused. She seems as certain as Susan did when she diagnosed me.

'For now, I'd like to keep seeing you,' I say. 'And then maybe I'll get a second opinion at some point.'

She nods. 'Of course. How have you been going otherwise?'

'Next week will be Deda and Jenny's Yahrzeits, the one-year anniversary of their deaths.'

'How are you feeling about that?'

'I can't believe it has been a year. I don't know. I'm a bit numb, I suppose. Also, it's strange that their deaths will always be tied together for me.'

I don't mention their Yahrzeits will coincide with a supermoon, which I've been obsessing about. According to NASA, this November's full moon will be the closest one we've had in the twenty-first century. A supermoon looks huge, I discover, because the moon has become full on the same day as its perigee: the point in its orbit when it is closest to earth.

* * *

On the day of Deda's Yahrzeit, I feel sad but I don't cry. I want to, but even if I had privacy, I don't think I would be able to. School is buzzing as the results from the US election start coming in that morning.

'Ms Bellamy, it looks like Trump might win,' one of my Year 9 students tells me, showing me the electoral college map.

'No way!' He explains his analysis to me, and I think he has a career ahead of him as a politician or an election analyst.

In my breaks that day, I keep to myself, ignoring the chatter about Trump.

Instead, I let painful memories flood through my mind, including a visit to Sydney when Deda didn't recognise me at all. I remembered the ways I had tried to cheer myself up. I'd walked to a flashy new shopping centre and looked at makeup in a few shops, wondering if covering my face would help push aside my sadness. I heard a commotion and looked around. A group of security guards were making their way over to a woman who was screaming. They pounced on her. I watched as police arrived and added to the throng around the woman, who was writhing on the ground and continuing to scream. I wanted to scream, too, but couldn't.

I had also wandered into a grocery store, hoping for something sweet to distract me. The plump, bright mangos for sale were soft and fragrant, unlike the hard, green ones back in Melbourne. I bought an oddly shaped mango and retreated to the hostel I had booked near Central Station. It was 36 degrees, and my tiny private room had no air-conditioning or fan.

Writing helped me process my feelings, so I'd opened my laptop and written out the interaction I'd had with Deda. It spilled onto the page and once it was out, I saved and closed the document. I ripped into the mango – I'd forgotten to buy a spoon or knife – and ate the sweet flesh, crying and shuddering.

The next morning, I'd boarded the first bus from Central Station with the word 'beach' in neon letters. I didn't really care which beach it was. The ocean had always brought comfort when I needed it.

I exited the bus as soon as I saw the first strip of turquoise through some trees, and made my way through a park and down some steps to Clovelly Beach. It's where I used to go as a child with Baba and Deda, for a dunk on a hot day. Deda used to sit on the sand in a prim linen shirt and tailored trousers, while Baba and I waded in the shallows, remarking at the different species of fish.

There weren't many people at the beach on a weekday morning. I stripped off my clothes and went in, smiling at a mother and her baby. Eventually, I left the water and sat on the sand, but then felt the need to return: to submerge myself again before leaving. As I lowered my body back into the water, I felt completely peaceful. I drew myself out slowly, reluctantly. I threw clothing on over my wet bathers and sat at the bus stop, trying to process my swim. I pulled a notepad out of my bag and wrote for a while. On the way back to the hostel, I listened to Jeff Buckley, whose music I often turn to when I'm sad – it helps me process my feelings.

I posted on Facebook about the experience later that day. *Sometimes, to contend with intense experiences, you need to visit a body of water, submerge, then surface, write a poem and listen to Jeff Buckley.*

My friend, Jenny, commented that I'd had a *Jeff Buckley mikvah*. A mikvah is intended to be purifying, to deepen one's spirituality and introspection. I realised my swim had felt like the Jewish ritual immersion, even if it didn't follow the religious requirements. Swimming always felt nurturing to me, but this swim was different. Though I hadn't consciously meant for it to be a healing mikvah, it had felt intentional. I had been intrigued by the concept of the mikvah since I married Rachel, as I'd grown up with the knowledge that Jewish women are meant to go to the mikvah before getting married.

Most of the mikva'ot in Australia are Orthodox-run. I've read accounts of immersion that describe the mikvah as transformative, evoking some sort of metamorphosis. I love the sound of transformation and metamorphosis, but first I'd have to get past the mikvah attendant, and assumptions around gender and sexuality.

Thankfully, a mikvah doesn't have to take place indoors. Oceans are valid mikva'ot. I have immersed myself, or been immersed, in oceans since I was a baby. In my life, water means play, ritual and rebirth, as well as self-care and self-soothing. It's a privilege.

Unlike organised religious rites, an ocean mikvah can take place on my terms, with the sound of the waves and birds, the smell of salt and seaweed, and a sense of embodiment and safety that doesn't require anyone's approval. I knew I might never find a formalised mikvah that suited me but that I would always turn to water to mark transition and change. Water carries me – my identity, my quirks, my questions – the way it has carried my grief and sadness many times before.

The following month, my family and I had travelled to Sydney together to see Deda, whose health was declining.

We stopped for the night in Mittagong. I realised during the drive that I felt unsure about how much to talk around my family. During my childhood, I was often called a chatterbox, so I felt sensitive about speaking too much. But it frustrated me to keep my mouth closed. I spent two decades with my mouth closed – part of that time with braces pulling my teeth in the right directions and the rest with an internal voice, a wannabe saviour, pulling my whole jaw tightly together for safety at school. I wondered if that was why I wasn't truly honest with Karyn, my family or friends, or even Rachel. Maybe I feared judgement if I unleashed everything that was going on inside.

In Sydney, we shared an apartment in Lane Cove, near Deda's nursing home. Deda had lost a lot of weight, and Mum suggested some foods he might like. Jess mentioned borscht, and his face lit up. Back at the apartment, we worked together in the kitchen chopping the vegetables we'd bought: beetroots, onions, cabbage, carrots, potatoes, garlic and dill. I liked to think we were imbuing the food with love and hopes for Deda's recovery. We tasted it. The punch of the garlic and onion, the earthiness of the beetroots and potatoes, and the dill, which always brought back happy times from my childhood, cheered me up. It reminded me of family gatherings at Baba and Deda's apartment, eating ruby red borscht – dangerously – on a lacy white tablecloth. Baba adding the right amount of dill and a dab of sour cream, delighting in our enjoyment.

We turned up with borscht in plastic containers, and Deda looked pleased. The nursing home mostly fed the residents bland Anglo food, and we had wondered if the lack of flavour was further putting him off eating. He went to try the borscht but we worried it was too hot, because of his medical issues. We fussed over getting the borscht exactly right. Mum and I stirred in some sour cream to cool down the soup and handed him a spoon of it, but he couldn't recognise the taste. It was too rich and creamy. Then Jess played around with quantities and managed to get it right. He smiled. 'Very tasty,' he said. He couldn't swallow more than a few sips.

When I'd headed to the airport to return to Melbourne, I sat at the gate for my flight, surrounded by people who seemed to be excited about flying. I felt guilty and scared that Deda would die before I came back. I called Rachel and cried over the phone.

'Baby, you should stay if you feel you need to.'

'At least I'll get to be with you. I miss you so much.'

'I miss you too. But do whatever is right for you, okay?'

The tenderness in her voice took me back to when I found out that Baba, Deda's wife, was dying, just over a decade ago. Back then, I had no way of coping with death. I was the bad friend who had pretended not to get the message when one of my friends lost her own grandmother. It was easier to play dumb later than to be real. 'I had no idea!' I exclaimed months later, after deluding myself that her grief had subsided. And then Baba had died, and I had to navigate a new low I hadn't been able to imagine before.

As I boarded the flight, I felt desperate for comfort. I messaged Rachel, who was at work, and then reached out to Sharon. Despite living across the world from each other, when shit gets real, we turn to each other for comfort.

That night, I lay in bed with one hand to my heart, awake for hours while Rachel slept beside me, my other hand in hers. I felt each beat of my heart against my palm. If I breathed deeply enough or slowly enough, the panic might go away, or so I had been told by my GP and my psychologist. I worried that my heart rhythm was irregular, that maybe my thyroid was acting up again.

The panic didn't go. I inhaled and exhaled, feeling the breath attempting to soothe my body. But it barely made an impact. My heart and ribs felt tight, unyielding. They didn't want to be soothed. They wanted to be tight, nervous, painful. The constancy of my pain was the only thing that seemed to soothe, oddly.

Another memory comes to mind: the day after Deda's death. After flying to Sydney, my family had piled into my uncle and aunt's car. Six of us needed to fit in the small hatchback, so my aunt lay across our laps in the back. We laughed madly, the way grieving people do. My uncle drove us straight to the Chevra Kadisha, the Jewish organisation responsible for looking after deceased people and handling burials. I stared at the sign at the front that said *Do not shake hands with the mourners.*

My cousin had organised for his family's rabbi to run Deda's service. When I found out he was Orthodox, I panicked and messaged Jenny. I'd first met Jenny through her partner Joel, who I went to school with from kindergarten (when he was my boyfriend) to Year 12. When I met Jenny for the first time, she said 'Oh, you're Joel's lesbian ex!'

At first, I'd thought of outspoken, feisty Jenny as 'Joel's partner'. We became good friends quickly, after she and Joel relocated to Melbourne for his new job.

I knew Jenny would understand my fears and be able to tell me what I needed to know about the rabbi handling Deda's funeral. She had interrogated most rabbis in Sydney, and now Melbourne, on their political views, especially on LGBTQ rights and their stance on Israel/Palestine.

'Which rabbi is it?'

When I told her, she replied, 'To add insult to injury.'

'Why?'

'Oh, he's a Chabadnik, that's all – you know the deal. Sexist, etc. etc. Drinks too much too.'

'Exactly what I imagined. Rach will be there with me. Time to confront my issues with Orthodoxy once and for all.'

'If there are difficulties, tell me exactly what happens and I will thoroughly enjoy tearing strips off him. I'll be virtual-hugging you all through.'

When we met the Rabbi, he asked each of us who we were so he could define our relationship to Deda. I didn't hesitate when I introduced Rachel as 'my partner.' He baulked.

The next day, at Deda's grave, Rachel stood by my side, holding my hand in front of all my elderly relatives. It wasn't to ruffle feathers or make a statement, but to help me get through the burial. When close family and friends were invited to come up and throw a spade of soil into the grave, Rachel joined in.

After Deda's funeral, Rachel and I went down to Coogee Beach. Rachel encouraged me to swim, right then and there in my bra and undies, while she sat with my clothing. I ran into the water, unfazed by the sunbathers and onlookers. The ocean felt warm and nurturing, and I frolicked in the waves, twisting onto my back and then front.

I thought about Deda and how much he loved the ocean. He used to drive to Bondi Beach, park his car and watch the waves. I never accompanied him for one of these trips. I don't know how long he spent there or what he thought about. Maybe he thought of his hometown, Odesa, the port city on the Black Sea.

That evening, Rachel and I stayed close together during Deda's minyan. I introduced her to some of my extended family, including some of the older women. I'd previously kept these parts of my life separate.

We talked to my cousin's kids. The older boy was a keen surfer learning surf rescue in the Nippers. He talked about how much he loved sport at school – the same school where PE had given me panic attacks. He seemed well-adjusted and I wondered if it was because he was a generation further down the family tree from our family's World War II traumas. It was interesting that while he was strong and sporty, so unlike me, we both loved the water. I wondered if my children would be like him, if I ever trusted myself enough to have them. I worried about my unpredictable moods.

After the rabbi recited the blessings, he asked if anyone wanted to say anything about Deda. Nobody offered to speak, until I did. I attempted to communicate my loss in a short speech about his kind, gentle and protective nature. He'd always reminded us that the speed limit near his apartment was 40 kilometres per hour, and to lock our car doors. He checked if we were cold no matter what the weather was like. And he fed and chatted to the birds, everywhere that he lived.

As the minyan continued, I realised I'd always thought that the affectionate nicknames Baba and Deda used for me – Rozhinke, meaning 'raisin' in Yiddish, Solnishka, meaning 'little sun' in Russian, and Malinkaya, meaning 'little one' in Russian – would be permanent fixtures in my identity. I wasn't fluent in Russian or Yiddish, but knew the words of endearment.

When we returned to the apartment we were staying in with my family, I messaged Jenny to tell her about Deda's funeral. We had a long discussion about Judaism, sexuality and death. She understood without me having to justify anything, and I cried and vented. Then she texted, *baby crying xx*. I didn't hear back from her, but was too distracted and sad to wonder why.

After a few intense days of grieving Deda in close proximity to my family members, I decided it was time for me to leave Sydney, but I wasn't ready to return to Melbourne.

Months earlier, I had booked a trip to Adelaide to attend a conference. It wasn't for work or uni; it just appealed to me, partly because of the name. It was called the Homosexual Histories conference, which sounded quaint and, frankly, adorable. I'd emailed the organisers to cancel my registration after Deda's death, but as the week progressed in Sydney, I started to think it was a good idea to get away.

On a 6 am flight to Adelaide, I stared out at the rippled layers of clouds beyond the window. I couldn't stop looking at them, taking photographs – unable to focus on my book or the in-flight entertainment – and thinking about Deda. It hit me that my grandparents' deaths had taught me how to grieve loved ones, and I saw this is a final act of love. I cried openly on the flight, not caring that the man seated on my left was looking at me.

When I arrived, I took a taxi to the conference venue and stored my bag at the registration desk. I made it in time to hear the Welcome to Country given by a Kaurna/Ngarrindjeri elder. I had never been to the lands of the Kaurna people and felt so pleased to be there, to let go of my grief, if only for minutes.

In the evening, I lay down at my serviced apartment near Chinatown, listening to music, when a message came in from Joel. He said there had been a terrible accident with Jenny's medication. She was brain dead. It was worded simply and succinctly, and I had to read it a few times to fully comprehend what had happened.

I called him, not knowing what to say or offer. He told me the basics through his shock. She had been in a coma for a few days, after overdosing on her medication on Tuesday night. That was the night I last spoke to her.

When we hung up, I thought about how furious Jenny would be. That she would miss out on critical, beautiful years with her young family. Also, that this had happened to her in Melbourne, a place where she had never felt at home. She'd missed her beloved Sydney beaches. It was beyond unfair; it was cruel.

Eventually, I had to stop.

Instead, I played a film reel in my head, focusing on her kindness, intellect and passion, and on how much she had loved Joel and her two young daughters. I took deep breaths, thinking about the way she was blunt as fuck but served hordes of friends dinners flavoured with love and warmth.

I called Rachel and sobbed, unable to speak after I broke the news. As she comforted me, she shifted into planning mode, deciding to take the train to Adelaide. She booked it as we talked and told me she would arrive the next day. She told me to do something nice that night to try to distract myself.

Outside, Adelaide looked normal. It wasn't dark yet, at nearly 8 pm, and I strolled through Chinatown, trying to think of something to do. Jacaranda blossomed all around the city. I paced the streets, filled with rage and sorrow.

I messaged Rachel's sister. Their family had lived in Adelaide when they first moved to Australia. I asked her if she knew anyone there who could get me drugs. *I don't*, she texted. *Why don't you go and drink instead?*

I looked around, madly, and saw a sign for adult entertainment. *I'm thinking more along the lines of strippers*. The thought of breaking my own rules, living outside of my usual brain and body, was the only thing that distracted me from my pain. I didn't do any of the things I wanted to. I went back to bed and cried.

I woke to the news of the Paris terror attacks. I couldn't stop reading about the victims killed and injured, as I waited for Rachel's train to come in. As people applied the French flag colours as a filter to their profile pictures, posted with the hashtags #JeSuisParis and #PrayForParis, I saw Islamophobic articles and sentiments spreading. I thought about how Jenny always posted a clear-eyed, no-bullshit summary of current events.

Rachel arrived that afternoon. Seeing and touching her calmed me down and reduced my anger. We hugged for a long time. 'What do you want to do, love?' she asked.

'Well, I was thinking maybe we should go to the parade.' The conference I'd attended had been deliberately timed to coincide with the Adelaide Pride March. I thought it might be a nice distraction. When we arrived, there was a Christian group protesting. Again, I thought of Jenny, and imagined how she would have reacted.

We spent a few days in Adelaide. Jenny's funeral was delayed: her body was still with the coroner. I didn't see any point in flying home early.

Each morning, I bolted awake at 5 am, showered and made a cup of tea. I felt impatient as I waited for Rachel to wake up. I wanted to talk to her. Instead, I called friends who were early risers. Ari was also devastated by Jenny's death and we discussed ways of remembering her.

When I spoke to Cameron, his response was different. He didn't know Jenny but had made assumptions about her death based on what he knew about her. 'An overdose is the ultimate attack on the body,' he told me. 'I've read enough coroners' reports to know suicide is the most common explanation.'

His comments compounded my grief, adding an element I didn't want to think about. After our call, I felt devastated. Why hadn't I argued with him? Perhaps I believed his professional experience in mental health made him an expert.

* * *

Jenny's funeral was held at Emanuel Synagogue, the shule she loved, where I had wanted Deda's funeral to be held. When I arrived, I saw the long hearse parked in the driveway outside the synagogue where I'd had my bat mitzvah. I approached Joel, Jenny's partner, and we both wept as we hugged.

Joel's eulogy was beautiful, poetic and rich with detail; he managed to make us laugh and sob in equal measure. He said, 'Jenny's life was vast and deep, restless and constantly forceful, like the ocean she loved madly. Jenny seemed to have many lives, glimpsed, like the ocean, from disparate perspectives, mysterious and never viewable in full, though bound up as one organism. Growing up, she visited the beach daily, regardless of weather – Coogee Beach, I should say, for none could substitute. She was at home in the water, and would use her buoyancy to just lie back and nap.'

We baked in the sun and thirty-seven-degree heat at the cemetery. Someone joked Jenny was turning us into pita bread.

Her minyan, held at Joel's mother's house, was packed with family, friends and people I knew from the Jewish community. The last time I went to that house, I'd told Jenny I felt uncomfortable around one of the old friends I was there to catch up with. She'd acted so awkwardly around Rachel, I thought she was homophobic.

'Trust me, I have interrogated each of these people about their beliefs,' Jenny assured me at the time. 'If anyone had expressed any homophobic sentiments, I would have kicked them out of the house.'

I smiled at the bittersweet memory.

After the prayers were recited, the Rabbi invited us to share a few words. I didn't want to speak; I wanted to keep patting the traumatised former pig-hunting dog Jenny had so loved. He had been hurt badly by humans.

When nobody agreed to speak, I stepped forward, just as I had at Deda's funeral. This time, it was because I could imagine Jenny using the opportunity for a monologue, either theatrical or political.

'I need to begin with a disclaimer that Jenny was never one to bite her tongue. Instead of speaking sentimentally about her, which she would hate, I will talk about the issues she was passionate about.' My hands shook but my voice was steady as I talked about Palestine, LGBTQ rights, and other social and political issues.

Later, I went to the beach to think about Deda and Jenny. I thought about Jenny coining the 'Jeff Buckley Mikvah', which lodged itself in my brain. I remembered Jenny once writing on Facebook: *Coogee is my best place, my home, my favourite place in the universe. I know every rock on that coastline. One day I'll become King of Coogee and then I'll throw all the horrible new bogan-gone-posh incomers out and I'll demolish all the buildings from the sea to Brook street.*

I wanted to think Jenny was the King of Coogee now, even if her body was buried inland, on the other side of Sydney.

After death, a Jewish body is washed, purified and dressed by volunteer members of the Chevra Kadisha, the Jewish burial society, in a process called tahara, which involves a flow of water analogous to a mikvah, followed by the words, '(S)he is pure, (s)he is pure, '(s)he is pure'.

I liked to imagine Jenny had so many ocean mikva'ot that the words, 'she is pure, she is pure, she is pure' echoed around her long before her own tahara and burial.

Back home, after the funerals, I felt my anger grow. I was furious with myself for not being there when Deda died and for not having been more physically present in Jenny's life. I believed I had failed them.

I raged at various people in my life for what I perceived as their lack of understanding and support. I wrote an article instructing people on how to talk to family, friends or colleagues when they lose someone they love, acknowledging I had once lied to my friend who was grieving her grandmother. I woke up before dawn most days and spoke to my closest friends for hours, often while Rachel was still asleep. Or I wrote. I ran out of energy in the afternoons and wept or slept.

I visited my family once a week, taking the train across Melbourne. I knew Mum wanted to see me more, but I didn't have more to give.

When I wasn't angry, I felt a sense of pride about some of the recent changes I had noticed in myself. I hadn't tried to hide my relationship from all the elderly relatives by pulling away from Rachel at Deda's funeral. I had brought up queer issues, refugees and Palestine in front of a room that included conservative older Jewish people, instead of saying sentimental things about Jenny that she would have rolled her eyes at. I was getting better at setting boundaries with my family and my in-laws and at trying to figure out what I wanted instead of giving in to what others wanted from me.

I had attributed this to mourning overshadowing my usual feelings and impulses. But I also wondered if I had finally moved on from feeling like I had to hide – if I had started believing it was possible to be open about my identity and have strong political views. That it wouldn't necessarily preclude the relationships I had with friends, family, my in-laws or the Jewish community. My new, hard, confident exterior could co-exist with my past self. And if people had a problem with that, it would no longer hurt me the way it used to.

**

A year after Deda and Jenny's deaths, near the end of my first year of teaching, I don't want to deal with my grief, or Trump becoming the next US president, so I focus on the upcoming supermoon. I look up when the last full moon and supermoon was so close to the earth and discover it was in January 1948. I wonder what Deda was doing then, just after World War II and a week after his twenty-second birthday. I hope he looked up at the moon, but I wouldn't be surprised if he hadn't. He had returned to Odesa after fleeing the Nazis, and found his family's home taken over, their possessions gone.

The next full supermoon will take place in 2034. I'll be fifty. If I get the chance to see it, I hope I'll be more settled then, and more able to follow the flow of seasons, moon phases, tides and my moods.

It's easy to distract myself like this: the news outlets I read are hyping up the supermoon, interviewing experts and telling the public where to gather in order to observe it. This includes east-facing beaches, mountains, tall buildings and hills. It all seems eerily appropriate. While Deda liked to look at the waves from his car, Jenny's dream was to listen to Tchaikovsky's Violin Concerto in D Major at the beach during a sunset and 'swoon with the sheer ridiculous beauty of it all'.

When I first found out the supermoon would take place on the anniversary of Jenny's death, I laughed. I thought she would have appreciated the symbolism. She probably would have had made some reference to paganism. But on the day of the supermoon, I change my mind: Jenny would have hated the idea of using the moon as a metaphor to mourn her. She hated hagiography, the idolising of the dead as saints. She would have been bemused at any attempts to view her death symbolically, rather than what it was: a waste.

On the evening of the supermoon, I see social media posts of people gathering at dusk and think of Jenny: she would have gone to Coogee Beach to listen to classical music, drink gin, and go skinny dipping.

I don't have it in me to go out. Instead, I go to the street and stare up at the sky. It's not an ocean view, but the natural world renews my reserves of hope, peace and calm. It's magic, just when I need it most. For a brief moment, I let go of everything else.

Chapter 12

The 2017 school year starts ten days after the Bourke Street Rampage, where a man drove his car deliberately into pedestrians on a busy city street in Melbourne. My students are disturbed by the footage they've seen all over the news. In Year 10 English, our first unit is on persuasive language, giving us an opportunity to delve into the attack. As I display a news article and listen to my students' responses to the emotive language in the headline, I'm proud of how savvy they are about the media – and of myself for persisting with this challenging career.

On my birthday, a week into Term 1, Rachel gives me a rainbow necklace. It takes me a second to recognise it as the one I admired at the new age shop in Carlton last year, when my mood was elevated.

I smile. 'Thank you!' She has a level of care and attention to detail that I believe I lack. I feel guilty and grateful at once, making it hard to feel I deserve Rachel's gift.

I'm teaching English this year. I'm so much more confident teaching texts, language and analysis than I was teaching Humanities. But I'm back to panicking before each class and I miss the period where I felt comfortable in the classroom. My imagination is good at creating worst-case scenarios, both in my nightmares and in the staffroom before class. Once I start the lesson, I realise that things are fine.

In the staff room, other teachers complain about the same behaviour challenges I face. Last year, I felt my struggles were unique. Now, I only have to give a student a pointed look, or threaten to hold everyone back to finish the lesson during the break, and I'm able to get things back under control. The main difference is that I am not constantly scared.

I catch a Year 8 student taking photos to send to a friend.

'No, Miss,' she argues, 'there's no photo. See?'

'Yes,' I reply, 'because you're using SnapChat. The whole *idea* is that it disappears.'

'Miss, I can't believe you know about SnapChat!'

As I get to know my Year 10 students, I get to know their politics too. When they present persuasive speeches, one of the girls argues there is no such thing as a gender pay gap. Some of the boys in the class cheer her on, and laugh as another female student presents a speech about feminism and the pay gap. While I might have been unsure about how to navigate this last year, now I sit back and allow the students to engage in deep debate, redirecting it occasionally if needed, only reining it in if it gets out of hand.

The school administration sends out surveys to students and asks for feedback on their teachers. In my first year, I could barely bring myself to look at how my students rated me. I was scared. This time, I'm excited to read them. I see lots of five out of fives, particularly under 'expertise' and 'approachability'. It feels good.

※ ※ ※

In Term 2, the warning signs of depression I felt at the end of Term 1 are returning. I want to stay in bed all day, and often do for as long as I can on the weekends. I stop wanting to see friends and family. At work, I plan my lunch breaks based on who will be around and whether I will be expected to talk to them.

Rachel gives me space when I tell her I want to watch TV all day. I watch episode after episode of *Friday Night Lights*. In one season, a character is diagnosed with bipolar disorder. I'm fascinated by the depiction, relating to some of her extreme and impulsive behaviour, but then they write her out of the show. I stop watching it and just lie in bed. Rachel suggests I make an appointment to see Karyn. I agree, though I'm reluctant.

Rachel and I are getting along well – unlike when my mood is elevated, when I'm blunt, sometimes to the point of cruelty.

'Do we only get along when I'm depressed?' I ask her.

'No!' she replies. 'What about all the months when you felt your mood was stable? We got along very well then, too.'

'I guess,' I say. 'But I feel so good and so energised when I'm manic or elevated. I worry that treatment of any form will end up taking that away.'

'I don't know what to tell you, love,' she says. 'Why don't you see what Karyn says?'

I send Karyn an email and tell her I am struggling and need to see her. I think about a sliding-doors version of myself where I don't have Rachel. I'm sure I wouldn't make the appointment, that I'd let things escalate until I needed urgent help.

On the day of my appointment, Rachel reminds me to leave the house on time to take the train. I walk up the busy city streets from Flinders Street Station, take the lift up to Karyn's floor (looking at myself critically in the mirrored doors on the way), then head to the reception desk.

A middle-aged couple is booking further appointments for marriage counselling. Despite how flat I feel, I eavesdrop on their conversation. Rachel and I tried one counselling appointment together, but it wasn't couples counselling. It was a session with Radhika, my previous psychologist. As it was on my turf, rather than a neutral or mutual space, I felt like I'd dragged Rachel in for an intervention.

The receptionist asks for my name.

'Oh no, didn't you get our message?' she says. 'Karyn is away sick. We called all the patients she had booked today to cancel.'

'No, I didn't get any message.' I check my phone. 'No missed calls.'

'I'm sorry about that.'

I start to cry in a way I find deeply embarrassing on one level, but don't care about on another. 'Are you sure she isn't in? I emailed her and she knows I'm having a hard time at the moment. It seems weird she wouldn't have contacted me.'

The receptionist offers to call Karyn to check. I hear parts of the hushed conversation, and the receptionist looks at me quickly once or twice. 'She's quite upset,' I hear her say.

She hangs up the phone and looks at me sympathetically. 'I'm so sorry about this, but Karyn says you don't have an appointment today. She says yours is next week?'

'No, that can't be right,' I reply, but I hear my own uncertainty. I'm usually so careful about dates and times. I take out my diary and flick through the pages, my hands shaking. I see it on the page at the same moment my gut lurches. I mixed up the date. She's right. There must be something quite wrong with me.

I continue to find comfort in Rosie and marvel at the progress she has made. Our walks are the only thing that come close to the mindfulness meditation various people keep telling me to do. We walk along the Merri Creek path, explore Yarra Bend Park and Edinburgh Gardens, and sometimes go further afield.

Rosie's solemn, sweet face is such a comfort. She still gets quite anxious, which she shows by tucking her tail between her legs, leaning into me or Rachel, and shaking. The greyhounds on the rescue organisation's Facebook page reportedly settle in quickly most of the time. Rosie's progress seems slower when it comes to her mental health: like mine.

The correct date for my appointment with Karyn rolls around. That morning, I can't quite get myself to dress and head into the city. I decide it will be a lot easier if Rachel comes with me. I briefly wonder if I am repeating the couples counselling I attempted with Radhika by bringing Rachel into my therapy space.

When Karyn calls me in from the waiting room, I ask if Rachel can come with me. 'I think she might have some helpful insights,' I explain.

Karyn nods. But it isn't even about the helpful insights: I am frightened by the notion of speaking to Karyn alone for an hour, and not sure what to say about how I'm feeling.

In the consultation room, Karyn apologises for 'the mix up' last week.

'It's not your fault,' I say. 'I was convinced I had an appointment with you. I don't know what's going on with me.'

'What *has* been going on with you recently?'

I talk slowly, quietly, about being depressed again. 'I hate it so much. I was manic, or elevated, so recently that I can remember exactly what it feels like,' I explain. 'And now, I don't have any patience with myself at all, and judge myself for feeling flat and shitty again.'

'What do you think brought on the change, the depressive state?' Karyn asks.

'I don't know if anything brought it on, necessarily,' I say. 'If this is bipolar disorder, then it's only natural I have a depressive period after being manic or hypomanic, right?'

Karyn explains that even in the case of a mood disorder, it's still likely that my depression was triggered by something.

'I don't know. Things were okay at school and between us,' I say, gesturing at Rachel. She looks uncomfortable, like she'd rather be out in the waiting room, and I feel bad. The anticipation of therapy is always the hard part – just like teaching. Now that I'm here, I feel silly for asking Rachel to come in.

I don't get any definitive answers to the questions I didn't realise I was seeking. At night, I turn to TV and the internet for external distractions to push away my feelings. I'm hoping for something to take up as a cause – to have feelings about something other than myself and my woes. I've done this in the past and it never works, never lasts as long as I need it to. I suppose this is why many people living with mental illness turn to drugs and alcohol, like I turn to sugar and caffeine.

Sick of social media, I head to the official greyhound racing website, which contains information about each dog, including their litter. I love reading Rosie's racing profile online and watching videos of her races, even though they make me sad, as we've heard she struggled. She didn't take to racing at all, which is hardly surprising for such an anxious dog. She has a Victorian Racing Offence against her name from a few months before we adopted her: 'Fail to Chase'. We think that's impressive.

I often read about Rosie's five littermates, noticing that two of the six dogs are based in Victoria and have the same owner listed on their records. It occurs to me to Google the owner's name. He has a profile on a free online marketplace, where his past advertisements say, *Free greyhound*. I've heard awful things about what happens to greyhounds given away for free. Some are cross-bred with pig-hunting dogs and are severely injured, or die when giving birth. Others are used as bait dogs for dog-fighting rings.

'Do you think I should message him?' I ask Rachel. I don't have to explain what I'm talking about; I've mentioned these dogs numerous times already.

'What would you say?'

'I don't know. I guess that when he retires either of her siblings, could he get in touch with us before advertising them online?'

'Okay, go for it,' Rachel says.

I'm glad to have her approval; I don't trust my own decision-making these days. I've started to realise some of the decisions I made last year, and the ways I found to put myself at risk, were a form of self-harm.

The next day, between classes, I see an email from the man who owns Rosie's siblings. He mentions her sister by name: Opal. 'She seems to have dropped a back muscle so will most likely be retired. Do you want her?'

'Yes, we do. When can we come and get her?' I don't think we can adopt another dog, since we're renters and only have permission to have Rosie, but I don't tell him that. He'll give her away for free to someone before we can help get her into a rescue program.

We reach out to local greyhound rescues and hear back quickly; they can't take another dog: their waitlists are full. Apparently the lead-up to winter sees many dogs getting dumped. Finally, we hear a positive response. One rescue organisation is willing to meet with us on the weekend, as long as we can pick Opal up from her trainer.

On Saturday, we head off early, as the trainer lives outside of Melbourne. When we get there, a man grunts at us from the front yard, where he's pulling out weeds. Unlike Rosie's adoption through a rescue organisation, this is the first time we've met a greyhound trainer. He's in his seventies and I wonder if he's seeking fame and fortune by training racing dogs in his retirement.

He leads us over to his garage, rolls up the door and there she is, tucked away at the back of the garage in a cage. She wags her tail as Rachel and I approach. Opal is white with black spots, like Rosie, who is at home, no doubt asleep on our bed.

We don't see any bedding or toys in the garage. It's late May, and there's already a sharp chill in the air that made us turn on the heating on the drive from Melbourne.

The owner tells us about her racing history. Rachel listens while I think about grabbing Opal and getting us out of there. Then I notice his eyes widen as he thinks of something. 'You don't want another dog, do you?' He gestures at a thin black greyhound in the cage next to Opal's.

We look sadly and say no, unfortunately we can't.

'Alright, then, have you got a leash for Opal?' The owner is all business.

'Yes, it's in the car.' Rachel and I look at each other briefly. Her look says, *Hurry up and get that leash so we can leave*. My look says, *I'm nervous leaving you alone back here!*

I come back from the car holding the leash. It represents so much – freedom, walks and happy, panting dogs. Rachel and the owner are standing over to the side of the garage in front of a contraption. He is talking animatedly. She glances at me, her expression suggesting she wants to change topic.

'Roz, do you want to see the walking machine the dogs use?' Rachel asks.

'Uh, okay?'

The man turns on the walking machine: a narrow treadmill for dogs. He demonstrates how it's used by flicking the switch and showing us how he connects a leash to the machine.

'They love it,' he says. 'They can't wait to get on it each day for their exercise.'

I am confused. There's a garden only metres away, but the dogs have to pee and poo in their cages and are only allowed out to run on the walking machine or to be taken out to train at 'the paddock', whatever that is. I try to hide my judgement.

He hands us Opal's vet records and a bottle of pills, explaining they stop her menstruating. 'Here are some spares.'

'We're going to get her desexed,' I say.

Finally, he unlocks Opal's cage.

Opal doesn't know us but that doesn't diminish her joy. She pulls on the leash, telling us it's time to go. As we farewell the man, she does her first freedom wee on the grass. She wags her tail as we leave.

Mood

We email our landlord, pleading to be allowed to have a second dog at the property. We emphasise how quiet Opal is, that the two dogs are sisters and that we don't want to separate them, that we are happy to pay an additional pet bond to give him piece of mind.

After we send it, I keep checking my email. I don't want to give Opal up. Her uncontainable joy at everything, despite what she has experienced in her life so far, is so beautiful and reassuring. And she already seems to know she's home.

Eventually, we hear back from our landlord: we have permission to adopt Opal. The four of us become fixtures in our neighbourhood – the queer couple with the matching dogs. People stop us to pat Rosie and Opal, comment on their rainbow collars or coats, and ask if they recognised each other when they were reunited. We tell them when we brought Opal home, she and Rosie sniffed each other head to toe, which they don't ever do with other dogs.

The hounds bring joy and companionship into an otherwise bleak winter. Some people praise us for adopting them, which makes us a little uncomfortable. 'Good on you!' they say, beaming. 'What an amazing thing to have done!' I want to explain that we have benefited from this turn of events, too. Sometimes, I think the dogs are all I have keeping me steady between the extreme spectrums of grief, anxiety and instability – it's much easier to appreciate them than the humans who make up my support network.

When my mood is low, new piercings soothe me. And now that I've joined the world of the tattooed, I have even more options for body modification. There's something about the pain, and the carelessness of committing to a tattoo on an impulse, that thrills me. I decide a second tattoo would cheer me up, or at least distract me from feeling sad for a bit. Rachel points out this sounds like self-harm, and I shrug. 'Well, at least it'll look good!' I say.

A tattoo artist I've been following on Instagram is doing a series of gemstones with bees, and I contact her about getting a tattoo of an opal.

'This can be in honour of Opal, our newest family member,' I tell Rachel. 'Like the tattoo I got when we adopted Rosie.' I can't stop staring at the beautiful, rainbow sparkly opal on my ankle. I take a photo of Opal the dog with my opal tattoo. I push aside the memory of leaving Rosie on her first night with us to get a tattoo. There's a lot I regret from that time. My preferred way of dealing with it is compartmentalisation and avoidance.

As it gets warmer in Term 3, I start wearing dresses and skirts. My classrooms don't have air-conditioning and on some of the early spring days, our rooms are stifling. One of my Year 7 students notices my tattoo and stays back at the end of class to ask me about it.

'Ms Bellamy, why are the opal and bee significant to you?'

I smile at her. 'I recently adopted a dog named Opal,' I tell her. 'And I like bees. I associate them with spring and summer.'

As I explain my reasoning, I start to think there's more to it. The tattoos represent change. The bee represents movement, which is something I struggle with in my stagnated depressive periods. It also represents being outdoors in nature, where I feel most centred and peaceful. It's also – perhaps most stereotypically, but quite meaningfully to me – about freedom.

Teaching involves a lot of movement, too: it's frenetic, and you're constantly trying to keep up with the curriculum, planning and marking. The profession doesn't leave a lot of space in your life; you need to be able to carve some out or you burn out. I feel like I'm getting close to that point, even though I'm only in my second year. It makes me feel a bit hopeless but also provides a sense of clarity. Maybe this isn't the right career for me.

When I began my application to become a fully registered teacher, rather than a graduate teacher, I noticed the question on impairments: 'Are you suffering from any physical or mental impairment, disability, condition or disorder (including substance abuse or dependence) which seriously affects your ability to practise as a teacher?' I still don't know how to feel about it.

I wipe the whiteboard and pack up my books to go. Near the door, I look back and out the window at the students already playing in the yard. I think about how far I've come: I'm no longer triggered by the loud voices and the locker fights near my classroom. Maybe I can cope with freneticism – but elsewhere, in environments that sustain rather than drain me.

Chapter 13

In Term 3, I'm teaching *To Kill a Mockingbird* to my Year 10 English class when the Unite the Right rally takes place in Charlottesville, Virginia. I watch the news all weekend, disturbed and distressed by the images of neo-Nazis, the tragic death of one of the protesters, the antisemitic chants of *Jews will not replace us*, and the white supremacist signs and imagery.

On Monday morning, as I'm preparing for my 9 am class, I notice teachers and students in the courtyard, staring up. There are giant swastikas painted high up on the walls of a building. It's next to my classroom.

I go into the staff room expecting a discussion about it, but everyone is busy making coffee, photocopying pages for their classes, chatting. 'Um, have you seen the swastikas?' I ask. It comes out meekly. I don't know how to say the words the way they feel. It would seem dramatic and ridiculous to them if I got worked up.

'Yeah, apparently some kids used the scaffolding to get up there,' a teacher tells me. She shares this dispassionately, like any other Monday morning gossip.

I think about how often I find swastikas on the desks at school, and sometimes the walls. Once, I reported them, and while I waited for the school to take action, one of my colleagues made a suggestion. 'What if you got cleaning products and sponges, and went into your classroom early to clean it off? Then the students would come in and see the visual of you scrubbing them off.' I winced, thinking about a Jewish teacher having to performatively scrub off swastikas as a learning opportunity.

A week passes, and I realise the giant swastikas aren't going away any time soon. I call my parents. 'You won't believe it. We came in after the weekend and there are huge swastikas up on the school walls facing the courtyard. I'm sending you a picture.'

'When will they remove them?' Dad wants to know.

'They said it's going to take a while. It's high up, so it's an occupational health and safety risk.'

'What about the risk it poses to you, and to any Jewish students?' Mum asks, furious. 'Seeing that every day must be very triggering.'

'I know,' I reply. 'But I'm used to antisemitism from all the schools I've taught at.'

'I mean it, Rozy,' she says. 'You might end up with complex PTSD.'

Clearly, she recently watched a TV program or read a book about complex post-traumatic stress disorder. Only later do I stop to think about what she said. I wonder why I am so reluctant to explore the impact. The only answer I can come up with is that I have enough traumas as it is – I don't want to claim any more. I feel sick with anxiety, almost constantly, at school. I find myself having heart palpitations when the students or staff mention the swastikas. At home, I get headaches and stomach aches, especially when I'm really dreading going back in.

When it comes to wounds, some of us pick at our scabs, while others cover them and hope they heal. But there isn't one approach that works with trauma. Ripping off Band-Aids and picking at scabs in therapy sometimes feels helpful, while other times I leave those sessions feeling devastated. As hours pass after my appointment, I replay moments and fixate on things that upset me. It doesn't feel good. But covering up mental health issues and ignoring them is even worse.

Meanwhile, the Australian media is buzzing about the Australian Marriage Law Postal Survey. As the Australian Bureau of Statistics starts mailing out the survey form, the 'No' campaign starts lobbying and advertising against the marriage equality movement. Whenever we drive outside of our left-leaning suburb, we see 'No' billboards with messages about how gay marriage will hurt children and families. We read nasty letters, articles and posts against marriage equality in the mainstream news and on social media. There is a groundswell of support from many Australians, and rainbow flags and the words 'Vote Yes' start appearing in the windows of homes and shopfronts around the country. But the queer community is negatively affected by the 'No' campaign. Mental health and crisis support services report a stark increase in crisis calls. We hear stories of the survey damaging relationships and connections within families. And the negative messaging has a widespread impact on mental health.

A study[1] conducted by psychologists at the University of Sydney a couple of years after the survey will find that more frequent exposure to homophobic campaign and media messages at the time of the Postal Survey was associated with increased levels of depression, anxiety, generalised stress and psychological distress. Many other studies conducted around this time will have similar findings.

The pro marriage equality sticker we put on our letterbox is torn off. We attend 'Yes' campaign rallies and remind everyone we know to post their surveys. I continue to read the 'No' campaign's material and view their advertisements, even though they upset me. The Australian Christian Lobby uses scare tactics, telling Australians 'radical gay sex education programs will become more widespread and compulsory'. It hurts to view these videos. I think of the kids I teach who have come out to me in secret. I can only imagine how this all must feel to them.

A colleague tells me she put up a 'Vote Yes' poster in her classroom and was asked to take it down and move it to the staff room. 'As opposed to the swastikas that have been there for four weeks?' I say.

My students want to talk about the Postal Survey. I have some leeway as an English teacher, since we talk about political and social issues when we study language and texts. But I also know there are topics teachers are expected to avoid in the classroom. We can talk about the media coverage of the issue, how journalists and politicians construct their arguments, even the emotive language used – but not our own feelings.

I find it hard to follow these rules. The topics I'm meant to avoid seem to come up constantly. The students are drawn to the weight of them. Sometimes the off-limit topics emerge before I can stop them: not safely tied to the curriculum, but free-falling.

---

1 Verrelli, S., White, F. A., Harvey, L. J., & Pulciani, M. R. (2019). Minority stress, social support, and the mental health of lesbian, gay, and bisexual Australians during the Australian Marriage Law Postal Survey. *Australian Psychologist, 54*(4), 336–346. https://doi.org/10.1111/ap.12380

I hear about my students' struggles and I want to share my own experiences. My students are hungry for stories. But teachers are not meant to talk too much about ourselves. We're meant to keep it professional, avoid the personal and stick to the content in the curriculum.

I ask my Select Entry Accelerated Learning class to write poems, and I keep the task open, unrestrained. My students haven't written this way in the classroom since primary school.

After initial hesitation, they begin to write, revelling in the freedom. A poem about anxiety and depression comes with a disclaimer begging me not to share it with the student's parents or year-level coordinator. But I have an obligation to report wellbeing issues, so I do. Another student insists her poetry about sexual assault is fictional, but I have to forward it onto the year-level coordinator due to concerns about possible child abuse. Her parents are informed.

The magic built with my students through the poetry exercise doesn't deflate or disappear; it shifts. I feel guilty: I defied their requests and treated them differently to the way I would have wanted to be treated as a teenager. But I need to protect them and ensure their safety. Teaching isn't about being their friend or parent, no matter how well we connect.

Sometimes, I wonder if 'duty of care' should mean something else; caring might actually mean listening to their words and absorbing them. Hearing young people the way their family and friends might not. Asking them about what it meant to write those words and how it feels to know somebody has read them. Focusing on the literary techniques, themes and ideas in their work – the tangible and abstract – instead of classifying, pathologising and labelling them. I don't want to dismiss something in their words they might not be ready to say out loud.

I continue to question whether I should be teaching. Referring students to their year-level coordinator or to the school counsellor doesn't seem to achieve much. A Year 8 student admits she isn't eating much anymore, and tells me that is why she thinks she is having headaches. I follow the usual pathways but don't hear if anything comes of it.

I feel stilted by the curriculum and educational policy. I look into other ways to make a difference with young people. I think about applying to a PhD program – a research project could be a great opportunity to focus on promoting wellbeing and mental health.

* * *

There is a spate of suicides in the queer community. When I hear about them, I research the person's life in detail and try to find ways to remember them. If there isn't much on social media about the person's death, I become transfixed. I'm disturbed by the way the death has been erased, physically and digitally.

Rachel keeps an eye on me, worriedly; I've become obsessed with suicide before. I guess it's a form of suicidal ideation: researching, absorbing other people's grief online and thinking about the dead person non-stop. Rachel points out that I keep reading distressing material.

'You seem particularly drawn to posts that aren't going to be good for your mental health,' she says. 'You're like a moth to a flame when it comes to trigger warnings.'

'Yeah, I know,' I reply.

'It isn't good for you, Boo.'

'I know.' It's all I can say, but we both know I continue to do things that aren't good for me. 'I'll mention it at therapy, I promise.'

When I next see Karyn, I tell her about my compulsion to research suicides. She asks a typical question for a therapist. 'Why do you think you do that, Roz?'

I respond with a typical answer. 'I don't know.' It's a lazy answer; one that refuses to delve into the ugliness.

'Okay. What do these deaths bring up for you?'

I know the answer but I'm embarrassed to say it. I'm drawn to these suicides because of my own suicidal ideation, which has turned into active planning at times. Sometimes, suicides by queers in ethnic communities bring up deep-seated fears I have around family rejection, abandonment and invisibility even after death.

Instead, I say, 'I'm wondering if it's part of whatever psychiatric issues

I have going on. I've been thinking I want to get a second opinion about my diagnosis. I was wondering if you could recommend any psychiatrists, since I had such a bad experience with the last one.'

'Actually, we have a new psychiatrist who works at the clinic once a week. I can follow up for you and see if he's taking on new patients, if you'd like.'

'Yes, that would be great.' I'm glad Karyn has made the recommendation this time, rather than Cameron. I feel a bit guilty about continuing to seek out a psychiatrist. Despite my frustrations with Cameron, I am still influenced by him. I respect him and trust him, and believe his conviction that psychotherapy is the only answer to my problems. My desire for a diagnosis gives me an excuse to move away from psychological treatment with Karyn, even though we are making progress. Perhaps I'm scared of making progress and where it will take me.

※ ※ ※

During my first appointment with Andrew, the new psychiatrist, I think about how young he is. He is around my age, thirty-three. He wears old-fashioned spectacles and a black tailored suit. I question his choice of outfit and wonder how relatable he expects to be in a suit. Or maybe he doesn't care about being relatable.

'So, what can I do for you, Rosalind?' he asks.

'I've been seeing Karyn, who I believe you spoke to, for almost three years now. She's great. But I wanted to get a second opinion on a psychiatric diagnosis.'

He asks me questions about my symptoms, my appointment with Susan, Susan's diagnosis, my psychological treatment with Karyn and Radhika, and my medical history. I explain why I have thought, from time to time, that I might have bipolar disorder.

At our second appointment, he tells me that he doesn't think I have bipolar disorder. But unlike my appointment with Susan, where I accepted her diagnosis immediately, this time I question Andrew's assessment. He hasn't seen me when I'm manic, I think. Come to think of it, neither had Susan.

A few things happen in quick succession with Andrew. He concurs with Susan: in his opinion, I have borderline personality disorder. He listens to me talk about some of the things causing me stress, which include current political events, and he says, 'I think you're taking this too personally.'

We talk about the events in Charlottesville. He believes there are extremists on both sides. He adds, 'I don't think it's a good idea to get too involved in political activism.'

He doesn't seem to understand that political and social events bring up past traumas, including intergenerational trauma, for me. Instead, he encourages me to avoid social media and the news as much as possible while I'm struggling.

It's infantilising. He doesn't seem to think that I've considered disengaging for my mental health. Of course I have, but ultimately decided it's too important to give up. I tell Rachel he is using my mental health issues to discourage my activism. She suggests telling him about the disconnection I feel from him. Outside his brick-walled room, this seems possible. I decide to tell him that I find his attitude towards my political beliefs judgemental and patronising. But once in his presence, I can't. I don't feel comfortable enough to talk about being uncomfortable.

I worry that his own political and social perspectives are impacting on his work with me, that perhaps he can't help me either. Seeing Andrew after my bad experience with Susan turns me against psychiatry. I decide the majority of psychiatrists are political centrists, that not many will understand the issues I care about. I question whether I should continue seeking psychiatric care.

It's not just Andrew I'm clashing with. Cameron and I are not getting along. When I'm depressed or stable, we get along fine, but when my mood starts to shift from depressive to elevated, and I'm comfortable expressing my anger, our relationship turns passive-aggressive. As winter turns to spring, the passive-aggression starts to hint at actual aggression.

One weekend, as we try to schedule a time to see each other, I make a joke about hiding any knives.

'Do I need to?' he replies.

Later, I find out he perceived this as a threat. I'm thrown by this and angry; I've never shown him any sign of violence. He tells me he was concerned for his wellbeing.

We fight over things that seem ridiculous. I use the word 'perfect' and he tells me there is no such thing as perfection. I try not to use the word in his company.

I turn up late a few times. One evening, when I apologise and explain what held me back at school, he smiles in a way I find patronising and says we make time for things we value and consider important.

'No,' I clarify, 'I do value our time together and see it as important. But I work at a government school and there's a lot going on outside the classroom.'

'What time do you officially get paid until?'

'That's not how it works. I can't get up and leave at 3.30 on the dot.'

'Well, you can, actually,' he says. I hold back a harsh retort.

Another afternoon, he offers to pick me up after my meeting at the end of the day. The meeting is scheduled to go until 4.30 pm, but of course it runs late. I start panicking. One of my colleagues asks why I'm so stressed. When I explain Cameron will get mad and tell me lateness means disrespect, he calls out to another colleague, 'Oops, sorry mate, I guess I've been showing disrespect for years now!' He turns back to me and raises his eyebrows. 'Your friend sounds like hard work.'

Unsurprisingly, things end badly with Andrew. I've been losing my voice a lot lately, which I assume is related to having to raise my voice all the time when I'm teaching. The next time I have an appointment with him, I have to cancel at the last minute. It's pouring with rain and fierce winds are whipping the trees.

I call the clinic. 'Hi,' I rasp, 'unfortunately I need to cancel my session.'

'Reason?' the receptionist asks crisply.

'I have lost my voice and can't speak louder than a whisper.'

About five minutes later, Andrew calls me.

'I can't talk,' I tell him. 'And coming into the city might worsen things.'

'We can Skype,' he says.

'No, it's not just about not being able to come in,' I explain. 'I can't use my voice.'

'We'll give it a go.'

'No.' It's only a syllable, but it has ramifications. When he answers, after a pause, there is a hostility in his voice I haven't heard before. It reminds me of Susan's anger when she fired me as a client. 'You'll need to pay for the appointment,' he says. 'You're a no-show.'

'Even though I can barely speak?'

'Yes. You're cancelling outside of the cancellation period.'

I roll my eyes. I'm done.

From time to time, after that call, I receive a phone call reminding me I have to pay for that last 'appointment'. It grates to think Andrew is blaming me and my borderline personality disorder for this dramatic ending to our therapeutic relationship. I'm sure he has no sense of being at fault himself.

***

Like last year, I call in sick on days when I don't feel capable of teaching. I'm disappointed in myself: I'd managed not to take sick days in the first two-and-a-half terms of this school year. My absences start accumulating around spring. This time of year – the lead up to Rosh Hashanah, the Jewish New Year – seems to have become a trigger for my mental illness.

I can't go in. I don't trust myself in the classroom, what I might say. Each episode of mental illness feels like a fracture, a break that spreads into other areas of my life and causes new problems, which are even harder to fix. My sense of self – already fragile – has to recalibrate among the pain and fear.

My students keep emailing and asking when I'll be back. A Year 10 student pleads, 'Please, Miss. Please. Come back. I'll do anything.' My pessimistic brain assumes that some students are just worried about how my absences will affect their grades, while others want me back because they get away with more in my classes.

I talk about it with Karyn and she says, 'You have a big impact on these kids.'

I want to believe her. I don't. I can only see this away from the classroom, when I'm well.

I'm sitting at my laptop on the couch, blanket around my shoulders. It's 4 am Monday, on the last week of Term 3. It's cold this early in the morning, even though it's spring now, and the single light doesn't add much warmth or comfort to the room. Rachel will sleep until our alarm goes off, like I used to. Rosie and Opal are still curled up in their beds. Our neighbours' houses are dark, and the trains haven't started for the day. The only sound comes from my fingers on the keyboard.

In three hours, I will have to dress and leave for work. I'm a bit anxious about going to school. On the weekend, I had my hair bleached and dyed bright blue and purple at a hair salon in Fitzroy. I then performed at a marriage equality fundraiser at Hares & Hyenas, the queer bookshop. I don't know how to merge the two parts of me: the Roz who had a full and colourful weekend and the Roz who has to go in and teach high school students today. Instead of finding an answer, I write for a couple of hours.

At work, my colleagues often look at me incredulously when I mention that I write. 'How do you fit in writing with your teaching and the rest of your life?' they ask. It is a difficult question to answer. I worry what they are actually saying is: 'It isn't possible to do it all. You must be doing something wrong.' I'm sure that I am doing it all wrong, but I manage to have some of my articles and essays published, and writing soothes me.

Writing nonfiction would certainly be easier if my mental health was under control, though. I censor myself as I write about my life experiences and slip into a removed tone that a friend once referred to as 'reportage'.

There are many people I might hurt or piss off if I tell my stories honestly. Deep down, I want to do it anyway. Writing has always been calming and nurturing to me, even though writing about some experiences can be painful. It helps me make sense of myself, and of living with mental illness. It will take a long time to get to a point when I feel free and ready to tell the stories I want to tell.

Sometimes, I let fear get the better of me. I don't say what I think. I censor myself in my writing or online, and I obsess over things I've put out into the world previously. Pieces of writing that aren't even online anymore, thanks to the rapid turnover of literary magazines and publications, play on my mind. I imagine them getting into the wrong hands.

I tell my uncle I'm worried about travelling to the US because of things I've said about their government. I imagine being locked up, caged.

'Well, why do you say those things?' he asks. The side of my family from the Soviet Union believe you should keep your mouth shut. Don't have people over unless you've tested them, checked they're trustworthy, that they're one of us. Never speak out. Never end up with your name, your identity, on a list. I've done all the wrong things.

His question frustrates me. I *have* to speak out, because – as history can attest to – people not speaking out leads to bad consequences. But I understand why he asked the question.

Despite this compulsion, I'm also afraid of the consequences of speaking out. I'm scared because of the things my parents told me, because of events their parents recounted, and because of what I found out through my great-grandparents' diaries. I suppose having these fears from a young age are exactly what my mentor teacher, Sonya, meant when she spoke about raising Jewish children with a 'victim mentality'. If anything, I was raised with a survival mentality. But the fear is deep and innate. I have to draw on bravado to mask it.

Chapter 14

Cameron uses the word 'grandiosity' one too many times about me. I'm furious. I interpret it as criticism of my ambition. It makes me feel like my desires are greedy, wrong and inappropriate.

Our friendship no longer feels equal, the way it once did. There's a hierarchy. We've ended up on different sides of the desk. He's the expert; I'm the patient: the broken one, the fuck-up.

Over tea at his house, at the start of the school holidays, he refers to a man he is dating as 'damaged'. It reminds me of when he referred to Dexter, the rescue dog Rachel and I had wanted to adopt, as 'broken'. I don't know how to tell him this, even though he's blunt when it comes to correcting my use of particular words.

Sometimes, I try to ignore his strong opinions on everything, like when he asked if Rachel and I were planning to have children. When I'd said maybe, he told me to hurry up: 'The clock is ticking. You might want to freeze your eggs.'

Fuck the clock, I wanted to say. I thought of the times Jess and I had discussed our eggs: the past and future generations stored like matryoshka dolls. I knew I was carrying the pain of multiple generations – from pogroms, starvation, Nazis and exile to imprisonment and suffering. I needed more time to process my family's past traumas, and my own, before bringing a child into this world to potentially endure more.

I spend the first week of the spring school holidays panicking about the upcoming wedding of a friend, at a Catholic church. We worked together for years, during which we became close friends, bonding the way people often do in bad jobs. While I feel comfortable around her, I feel uncomfortable around her family: I've noticed the way her mother looks at me, her daughter's one gay friend.

In the lead-up to the wedding, which is due to take place during the Australian Marriage Law Postal Survey, it was announced that the American rapper Macklemore will be performing the song 'Same Love' at the rugby Grand Final in Sydney. The performance happens to be on the same night as my friend's wedding.

In my elevated state, it's hard not to believe his performance at the Grand Final contains some greater significance. Rachel and I had chosen 'Same Love' to be the last song at our wedding reception, and it had played as we hugged our guests at the end of the night. We had first heard the song in 2012, the year we got engaged, when we turned on the car radio and heard lyrics about queer identity, right-wing conservatives, homophobia and fighting for equal marriage rights. Back then, we had lived on the south side of Melbourne, away from the majority of the queer community, and listened to the song in silence. We had never heard anything like it on commercial radio.

The song is associated with the marriage equality movement in the US, and there's already a backlash about the Grand Final performance. The conservatives are calling it too political in the lead-up to the marriage equality vote.

At the church, on the morning of the wedding, I am tense, waiting to see if my friend and her husband mention marriage equality at some point in their ceremony. They don't, even after the bit where the priest says, 'Marriage, according to the law in Australia, is the union of a man and a woman to the exclusion of all others.' Even though I'm prepared for the word 'exclusion' and know it's a mandatory part of the service, it feels offensive, even laughable.

Several of my friend's pre-wedding events had clashed with marriage equality protests, and I had struggled with how she'd ignored them. Then she asked me to be an MC for the reception, along with my sister, while other friends were asked to be bridesmaids. With my bleached and colourful short hair, and the matching power suits Jess and I have chosen to wear for our MC duties, I clash with the traditional, heteronormative aesthetic of the wedding. I feel a bit like the unpaid entertainment.

During the reception, which takes place at a boutique venue in a leafy upmarket suburb, I announce to Rachel and my friends over the shiny silverware that I'm going to watch Macklemore's performance at the rugby final. Most are supportive, but I notice a few looks. I wonder if I'm being dramatic. Regardless, I stream the performance on my phone. A friend and her husband cheer me on.

Later, I stack the DJ's request list with the gayest anthems I can think of. Soon, the Village People's 'YMCA' is playing – which actually attracts some of the bride and groom's families to the dance floor – followed by Lady Gaga's 'Born This Way'. I dance with Rachel and stay on the dance floor with her during the slow, romantic songs. I think about how we used to be too shy to slow dance in front of a mostly straight crowd, and lean in even closer.

By the end of the night, I'm feeling overwhelmed. I'm losing my voice, which usually happens to me at weddings because of having to shout over the music, and I'm starting to cough. We form a circle to farewell the bride and groom. I try to hold it together but whisper to Rachel that I'm going to be sick. I run to the toilet just in time to throw up.

After the farewell circle, we're getting ready to leave and I have to run back to the toilet. I barely have time to tell Rachel and Jess I need to go. When I'm in there, I vomit more intensely than I ever have before. I sob, while Rachel and Jess comfort me from outside the cubicle.

On the drive back northside, we attribute the vomiting to my stress about the event, and stop to buy McDonald's fries and lemonade for the way home. I try to forget about how the night played out.

***

In bed, I turn to Rachel. 'I'm so glad that's over. The whole thing felt so heteronormative and conservative. I kept thinking about our wedding.'

'Ours was amazing,' she replies.

There's a stereotype, particularly in the US, of the 'U-Haul lesbian', referring to queer women's tendency to fall in love and move in together after one or two dates. I had done one better: I spotted my first potential wedding location before Rachel and I became a couple. I had visited a park in Spain that seemed like the ideal place, from the slanting sun on that cool autumn day to the clear blue sky behind the flowers and fountains. We'd been emailing each other for only two months and I felt pretty sure I was falling in love with her. While Spain had been the first country to legalise same-sex marriage, the idea of getting married over there was a bit too complicated and expensive.

When we got married in Australia, in 2013, our celebrant had informed us she couldn't call the ceremony a wedding or use terminology like 'wife' and 'marry'. These words meant something to us, but asking her to use them would risk her being de-registered and having our certificate voided. Instead, she had to refer to it as a commitment ceremony, but we could continue to call it our wedding.

On our wedding day, our celebrant met us before our ceremony with an idea. 'What do you think of me asking the guests to stand along each side of the aisle as you walk down it?'

We looked at each other and nodded. 'I love that,' I said. We had been feeling nervous about walking down the long aisle to the verandah where our guests would be waiting. This sounded communal and inclusive: the way we wanted to start our marriage.

'Okay, I'll let them know.'

The verandah was one of the selling points of the venue.

Before we settled on it, we'd inspected a boutique vineyard. We had driven up the lush driveway, passing rolling hills that would provide an ideal wedding ceremony backdrop, and I'd touched Rachel's arm. 'This is it.'

We'd parked and headed inside, where numerous couples were having wine tastings.

The man working there looked up at us. As he sized us up, I became aware of our casual clothing.

'We wanted to enquire about having our commitment ceremony here,' I said. We had started using that term, instead of wedding, because whenever we mentioned a wedding, people seemed to get confused and thought one of us was the bride's friend.

'Yeah, sure, just a minute,' he said. He returned to one of the couples having their tasting. Eventually, after making a large sale, he returned to us. 'Did you want some information?' he asked.

'Yes, please.' He led us around the property quickly, giving what felt like an abridged version of his spiel. When I asked a question, he sighed.

By the time we left, I was sure he hated us. 'What was his problem?' I asked Rachel.

'He decided straight away that we weren't serious about booking, or weren't the right type of couple, and then didn't put any effort in.'

We looked at a few other venues, which weren't available or affordable. Finally, I told Rachel that I had noticed another vineyard listed online, but there didn't seem to be any information about it. 'Should we try it?' I asked.

'We may as well.'

I called the number and a man answered in a booming British accent. Before I had given him much detail, he encouraged us to come by for a visit. 'Do come on over.'

We drove out to the vineyard, which involved driving down a remote country road for some time. I was starting to get misgivings when we saw a sign for the property.

The property itself was old and filled with eclectic objects. 'Come in and make yourselves comfortable,' the man said. 'Now, you said on the telephone that you want to have a wedding here?'

'Yes.' I looked at Rachel, wondering how this man would respond to our relationship.

'Which one of you is getting married?'

'Uh, both of us.'

'Oh, two weddings?' he exclaimed, and chuckled. 'Yes, we can accommodate that.'

He hadn't even asked for the date. I assumed he didn't get too many bookings; it looked like he was struggling with the upkeep of the property.

'No, just one wedding,' I said. I was about to explain it when his wife piped up from the back of the room.

'I understand,' she said to us, and then turned to him. 'They're getting married to each other.'

'What?' He looked confused.

She walked over and introduced herself to us. 'Let me show you the verandah, since I imagine that's where you'd like to hold the ceremony.'

We nodded eagerly and followed her outside. The verandah faced a series of sloping hills and acres of vines. A lush grapevine trellis hung overhead. Two glossy horses grazed near the verandah. It looked like an ideal setting, despite needing a good clean.

Her husband followed us outside, still confused but warming up to the situation. 'Now, you'd probably want the ceremony to take place over here,' he said, gesturing, 'and this pathway would make an aisle. The carpark links to the pathway, so the bride,' he looked from me to Rachel, still not quite sure which one of us was the bride, 'could enter there.'

He led us out to a little cabin away from the aisle that looked old, rundown and forgotten. 'This is a little room, if any guest needs to stay the night,' he said.

'Oh, they've all got their accommodation sorted out,' I said.

'Yes, yes, but if you have any drunken guests who misbehave, this is a good place to put them,' he said with a wink. 'If any of the young men make a pass at you, for example.'

'That won't be an issue,' we said in unison, smiling. 'We're pretty sure our guests won't do that,' I added.

'You never know what will happen when drinking is thrown in the mix. Either way, this room is available if you need it on the night.'

Rachel thanked him, and we glanced at each other. The room was terrifying.

We walked inside and looked at the wines for sale.

'What did you think?' the woman asked.

'It's really lovely. Can you check your availability for us?' I asked.

'Yes. What date is your wedding?' She opened up a dusty old diary and flicked through the pages.

'March tenth.'

'Yes, that's fine.' She picked up a pencil, as if to write it in on the otherwise blank page.

'Can we speak to each other and then give you a call?'

'Yes, yes, of course.'

We bought a bottle of wine and headed back to the car park. Once we were back in the car, we started laughing. 'That was hilarious,' I said. 'I kind of love the venue.'

When our celebrant had the idea, on the afternoon of our wedding ceremony, for our guests to meet us along the aisle, she inadvertently found a solution to something I had been worrying about: who should walk down the aisle, and who should wait to receive them? When binary gender roles are removed, these things take thought and planning. During our ceremony planning sessions, she'd suggested one of us walk down the aisle first, then the other follow to join them up front, where the celebrant would marry us. I had been uncomfortable about it, as I was so focused on what people would think and what norm they usually encountered at weddings. But once we added in the detail of our guests lining the aisle, it felt loving and intimate, instead of awkward, as I'd feared.

'Are you ready to start?'

When we nodded, our celebrant headed back to tell Rachel's sister to start the music. It was completely quiet out in the hills and when our chosen song's opening chords began to play, I felt a shiver down my spine.

We had chosen 'Crystal' by Stevie Nicks, one of the songs we listened to on repeat when I first visited Rachel in the US. I teared up hearing the first line, about trusting your first initial feeling about someone, as we prepared to walk down the aisle. Part of the magic of the song was its reference to the love that had 'finally, finally found me'.

Rachel's father took her arm and they started walking down the aisle. Then it was my turn. Dad and I linked arms. I couldn't stop beaming down the aisle at Rachel, who had turned around and was waiting for me at the little archway we had set up at the front of the verandah. I was stunned by how beautiful she looked in her ivory wedding gown and shawl; flowers in her long, side-swept hair. I was wearing a silk ivory gown and had my hair pulled up and pinned with paper flowers made out of dictionary pages: a nod to my love of words. We had thought about every last detail for our wedding day, and it had paid off. Our guests stood along the aisle, wiping tears and taking photos. Little bottles filled with flowers, hanging from shepherd's hooks, lined our way.

When we reached the verandah, I joined Rachel and took her hand while our guests were seated. I looked around, amazed by how beautiful everything looked. We were standing under an archway decorated with vines. Crystals and little orb-shaped glass vases with fresh flowers hung from the roof of the verandah. Hills rose in the backdrop, and horses strolled past behind a nearby fence.

The ceremony flew past, even as I tried to take in every moment. We had created exactly what we wanted; it was ripe with personal details and stories. Our celebrant had tied all we'd shared about our relationship into a romantic and entertaining story.

'Rachel, do you take Rosalind to be your partner in life and in love?'

'I do,' she said, turning to look at me, her eyes shining.

'And will you continue to love, honour and respect her, and support her in life and friendship with honesty and sincerity, through good fortune and adversity, as long as you both shall live?'

'I will,' Rachel said.

Our celebrant asked me the same questions. I gazed at Rachel, feeling a sense of peace and love as I said, 'I do.'

Then it was time for our personal vows. I read my words as calmly as I could, hoping Rachel could hear the love behind each one. I finished off by saying, 'I will love you unconditionally throughout our lives, regardless of whether things are easy or hard. I knew when we first started to know each other that we were destined to be together for life. My life is brighter, happier and so much more colourful for knowing you. This ring is a symbol of my enduring love, respect for you and faith in our relationship.'

As expected, Rachel's vows had me tearing up after the first line. 'Rosalind, ever since I met you, I have been enchanted by you. You are the light of my life, a constant source of happiness and joy for me and the inspiration behind everything I do and every achievement I have.'

We stared at each other and squeezed hands. As she finished, I glanced at our guests for a moment and saw many wiping tears from their eyes.

'Dear Rachel and Roz,' our celebrant said. 'These rings have been warmed and blessed by all those present here today with all their hopes for your continued happiness and joy. May these rings always belong to each other's hands and your love always to each other's hearts. I invite you now to exchange the gift of your rings.'

We placed our wedding rings on each other's fingers.

I felt for Jess, who had to read a poem – 'I carry your heart' by E.E.

Cummings – in the middle of the most emotional part of the ceremony. She read powerfully, her voice emotional.

Finally, our celebrant explained our two certificates: the Australian Certificate of Commitment and our beautiful Ketubah, a Jewish wedding certificate. Among the other decorations on the signing table, we had a bulb of garlic with a ribbon tied around it, as a nod to meeting through *Buffy the Vampire Slayer* and our love of garlic in food. When our parents were called up to witness and sign the certificates, we hugged and kissed them, and I felt moved by our parents' love and pride.

'And so, without further ado, dear Roz and Rachel, it is my very great pleasure to formally acknowledge this binding and precious union as a commitment in love and a partnership for life, and of course you need no permission from me to kiss your lovely partner. Congratulations!'

We had worried about kissing in front of everyone, but had no trouble at all, and kissed passionately as though nobody was there. It was natural and joyous. We followed the kiss with delighted laughter.

I looked at Rachel, then at our family and friends. After spending much of our twenties hiding our queerness from many people in our lives, our relationship was laid out for all to see. And we were okay.

'Congratulations! Photo, please! Hold up your rings!' Jess held up her phone. 'Can I tell social media you two are married now?'

'Go for it,' Rachel said, and I grabbed her hand.

* * *

Talking about our wedding, late at night, after throwing up at my friend's wedding, makes me nostalgic and wistful. I don't feel sick anymore, just sad. I thought things had changed more in the four years since our wedding. But after the wedding we just attended, I'm worried about how Australians will respond to the Postal Survey.

I look around our bedroom, where framed photos from our wedding hang on the wall, and pull our dog-patterned quilt cover up around us.

'I just wanted her to mention marriage equality. It would have meant a lot to me.'

Rachel squeezes my hand. 'I know. I'm sorry. If it helps, our marriage will most likely be legally recognised soon.'

'We'll have to get married again,' I say, only half joking.

'Yes, let's do it,' she replies, leaning in to kiss me.

A week later, when Term 4 begins, I'm relieved to see the swastikas have finally been painted over. It makes going to school easier. I continue to have issues with my throat though. I cough so hard I vomit: sometimes when I'm out walking, which I attribute to hayfever, but other times when I'm driving or at home. My GP refers me to an Ear Nose and Throat specialist.

The specialist, a kind and direct doctor, is concerned by what she sees, and tells me she needs to do an endoscopy. She inserts a thin tube with a camera on the end through my nose, and it runs down my throat, tickling everything it passes along the way. She removes the tube and looks at me.

'There's a growth on your vocal cords,' she says. 'It could be nothing, but we need to check it again in a few months to ensure it hasn't grown further and that it isn't anything nasty.'

I can barely speak during the appointment because I used up my voice teaching earlier in the week. I manage not to cry until I've left the clinic.

Cameron and I make a time to talk about our friendship after a series of further arguments. On our phone call, I try not to say anything that will lead us into a fight. 'Our friendship is unique and really important to me,' I tell him as I stare into shop windows on Collins Street.

'I have *lots* of special friendships,' he replies. 'I think it's grandiosity that makes you believe our friendship is unique.'

I grit my teeth. 'I was trying to say it is special.'

While I'd like to avoid him for a while, I need his help. My GP has told me directly she's not sure who else to refer me to. When she said this, I wanted to give up on trying to manage my mental health, but I knew I had one unexplored option available.

Despite feeling mortified, I decide to ask Cameron if he has any recommendations. We may not be getting along, but he is better connected in the mental health sector than my GP. Cameron tells me about a psychiatrist who specialises in psychotherapy. They know each other professionally but there are enough levels of distance between them; we won't be breaking any boundaries. I email the psychiatrist, John, and I'm relieved when he replies to say he can see me. We make an appointment for later that month.

When I next see Karyn, she tells me, 'Be kind to yourself.' I try.

On some nights and weekends, when I can't remove my school laptop and student work from my backpack, I think, *It's okay if you don't manage to get any work done.* Sometimes I also think, *It's less okay if you feel like self-harming or think about suicide.* I tell myself that even suicidal ideation can be managed.

Karyn recommends exercise, which is meant to help alleviate some of my symptoms.

'How do you make yourself exercise when you're depressed?' I ask. To me, this is paradoxical – a Catch 22 – but she doesn't seem to think so. She continues to remind me to exercise, to my amusement and, occasionally, outrage.

My parents express concern. Like Karyn, Mum mentions exercise, good food, yoga and relaxation.

'Why don't you come visit us?' Mum asks. 'Come for a weekend, or longer if you're taking time off. We'll make delicious meals and you can swim at the beach. When was the last time you went to the beach? You love the ocean and it's so healing.'

I agree to visit but don't book my flights. I'm too squirmy and energetic to be with them. I'm not looking for peace and quiet, but drama and action. When Ari tells me to visit him in Sydney, I jump at the idea of going there instead. He has a new boyfriend and it would be fun to spend some time with them. I imagine us going out clubbing and barely sleeping. I don't focus on the fact that he works full-time and we're in our thirties now; most of my friends aren't into partying anymore. I don't even know if I'm into partying. Maybe I just like the idea of it.

I start being more open with Karyn than I have been in a long time – or possibly ever. Perhaps because I'll be seeing a psychiatrist soon, and I'm not sure if I'll continue to see Karyn as well, I feel less inhibited around her.

'I've been thinking about my gender identity lately,' I say.

Karyn waits for me to continue. When I don't, she asks what I have been thinking about it.

'Teaching isn't the best environment for figuring out things related to identity, but I've started to realise that I don't really fit into a binary category of gender. I don't see myself as a man or woman, most of the time. I don't think I'm cisgender or transgender, just like I'm not gay or straight. I think gender doesn't play a part in my attraction to people because sexuality and gender are not binaries for me.' I say all of this in a rush, looking at her briefly and then staring at the wall as she takes it in.

My gender varies depending on the day, my mood, my hormones, my feelings. Sometimes what I am is undefinable, but when I first heard the term 'non-binary', it made sense. I might be male or female, or both; maybe neither. I can dress, fuck and identify however I want. Nobody should have to adhere to a gender binary, unless they want to.

'What about when you were growing up?' she asks.

'I didn't have the words for it when I was younger, but when I was a teenager, I played around with gender a lot. I loved dresses and skirts, sometimes, but when I wore pants, I wasn't just a girl wearing pants.'

'Do you remember a time when an outfit you were wearing felt right for you?'

'Yes.' Memories come flooding back. 'I was in Just Jeans, trying on brown corduroy pants and a royal-blue velvet shirt. I felt incredible in it. There was something specific about that outfit.'

I try to force the memories to shift into focus. I remember leaning forward, one hand on my hip, tilting my head as I looked myself up and down in the mirror. I remember admiring myself in photos where I was wearing that outfit, feeling closer to butch and masculine than I did in any other clothing. I remember running my fingers along the velvet material and feeling attractive for the first time in my teenage life.

'Have you talked to anyone about it?'

'Yes, I talk to Rachel about it, and a couple of my friends. They've been supportive and are there for me in whatever way I need, but it feels like my own personal journey. I want to explore it more. It's terrifying, because it's another way I'm different, and another way I might be rejected or hurt. But it's also exciting.'

I can't pinpoint when exactly, but during my thirties, 'female' stopped fitting me. I haven't thought about it much during my time teaching: I have enough to worry about.

When I try to understand the evolution of my gender, I think about my childhood. My parents told me, when I was a teenager, that they would have named me Richard if I'd been a boy. *Dick*. I found this funny, but later, I was perplexed. I wondered what Dick's life would've been like at my school. If the kids were so nasty to me – a closeted, cis-appearing girl – what would they have done to him? Would Dick still be here?

I tell Karyn the realisation about my gender identity is confusing, but also makes me feel less alone. I'm starting to find communities I fit into. I often wish that back at school, I had known there were alternatives. That there was language that fitted me. Instead, I had grown up with an image of femininity as the desired template. It didn't feel right.

In the lift after my appointment, I imagine how all the people around me would look at me and treat me if I were completely myself. If I presented myself the way I wanted to. If I became visible as what I see trolls on the internet calling non-binary people: 'freaks'. Society rewards people whose gender matches the sex they were assigned at birth. Those who do not fit within the gender binary are erased, misgendered. We only find understanding in specifically curated and chosen community.

At our next appointment, Karyn says she still doesn't think I have borderline personality disorder. But, strangely, I *want* her to believe the diagnosis is correct. I feel like I have hidden myself too well from her, that she hasn't seen the 'real' me. (I've accused Rachel of that, too.) I want Karyn to see my dysfunction in a way she never has.

'Last year, around September,' I tell her, 'I put myself at risk in multiple ways. I was totally out of control.' I describe some of the behaviours and out-of-character decisions I made, like breaking up with Rachel and telling everyone.

'Also, I asked her to be the go-between with my family during an episode of mania and made her intercept all my calls, then accused her of being controlling and abusive for doing what I asked.'

'Do you still think she was controlling and abusive?' she asks.

'No, she never has been. Even at her worst, she's just bossy and opinionated. I wouldn't make it to my appointments with you or my GP without her. She has to remind me to take my meds every day, too. If anything, I am the one who has acted abusive at times. I've yelled at her, called her names and sworn at her. Sometimes, I feel violent and have to work to control my anger.'

Karyn seems shocked as I speak. I realise I have seen her as a parent, in many ways, and have only told her things that feel appropriate to tell a parent. It's just like one of the maladaptive schemas she told me about, not long after I started seeing her: unrelenting standards. My perfectionism has played a significant role in my therapeutic relationship with her. I've wanted to amuse and impress her. I've been curating the information I share with her in order to please her, or seek her approval. It's embarrassing; I feel ashamed.

Despite my confessions, she tells me she still doesn't believe I have borderline personality disorder. Perhaps she never will. It might be her training or her previous experience working with severely mentally ill patients, or perhaps – as my ego would like to think – I did too good a job of convincing her otherwise.

Still, now I've veered away from the script and been truly honest, I feel like she will never see me the same way. And maybe that doesn't matter, since I most likely won't be seeing her for much longer. But I keep thinking about the way she would have seen me before my revelations – our rapport, the sense of appreciation she had for my jokes, the soft, kind approach she took with me – and I wonder if telling her the truth was my attempt to ruin that.

Chapter 15

I'm waiting to hear that my position will be made permanent. I've been on two one-year contracts, and the state government recently brought in an agreement requiring teachers in my position to be made ongoing.

I'm aware I need to be more professional and reliable. I show up on time each day to teach my classes, even when I'm losing my voice or have terrible anxiety. I don't want to give the school any reason not to translate my contract into an ongoing position. It's not clear if they can refuse to do so, but I avoid mentioning my mental health to the school principal or my mentor teacher in case it affects my chances.

Rachel and I take out a loan and buy our first car, a shiny red sedan that was the model on display at the showroom. At night, we drive around with Rosie and Opal. Soon, our car is covered in dog fur. We joke that the car belongs to the dogs, not us.

Some nights, we talk about leaving Melbourne: driving until we feel better, whenever and wherever that would be. We take the Eastern Freeway or the Westgate, once or twice driving down the Frankston Freeway towards the Mornington Peninsula, but always end up getting tired and deciding to come home.

When we get home from these drives, I feel relieved but disappointed. I can't help thinking it's possible to find the peace and comfort we're both seeking elsewhere.

One night, we stop at a 7/11 in Brunswick. It's a warm night. Cicadas have just started buzzing their chorus. We buy ice cream for us and a packet of sliced chicken for the dogs. When we get back into the car, I realise I don't feel quite right. My heart feels tight. I know from last year that it's probably a panic attack, but my throat is tight, too. I'm losing it.

The panic escalates quickly, though I'd hoped naming it would make it go away, somehow. I start coughing, almost hard enough to vomit.

'I need to be checked out,' I tell Rachel.

'Okay, if that's what you think you need. But it's late. Wouldn't you rather go home and sleep there? You can speak to your GP tomorrow.'

Her suggestions make sense but I shake my head. 'No. I think I need to go to the hospital.'

Rachel nods. She knows better than to argue.

This time, we're much wiser. We don't involve an ambulance. We stop at home to drop off the dogs and make sure they have plenty of water and food. Then we drive to the same hospital I went to last year and park in a nearby street.

I'm so calm explaining my symptoms to the triage nurse that when I insist I need to be assessed by the psychiatric triage team, she asks me to take a seat in the regular emergency department. I'm disappointed.

The way I feel, I'm sure I need to be seen by a psychiatrist. But I'm not yelling like the woman who walks in after us. And I don't swear at nurses and doctors like the man in the cubicle next to me.

Like last time I went to hospital, the doctors focus on the physical symptoms first. They confirm there is nothing going on physically, apart from my issue with my vocal cords. My anxiety feels out of control, so I'm given a Valium, along with the doctor's strict instructions to take a week off work and stay on bed rest.

I am institutionalised – but in the school setting, rather than a psychiatric institution. I'm trying to treat my issues with exposure therapy, but it doesn't seem to be working.

I don't manage to stick to the bed rest longer than twenty-four hours. It brings up things I heard as a child about Baba's sicknesses. She spent a lot of time confined to bed, the causes of which I still wonder about. Bed rest makes me think of *The Yellow Wallpaper* by Charlotte Perkins Gilman, in which a young woman is prescribed rest and deprived of all mental stimulation until she has a mental breakdown. I read it at university. I associate bed rest with deprivation and isolation, with danger rather than safety.

When I call my parents, I don't know how to respond when they ask what is wrong.

'But you have such a lovely life!' Mum says. 'You have a beautiful wife and two lovely dogs. You're smart and hard-working. Try not to worry so much!'

'Unfortunately, mental illness doesn't care how wonderful my life is,' I reply.

'I still don't understand why you aren't coming to stay here for a bit. It would be good for you.'

I don't offer any reasons. I say, 'You won't be able to handle me.'

'What does that mean?' Mum asks.

'I don't even think I'll be able to sit still on the plane for two hours to visit you. I'll be going out of my mind.' I ignore her concerned response.

Every time I feel like I need to express my energy physically, I make unnecessary purchases, or get a haircut or piercing. The local body modification studio gets to know me well.

* * *

Two days after the trip to the hospital, I book a one-way flight to Sydney. I fly there three hours after making the booking. I book one night in a single room at a hotel in Potts Point. I don't bother planning ahead for the other nights. When Rachel sends me a message asking where I'll stay the other nights, I reply, 'I'll figure it out.'

I have an ulterior motive for my trip. According to photos on her Instagram account, my old school bully, who lives in Los Angeles, is in Sydney. I reach out to Dara with a private message without spending much time thinking it through or perfecting my words, the way I usually would. I imagine countless therapists, past and present, shaking their heads. She replies immediately and sounds enthusiastic about seeing me.

We meet at a dumpling restaurant in Potts Point on my first evening. We're both nervous, but exclaim when we see each other and even hug. It's a lovely warm evening, and I feel grateful to be back in my hometown. Dara and I sit outside, facing the street, and sip cocktails as we watch passers-by. Our conversation – about work, relationships, family, our dogs – flows so smoothly I almost forget the context. To anyone who might look at us, we are just old friends catching up over dinner.

Rueing her most recent relationships with men, Dara laughs and says, 'Maybe *I* should try being with women!'

After we finish eating, shit gets real. 'Do you know why you did what you did to me?' I ask.

'No. I've spent years trying to make sense of it. I still don't know.' She looks at me imploringly. 'Will you be putting this in your book?' she asks. She says she's been reading my writing for a while.

'I don't think so,' I reply, unsure if that's true. The question, which I've been asked by other people, too, implies guilt. It's not surprising which people are most scared of being written about. Later, when I decide to write about them, *I* feel guilty. I try to remind myself it's what happened to me – which is my way of reconciling anything compromising or difficult in these pages.

She insists on paying the bill. 'It's the least I can do,' she says. She tells me she has a present for me. It's a brooch in the shape of a human heart. Not a love heart, but a realistic organ. I tell her I love it, and she says it's from an art gallery in New York.

I walk her to her car and she asks more questions about my writing. I tell her I studied with the writer Cheryl Strayed. 'Do you know her writing?'

'Yes, I saw her on *Oprah*,' she says.

'She's amazing,' I tell her. 'She has been really encouraging.'

'Oh my God, Roz! That's huge!'

It feels so strange, and like a role reversal, to have Dara looking up to me in some way. During our childhood, I felt I could never live up to what she wanted from me. She was always correcting me, judging. I wonder why I felt the urge to see her on my first night here, especially so soon after going to the hospital for a panic attack. Perhaps I need Dara's approval – which she now offers readily, apologetically – after shifting the way Rachel, my family and now Karyn see me.

When I head back to the hotel, it takes me a long time to calm down. I can't stop thinking about Dara. What does it mean when your dark and abusive side comes out so early in life? It started when we were only just out of kindergarten.

She first apologised in Year 12 for bullying me so viciously. Before our final exams, she approached me, teary-eyed. 'I have been trying to work up the courage to do this for years,' she said. 'I want to ask your forgiveness for what I did.'

Her plea for forgiveness was surprising but it made sense. Between Rosh Hashanah and Yom Kippur, Jews are meant to atone for our sins. As apologies are mandated by holy texts at this time of year, I didn't take hers seriously. Trauma isn't seasonal and it certainly isn't about God for me.

That first time she apologised, I told her I forgave her. She cried with relief. But later, in therapy, I realised I didn't have to tell her I forgave her. Because I didn't. I'm still not sure if I do.

I decide to go out. I feel anxious after seeing Dara but also have a lot of adrenaline. I try to think of what I can get up to that would let off steam, even if it's not a good idea. While I'm in Sydney, I want to give in to that feeling I've been having that I think of as manic: no restrictions, no conscience, no rules. I can do whatever I want, whenever I want. If I normally spend too much time thinking about every action and decision, I'm now firmly in the other camp. Reality feels like something I can shake off, though I'm not sure I have that kind of control.

I make decisions while I'm there without considering any of the possible consequences. My trip is not what the doctor recommended.

It turns I'm even better at fucking things up away from home. I live on the fly, with no return flight or accommodation booked. One night in Sydney, I go to my friend Ari's place, thinking I will stay there, and I drink with him and a friend. Eventually, the friend gets up to leave. Ari doesn't say anything about me staying there, so I get up to leave too. I'd stored my small bag at the previous hotel, and I figure Ari assumes I have accommodation sorted.

I go out for hours, feeling untethered, doing whatever I want. At 1 am, I start calling hotels. They're all booked out except one, which has a penthouse available for thousands of dollars. Even in the state I'm in – dishevelled and exhausted – I decide that's too expensive.

Mood

I wander around Chinatown and sit down to eat crispy noodles at 2 am. I eventually find a backpacker's hostel with room in one of their dorms. I unlock the dorm and try to be quiet in case there are roommates trying to sleep. I'm still too alert. I replay some of the events of the night. Like an Uber driver telling me why he was pro-Trump, while I listened avidly and asked questions. I can't calm down.

I put in headphones and listen to music. I play Taylor Swift's break-up songs when I'm depressed and Beyoncé's revenge songs when I'm manic. As I listen, I realise I've been thinking of myself as Beyoncé in the music video of the song 'Sorry' – yellow dress, stunning hair, baseball bat out – but I'm more like Jay-Z, sneaky and untrustworthy. I'm not looking for revenge. I'm just angry at everyone and everything.

My hostel roommates sleep around me and I'm aware of the silence, my heart beating so fast it feels unhealthy.

The next morning, I have a quick shower in the shared bathroom. I wish I'd paid the extra five dollars to rent a towel to dry off with.

When I get back to my now-empty dorm, I speak to Cameron. I tell him about my trip and he is surprised to hear what I've been getting up to.

I call Rachel next, once she's awake. When she finds out I didn't have a room sorted until the middle of the night, she's disturbed. 'Tell me next time, please!'

I mumble my agreement and she reminds me to sort out tonight's accommodation.

The next time I call her, I am in a Starbucks, crying. 'I need somewhere to stay but am losing it,' I tell her. 'I can't focus on anything.'

Rachel tells me she is worried about me. She keeps me on the phone for over an hour, making sure I'm okay, and books me a room at the nearby Sheraton hotel. It's more expensive than we'd normally book, but it's just a block away from the Starbucks and she wants me settled somewhere close.

I swan around the Sheraton feeling like a rich housewife. I meet an older woman, Leslie, in the hotel's pool. She lives in Sydney and isn't a guest at the hotel, but is using the pool because she has problems with her back. She used to be a teacher and we can't stop talking about the education system. We make plans to have a meal together the next day.

That night, I'm meant to meet my friend Michael and his wife Marija for dinner in Newtown but don't feel up to it. Selfishly, I don't want to leave my five-star lodgings. I've had a bath in the marble bathroom, sampled chocolates from the truffles I found in my room as a welcome gift, and am now lying in the king-sized bed in a robe, looking out the wide windows at Hyde Park.

Rachel contacts my friends and they offer to bring dinner to me. I tell Rachel I'm nervous about seeing them because they know I'm in a bad place. I try to cancel.

'It'll be fine,' she tells me. 'They're so nice. It'll be good for you to see friends.'

They meet me with Indian takeaway and cake, and don't ask questions. I feel guilty for having tried to cancel. They hug me at the end of the night, looking worried. I keep hearing Rachel and my family and friends are concerned about me, but I don't believe there's a problem. Other than the moments when I feel like my behaviour is out of control, which I am able to compartmentalise and repress as needed, everything seems normal. I think I'm fine.

I arrange to stay with my friends Hannah and Carl. I've known Hannah since we were babies. That night, they cook for me and ask questions, gently. Carl tells me about a former colleague who has bipolar disorder. 'She wrecked her marriage,' he says, looking at me with concern. 'I think she's doing a bit better now.'

I wonder what aspect of my demeanour made Carl share this.

In bed later that night, I book a flight home for the next day. But when I wake up, I realise I don't feel capable of getting to the airport and going through the rigmarole of travel.

Hannah makes me porridge with fresh berries on top. I feel cared for and safe; I didn't realise I had been craving that. She asks me about my dinner with Dara. 'I was really surprised you decided to see her,' she says. 'I was worried for you.'

'It was fine,' I say. I tell her Dara gave me a gift.

'What is it?'

I get the brooch from my suitcase in the spare room. Hannah examines it, looking thoughtful. 'What are you going to do with it, Roz?' she asks.

'I don't know.'

'Do you want me to deal with it for you?'

'Uh, okay. Thanks.'

She puts it away in a cupboard.

I text back and forward with Leslie, the stranger I met at the hotel pool, and we make plans. In the afternoon, I take the bus back to the city and meet her at the Sheraton for afternoon tea. She knows the staff at the cafe and keeps waving her hand to order more drinks and snacks.

A waiter tells us the kitchen is closing and says we will have to move to their restaurant upstairs if we want to order food.

'That's fine,' she says grandly.

In the restaurant, she segues into talking about Jesus. I keep asking questions, when normally I'd make an excuse and get the hell out of there.

'I could never convert to Christianity,' I say when she finishes her sermon.

'Why?' she asks.

'After everything my family went through because of being Jewish. I could never.'

'At some point, you have to make your own decisions,' she says. I broadly agree, but the conversation is making me uneasy.

At the end of our meal, Leslie sits back and waits, so I pay the large bill with a sinking feeling.

It's time to go home.

Chapter 16

When I return to Melbourne, I act out in various ways. I put myself in the way of harm, deliberately. I repeat mistakes I made last year and add new ones into the mix. I drive too fast and only slow down to avoid being fined. I don't put on my seatbelt when I drive and put up with the warning beep. I steal grocery items from the supermarket.

I lie to Rachel often, taking advantage of her trust. I make excuses and go out. Occasionally, she catches me out in a lie. I just make sure I'm sneakier the next time.

Like the previous year, everything unravels fairly quickly, dramatically. In November, I find out my uncle, Dad's brother, has died in Sydney of terminal cancer. Our immediate family has been estranged from his family for years, but Dad's grief is still acute. I don't know what to offer him in the way of support or condolences from a distance, let alone how to handle my own grief.

Rachel tries to offer support, but I tell her I need to go out. Alone.

Later that evening, she tries calling me and I don't answer. She tries again and again. She uses Find My iPhone while I'm driving. I only pick up when the beeping gets loud enough to irritate me.

I speak to Rachel in between the bad decisions I make that night. She's a lifeline, through the fog of grief and pain, but I don't take the safety she offers.

'I think I'm in the city,' I say, and she tells me to come home, but I don't.

That night, I make decisions quickly, without thinking.

Later, the whole night feels foggy, like when I binge-watch TV late at night and then can't remember the plot the next day. But I remember something bad happened; I'm just too ashamed to tell anyone. Instead,

Mood

I store it in my memories, compartmentalised and insulated, to return to one day when I'm ready. Now isn't that time.

I call Sharon and we end up talking about my mental health. 'Do you think I should tell my parents about what's going on? What would you want to know if it was one of your kids? And how far should I go?'

'I would want to know details if their lives were at risk,' she replies.

This perturbs me; my life *is* at risk.

The next time I call Mum, I tell her I'm out of control. She listens for a while and then tells me she is worried. She adds, 'Your sister is also worried about you. When I stayed with her, I found out she keeps her phone on loud every night in case you need her.'

I tell her I appreciate that but wonder why she hasn't mentioned it to me. I feel annoyed at Jess, momentarily, for not offering more, and then feel petty. She's been one of my main sources of support for years. Now, I think of myself as greedy for the time when no amount of care was enough.

I call Sharon back and she listens to my worries and complaints. 'You can call me any time,' she says, when I ask if it is too much.

'Thank you. I appreciate that,' I say. And it's true; all I really want is for someone to listen to me complaining. 'You know, I think all of this will make me a better human once I fix the problems I've created.'

'Absolutely,' she says. I wonder if she's humouring me.

'Then again, maybe I'm just a very manipulative fucker,' I reply. 'It's possible I've even fooled myself.' And though I spoke in hypotheticals, I knew it was true.

* * *

I go to see my new psychiatrist, John, for the first time, a month after making the appointment. Waiting outside his consultation room, housed inside an old terrace building in Brunswick, I take stock of what I want to talk to him about. I am quite sure I have a mood disorder, based on extensive internet searches and reading – I'm just wondering whether I have cyclothymia or bipolar disorder – and I'd also like to know whether Susan and Andrew were correct to diagnose me with borderline personality disorder, or if Karyn was correct to disagree. I'm very focused on getting a diagnosis – what I regard as a label that will help me figure myself out – or at least a definitive explanation of why I have certain symptoms.

In the session, John says, 'I don't like to rush into diagnosing patients. I'd rather start by getting to know you and ruling out possible diagnoses.'

'That sounds good, actually,' I say. 'I've seen three other psychiatrists and they have all said different things.'

While we talk, I stare at his many certificates on the walls, avoiding eye contact when he asks me a difficult question.

After seeing John, I start to delve into my old writing and it hits me; underneath all my perfectionism and subjugation is rage, sharp enough to cut skin. The fury of seeing my former bullies climb various ladders in their personal and professional lives: Dara is rich as fuck. They all are.

Did I hit a ceiling because of the various traumas I've experienced – the childhood bullying, the intergenerational trauma in my family, and the experiences of discrimination related to my gender, sexuality and religion? *That sounds right.* My twenties were a write-off in many ways, spent in bad jobs and therapy. One night, at 2 am, I wake Rachel and say, 'I realised there's a trauma ceiling.'

'What do you mean?'

'You know the glass ceiling for women and the pink ceiling for queer people? A trauma ceiling is whatever systemic issues stop traumatised people from living their full lives. Ambition is labelled 'grandiosity', which is considered another symptom, and others pass you by while you're stuck in therapy limbo. Professionals use our trauma to figure out our symptoms, but our ambition? Apparently that's just mental illness.'

Rachel just nods. She's used to my middle-of-the-night hypothesising.

The next time I speak to Mum, I tell her I've been thinking about the idea of a trauma ceiling I need to smash. She says, 'I'm not sure about 'smashing' it. I imagine you growing up around it and beyond it like a vine or a creeping fig.'

Maybe she's right. Our ancestors – particularly the women – didn't get a chance to break through any ceilings. Maybe the best coping mechanism is to find ways around and over it instead.

Mood

Trauma makes it hard for me to teach. It makes me afraid to explore my gender and express it, including telling people I'm non-binary and asking them to use they/them pronouns for me. My hesitation and fear make me feeble and fragile. They make me obsess about the dead and wish to be with them. They make it necessary to seek deliberate ways to be happy and content, because my default state is anxious, frightened, overwhelmed, lost. They make ambition feel too ambitious. They make me feel like an imposter. They make giving up feel like the only choice.

They make me see my bullies as lucky, as safe, as protected. When I rant about my bullies to John, he says, 'Let me guess, they're all CEOs now.'

I laugh. 'Yeah, pretty much.'

My investigation into my mental illness is ongoing, and involves living with and in the questions throughout my life. One of the possible answers – not a cure, but a balm – is writing. It's hard to write during depressive periods but even jotting down words, phrases and quotes or recording voice memos, where I rant about something for a few minutes, is cathartic. Sometimes, it's all that gets me through.

I decide to write more when I'm 'up'. I haven't written much during my elevated moods because I'm usually busy causing trouble. When I'm stable again, I write about other things and forget to process what it looks and feels like to be manic.

I examine my writing from my last manic period: *I'm noticing symbols and patterns that I'm usually oblivious to. Calendars repeating the same events, companies using the same templates and plans year after year, and even plants coming in and out of season, and it begins to intrude on my thoughts, dreams and imagination. I begin to obsess about certain times of year, just like I used to associate my moods with seasonal change. My grief is tied to wattle at the end of winter and jacaranda as spring turns to summer, both of which I associate with loss. Corporate promotions, like McDonald's Monopoly, start to take on a dark, forbidding shape. The symbols become a permanent part of the calendar, which is a strange and stressful thing to process. Seasons themselves have become swallowed up by the relentless market. Summer is not a season but a product range, a scent and a series of sales. I notice everything when I'm manic. When I'm depressed, I couldn't give a fuck.*

My 'manic writing', as I refer to it, isn't bad; it's concentrated, undiluted. I try to analyse it and then I realise it can sit on its own. It doesn't need to be analysed.

The way I feel in different mood states can be ephemeral, lasting as long as the mood and then transforming into something entirely different. Other times, I recognise my mood state from the way I sound in my writing. It's strange how familiar they are when I feel so different. Rationally, I know they are written by the same person, but in my mind, they're all different authors, and I'm genuinely surprised by the commonality.

Whatever my diagnosis is, and whatever diagnoses mean, I want to be transparent: to tell people about my mental illness and why it sometimes makes me want to die. I'd like to be able to help people by sharing how I get to the other side when it feels impossible. Writing is only part of the solution for me, though; I can't figure everything out through words alone. I know I need something more, some larger structure that will hold the pieces together around me.

* * *

For a little while, I pay to see both a psychologist and psychiatrist, feeling silly for doing so but also appreciating what each has to offer. John and Karyn know about each other, but it still feels weird, like I'm sneaking around behind their backs. I start cancelling or postponing my appointments with Karyn.

I tell John more than I've ever told Karyn. I'm less embarrassed around him. I tell him I have treated Rachel badly lately. I tell him I forgot about her own medical issues and only focused on my own, even when she needed me. I tell him some of the cruel things I've said to her, how untrustworthy I've been, how much pain I have caused her.

John rules out cyclothymia, a milder mood disorder. He says it will take him a few more appointments to rule out other conditions. I fight my curiosity and desire to be labelled. Instead, we talk about my symptoms.

After seeing me in different mood 'states', he is considering prescribing an antidepressant and a mood stabiliser. I'm nervous about taking medication, but finally feel ready.

When I'm manic, I want to ride the wave even though I know I'll get dumped when I come out of it. I want to live everything to its fullest rather than remembering or realising that it will lead to a huge depressive crash. Sometimes, I am aware but don't care that the crash is coming.

While hypomania and mania are so alluring when I'm under their spell, the comedown is awful. I feel jittery and my hands shake. Working as a writer can be hard to balance with a mood disorder. Every time I have a professional win, I flood with adrenaline. When it runs out, I feel empty and depressed. I crave validation and want my ego to be boosted.

Rachel and I return to Adelaide for the Homosexual Histories conference, almost two years to the date of the last time I attended. I think about Deda and Jenny a lot while we're there. It's the second Yahrzeit of their deaths.

We fight most of the time we're away. Rachel confronts me about some of my behaviour and I try to explain it. 'I can't process my existing trauma so I guess I add new traumas to the mix instead.'

She nods. She's patient, even if she's – rightfully – pissed off and hurt.

After we fly back to Melbourne, I'm driving home through Brunswick when the barriers come down at the open rail crossing ahead of us. The car in front stops, we stop and the car behind us stops, but the next car doesn't. It hits the car ahead, which has a domino effect. All the while, the railway crossing alarm screeches.

I don't think too much of it – I'm not at fault – but then I have another crash. Each time it's the same – I'm hit from behind. I wonder if I'm stopping too suddenly or too late. When I tell people about the accidents, I sense they blame me. To have one car accident may be regarded as a misfortune, but to have multiple crashes in a short amount of time looks like carelessness.

Our miserable, terse trip to Adelaide is followed by the results of the Australian Marriage Law Postal Survey.

On Monday, the day before the announcement, I message a non-binary colleague about how nervous I am. They email our school principal about the impending result and tell her it may impact staff as well as students. She replies she'd not thought of this and will speak to someone in wellbeing. She tells my colleague she supports staff not coming into school that day. My colleague decides to stay home.

I go to school as normal on the day of the results, feeling oddly compelled to be there. Before school, I'm interviewed over the phone by ABC Radio about an article I'd just published about why marriage equality isn't the biggest issue facing queer people. I go into it knowing I'm meant to talk about how I'm feeling, but instead end up talking about how we shouldn't judge people of multi-faith and multicultural backgrounds who responded no. When I hang up, Rachel says, 'You spoke very well.'

'Was I too nice to *no* voters?' I ask.

She considers this. 'Not *too nice*. But you did campaign for their side a bit.'

At school, I look down at the colourful outfit I've chosen to wear. We aren't allowed to wear political paraphernalia, as it is a government school, but my rainbow lanyard is from the teachers' union, so it's allowed. I've worn it to school throughout the campaigning. It serves as a beacon; queer and questioning kids and allies come and chat with me, though other kids take it as an invitation to make homophobic and transphobic remarks. A Year 12 student approached me during a recent yard duty and asked how I voted. Then he told me about having a wet dream, about how he ejaculated all over his sheets, and then looked at me, waiting for my response. I walked away and headed to the principal's office. He was removed from class during last period and given a warning. But as usual, there weren't any real consequences.

My heterosexual colleagues brim with enthusiasm. They want to talk to me about marriage equality, but I slip away and head to my classroom.

I'm teaching my Year 10 class during the announcement. I've planned revision on persuasive writing in the lead-up to their exams. They've been studying various op-eds over the last month, on all sorts of topics, and I include articles from a range of political perspectives. The boys in the class who like to talk about Breitbart are surprised and pleased when I let them study a Breitbart article. 'As long as you annotate it and analyse it, I don't mind.'

Towards the end of class, I open a news website that will stream the announcement. 'The result of the Postal Survey is about to be announced,' I tell my students. 'I'm going to play it in case some of you would like to watch it with me. If you'd prefer not to watch, that's fine, but please be respectful. The outcome may affect your fellow students in this class. It also affects me personally.' Some of my students look at me in surprise.

We find out that 61.6% of Australians responded yes, and some students clap. I call Rachel when the bell rings. We are thrilled by the result, but as we hear people around us cheering and music playing – maybe where she is, or maybe in the yard near my classroom – we fall silent. We're aware of the work ahead in our marriage.

* * *

John diagnoses me with bipolar II disorder and borderline personality disorder. I'm a bit shocked to have ended up with two disorders; I'd been hoping for a maximum of one, and for it to be bipolar disorder. It turns out there's a lot of overlap between them: from common symptoms (like impulsivity, risk-taking behaviours and emotional dysregulation) to high comorbidity (a meaningful number of patients diagnosed with both disorders).

A 2013 comprehensive, systematic review[2] of studies examining the relationship between bipolar disorder and borderline personality disorder found that ten per cent of patients with borderline personality disorder had bipolar I disorder and another ten per cent had bipolar II disorder. The review also found that twenty per cent of bipolar II patients, and ten per cent of bipolar I patients, were diagnosed with borderline personality disorder.

A 2017 study[3] found a genetic link between the two disorders, which

---

2 Zimmerman, M., & Morgan, T. A. (2013). The relationship between borderline personality disorder and bipolar disorder. *Dialogues in Clinical Neuroscience*, *15*(2), 155-169. https://doi.org/10.31887/DCNS.2013.15.2/mzimmerman

3 Witt, S. H., Streit, F., Jungkunz, M., Frank, J., Awasthi, S., Reinbold, C. S., Treutlein, J., Degenhardt, F., Forstner, A. J., Heilmann-Heimbach, S., Dietl, L., Schwarze, C. E., Schendel, D., Strohmaier, J., Abdellaoui, A., Adolfsson, R., Air, T. M., Akil, H., Alda, M., ... Rietschel, M. (2017). Genome-wide association study of borderline personality disorder reveals genetic overlap with bipolar disorder, major depression and schizophrenia. *Translational Psychiatry*, *7*(6) e1155. https://doi.org/10.1038/tp.2017.115

the authors believe requires further exploration in future studies. In a 2020 study[4], patients with both disorders – compared with patients with bipolar disorder only – had more childhood trauma, psychopathology in first-degree relatives, suicidality and hospitalisations. Research in this area highlights the importance of accurate diagnoses and of distinguishing between the two disorders, as treatment varies.

John and I decide, together, that I will come in regularly for psychotherapeutic treatment. He also prescribes an antidepressant and a mood stabiliser. I fill the prescriptions and start taking both medications. It makes a difference when I trust the psychiatrist; I'm willing to follow their advice.

Being mentally ill has its own coming-out process. I speak to my parents about it when I'm driving back from one of my appointments with John.

'I'm glad you're seeing someone you like,' Mum says. 'Has your psychiatrist said what he thinks is going on?'

'Yes, he has given me a diagnosis,' I reply. Even though I usually avoid mentioning therapy around my parents, I feel relieved about my progress with John and this prompts me to divulge. 'He believes I have bipolar disorder. And borderline personality disorder.'

'Borderline personality disorder?'

I realise it comes as a shock to them, while I've had time to adjust to Susan's original diagnosis. 'Yes. There's quite a large range in that diagnosis. There are more severe cases and then mild forms.'

'What are the signs of having it? Why did he give you that diagnosis?' Mum asks.

'Inappropriate anger. A fear of abandonment. Impulsivity. Difficulty in relationships. Instability.' I don't mention the one I think about the most: an unstable sense of self.

Dad has been silent for most of the call but he says lightly, 'A lot of people have those traits.'

'Yes. But you need to meet five or more criteria to be diagnosed,' I explain.

---

4   Zimmerman, M., Balling, C., Chelminski, I., & Dalrymple, K. (2021). Patients with borderline personality disorder and bipolar disorder: A descriptive and comparative study. *Psychological Medicine*, *51*(9), 1479-1490. https://doi.org/10.1017/S0033291720000215

'What causes it?' Mum asks.

'Trauma.' There's a lot more I could say about potential contributing factors, but trauma is the only one I'm comfortable mentioning. It's vague and doesn't reveal much. While I find it easy enough to mention trauma, I'm aware the t-word is probably shocking for my parents. There's an awkward pause.

I'm using that word as a stand-in for so much else. Some studies support the theory that there are genetic causes for clusters of borderline personality disorder in families, which are not caused by shared environmental factors. But genetics is certainly not the only contributing factor.

Childhood environmental factors like neglect and abuse – sexual, physical and/or emotional – and having a relative with mental illness or substance use issues have all been connected to borderline personality disorder. Changes in parts of the brain and neurotransmitters have also been linked to borderline personality disorder, but it has not yet been established whether these are a cause or a consequence of the disorder.

'What is the treatment?' Dad asks.

'Psychotherapy, for both disorders. And medication for bipolar disorder. I've been taking it and it seems to be making a difference.' I wait to see if they will say anything. My family is hesitant about taking medication, sometimes. I was raised to drink water if I had a headache, to take Vitamin C, eat chicken soup and get a lot of rest if I had a bad cold, and to take pharmaceutical medication only if I wasn't getting better.

I can tell my parents have more to say but they don't. I'm glad they hold back. While I appreciate how much they care, I increasingly feel that my journey with mental illness is mine alone.

Once I realise that, I begin to work on bringing better boundaries into my relationship with my parents. I resist turning to them as though my life depends upon it, as it once did.

On another call, Mum recommends the TV show *My Crazy Ex-Girlfriend,* which features a borderline personality disorder journey. I decide not to watch it. I'd rather read personal accounts of severe mental illness, and I find great companionship in books like Kate Richards' *Madness* and Bassey Ikpi's *I'm Telling the Truth, But I'm Lying*. Richards' account of her experiences of mental illness is so shocking that her recovery seems extraordinary. Her writing is enough to shake me out of my inattentiveness and complacency at the time. Ikpi's memoir captures what it is like to live with bipolar disorder, down to the minute-by-minute experience. It's so satisfying to read something I relate to so much, to know that even one other person in the universe understands my experiences.

Even if a TV show gets it right, I have no interest in subjecting myself to fictional depictions of borderline personality disorder. I've read crime fiction where the author casually refers to 'borderlines' to describe the worst psychiatric patients or to stigmatise certain characters, and it hurts every time.

When I tell others my diagnoses, some react the way Karyn did. They don't believe it, especially not about having borderline personality disorder. Rachel's family members, who have personal experience with severe borderline personality disorder, say they can't imagine the label ever fitting me.

Some people tend to 'diagnose' anyone difficult or abusive in their lives with borderline personality disorder. The people who do this tell me I can't possibly have it. They mean it in a positive way, but it strikes me as a form of gaslighting. It makes me question my treatment. I'm easily influenced; whenever someone tells me certain symptoms or behaviours are just part of my personality, I see my issues as unavoidable, untreatable.

Therapy sessions with John are an essential part of managing my health, and Rachel, my family and my friends provide support, love and care.

I love to challenge the societal hierarchy that places individualised care above community forms of care, and I'm thrilled to see books being written that challenge the notion of finding the right doctor in order to heal. My context, though, as an introvert resistant to asking for help, and as someone with the privilege to seek out what I need and reject anything that doesn't work for me, makes individualised care desirable and workable for me.

I'm still unsure how to feel about my diagnoses, but having correctly diagnosed myself with bipolar disorder makes me feel validated. I turn to writing. I write about the feeling of being in my body. When I'm manic, I feel every sensation. I am preoccupied with physical feelings, unlike therapy, which is so focused on the cognitive. I feel my skin and nails when I rip them. My lip when I bite it. Other people's emotions when I hurt them. The crunch of glass when I crash into someone's car. The sound when someone crashes their car into mine.

I write in the Notes app on my phone, which has become my diary, *I view everything through an apocalyptic lens when I'm down, so how am I meant to be optimistic about fixing my relationships?* But when I'm depressed again, I do exactly that. I apologise to people and try to address the mistakes I made while I was manic.

Eventually, I go back for the second endoscopy. By then, I'm convinced the growth on my vocal cords is cancerous and that I'm going to die. I think I might deserve it after wishing for a terminal illness when I was suicidal last year.

But when I go in, this time bringing Rachel with me, it's good news. My vocal cords are damaged due to acid reflux and asthma. Using my voice so much has exacerbated my condition. I have prescriptions for reflux medication and an asthma preventer inhaler that contains corticosteroids. I have a referral to see a speech pathologist. I need to rest my voice as much as possible.

It's not cancer.

It's such a relief. We decide to go from the clinic to a local Italian restaurant for a celebratory lunch. The restaurant is decorated for Halloween and there are plastic skeletons and fake spiderwebs on the walls.

'Maybe we can move on now,' I say after we order our meals.

Rachel looks at me and I see the hurt in her eyes.

'I don't know about "moving on", necessarily, but we can work on things,' she says.

'I'd really like that,' I reply. 'I'm willing to do whatever it takes, love.'

'So am I,' she says, looking down at the table and then back up at me.

A waiter delivers our drinks but I don't reach for mine. 'I want to learn how to control my anger and make sure I don't speak to you the way I have during some of the worst manic episodes.'

She nods. It's tense between us, but for the first time in a while we are both hopeful.

* * *

In November, I find out I've been accepted into a PhD program at my dream research centre. It's very good timing, as I've discovered the school is only offering one ongoing role. The school principal informs me and my colleague we will both have to apply and interview for it. I think about applying, but I don't think I can go through with the interview. I don't want to compete for the role when I'm not certain I want it.

I feel a sense of shame about not 'sticking it out' with teaching: I had hoped to teach for at least three years. Part of that was wanting to prove to myself that I could do it.

I compare myself to Lisa, my friend at the same school. She's thriving as a teacher. We both taught the same students this year, in different subjects. I watched her ease, comfort and humour in the classroom. We went on an excursion together and I couldn't help but envy the way she provided boundaries and ensured their safety without getting anxious. She has become besties with one of the other graduate teachers, like I feared when I started the job. I see a bright future in teaching for both of them, but it's not for me.

I tell the principal I won't be applying for the position. I mention the PhD and my health struggles, and tell her I will finish up at the end of the year. She sounds surprised, and keeps asking me if I'm sure. I tell her I am, but I feel a lot of doubt, guilt and relief. When I hang up the phone, I sob. It's the hardest I've cried in a long time.

In my final days of teaching, I receive farewell cards and gifts from my students. One of my Year 10 students writes: *You are a truly amazing teacher and I have learnt so much from you. You have helped me find my path and decide what I'd like to do going ahead.* I read his words over and over again, trying to take them in and believe them.

A Year 7 student's mother hands me a gift and says, 'Good luck with your PhD! My son is very sad you're leaving. You're the only English teacher he has ever liked.'

Another student writes, *We will miss you, Ms Bellamy, but hope that your vocal cords get better.*

The notes make me emotional. They make it clear that despite what my inner voice often told me, I built relationships and made an impact. I will miss my students so much. I wish I could stay, for them, but I need to take care of myself for now.

I start to think of my vocal cords as my metaphor, excuse and saviour. Later, I leave the school for the last time – and with it, teaching.

Chapter 17

Living with bipolar can bring extreme highs and lows, but on medication I mostly live in the in-between. The in-between can have hints of depression and mania, but not enough to feel like I can't get out of bed or that I'm going to do something dangerous. It's controlled, and I feel balanced unless something happens to throw me off. It's how I imagine mentally healthy people experience life.

After starting my PhD in 2018, I spend a lot of time researching mental illness. Part of it is for my PhD research, but I end up down a lot of rabbit holes, fascinated by my reading about mental health. I develop strong feelings about the *Diagnostic and Statistical Manual of Mental Disorders* (DSM): the way it pathologises normal human responses to trauma and oppression, and for decades associated sexual and gender diversity with deviance and disorder. I read about racial disparities in mental health: those from racial and ethnic minority backgrounds are far less likely to receive treatment, are more likely to encounter discrimination in a range of institutions, and face a range of negative health outcomes related to racial discrimination. Many psychiatric and medical treatments were designed based on beliefs around biological determinism and racial inferiority, which were considered justification for testing medications and procedures, including sterilisation, on groups of people.

I am also aware I was desperate to be given a diagnosis – I thought it would be a magic fix. And it has been helpful: many of the changes I've implemented in my life have been possible because I know more about the way my brain works. But a lot is suspect about the process of diagnosis – and about psychiatry in general. It's concerning to me that without Cameron suggesting John, I might still be resigned to a steady flow of Susans and Andrews. I think about those who can't afford to seek out second, third and fourth opinions – how they might receive a complex and severe diagnosis, the way I did, after one appointment, and not receive adequate support and resources; how they might end up feeling completely unheard and misunderstood, and not know where to turn next. There is a link (that goes both ways) between mental illness and homelessness, unemployment and the criminal justice system.

I sought out psychiatric diagnoses and individualised, personalised care when I craved having a sense of community around me. So I connect with others with mental illnesses and disabilities, and learn about disability justice, a social justice movement that focuses on improving access and inclusion for disabled people. It also explores how ableism – discrimination or prejudice against those with disabilities – relates to other forms of oppression such as race, class and gender.

I become much more open about my mental illness, and begin to understand it as a disability – it impacts on the way I participate in everyday life and sometimes compromises my ability to function. I build friendships within disability activism circles, where we discuss systemic issues, stigma, and sustaining others in the community through mutual aid. I begin to question the word 'disorder', which appears twice on my medical record. I read widely about neurodivergence and start to admire the beauty of seeing the world in different tones and colours, rather than judging myself for not fitting into society.

***

I have another episode in the spring of 2018. When I become manic this time, I can't blame teaching. I repeat many of the same behaviours: lying, disappearing, doing whatever I want, regardless of the consequences. A former colleague sees me somewhere she shouldn't have and I lie that it wasn't me. *You have a doppelgänger, then,* she texts.

I still can't write about everything I did. I want to claim responsibility, and I am willing to share everything on the page that's mine to share, but I am better at keeping promises now. Memoir can be many things, among them a confessional, but re-establishing rules and boundaries for my relationship was one of my most important ways forward.

I am aware of the irony of not including my worst behaviour in a book about mental illness. I want people to read about my actions during some of my manic episodes and be able to recognise behaviours and symptoms and seek support and resources. Can that still be achieved without 'the whole truth'? I've tried to give you everything, but I'm not sure I can keep my promise to Rachel while including every episode or relevant event.

I confess my behaviour to my friend Phoebe, who now lives in London. I tell her I've become an incredibly shitty partner.

'Oh Rozy! Well done for talking about it and for recognising it. Do you need me to be supportive or tell you you're shitty?'

'I don't deserve any praise, but thanks,' I say. 'Tell me I'm shitty. Everyone has sided with me so far.'

'You're shitty,' she says.

'I've really fucked with Rachel's head. Like what Dara did to me at school. It's that cycle of abuse, I guess.'

'So you're saying that you can blame it on your mental health but the bottom line is you know better?' she asks.

'Yes. I know better but all my empathy and common sense goes.'

'And I assume you've been talking to someone professional about this?'

'Yes, a psychiatrist and a psychologist,' I reply.

She acknowledges I have sought help and that I recognise my responsibility for my actions. She says she respects what I said about needing people not to side with me. In her view, we live in a world where we're constantly being told we are who we are and that's okay. But Phoebe suggests we should all aim higher – not for perfection, but to be better versions of ourselves.

'I guess the bottom line is, who do you want to be? How do you break the cycle? How do you become a better version of yourself? What are the variables you are able to control?'

'Currently I have to be afraid she's going to leave me before I try to do better.'

'So that's the cycle? You fear she'll leave and this causes you to self-sabotage, which gives her a reason to leave, and then you try to get her to stay?'

I nod, embarrassed by the description.

'What's your communication like during these times?' she asks. 'Are you able to express your feelings and hear her out, or do you become defensive?'

'Yes, that's the cycle. I'm nasty until some time passes and I calm down and suddenly realise all the awful things I said in a fight. *Then* we talk properly.'

I reflect on Phoebe's words after our conversation. Aiming higher, not for perfection, is good advice. I'm relieved she told me my behaviour isn't okay – even though I've been hurt in the past, even if I'm mentally ill. I know it's not okay.

I also keep thinking about the comparison I made between Dara's bullying and the way I treated Rachel. Maybe my cruelty was a test to see if Rachel would still want to be with me. Maybe I wanted to know how far I could push my relationship, to know what it's like to have all the power and control. To know how it feels to be the bully rather than the victim. And now that I know, I worry I have become Dara.

At my next therapy appointment, John and I talk about my recent struggles.

'I remember how depressed I was after I started my PhD at the start of the year.'

He nods.

'The fact that I still get depressed drives me crazy. It's November; nearly a year since I finished teaching. I'd hoped things would be a lot better. And they are. But now I'm realising I'll always have periods of depression, or the tendency to feel depressed, even when nothing bad is happening in my life.'

I tell him about my university student card, how I hate looking at it. The photo is a helpful reference point to remind me how I was doing in March. I look washed out and sad. I still had a streak of bleached hair from when I had dyed it blue and purple during the marriage equality debates. The colour had faded at the time of the photo, and my bleached hair had turned a miserable shade that reminded me of algae. As the heat had subsided late that autumn, so had my motivation and enthusiasm. John had tried to address this at the time by raising the dosage of my antidepressant. My depression faded away for a month or two and then I had another manic episode.

We discuss the things that have changed since March, including my new role as an editor at *Archer Magazine*, a magazine about sex, sexuality, gender and identity. Since beginning the role, in the most supportive workplace I have worked in, I have become out and proud about being non-binary. I'm also far less anxious.

At this appointment, he adjusts my medication again. This time, we get it right. It makes a huge difference. For the first time, I feel stable and know how to manage my conditions.

* * *

In 2019, a relative dies suddenly. We were distant cousins and didn't see each other enough but I really liked him. I want to fly to New York for his funeral but can't make it there in time, as Jewish funerals happen very quickly after death. My grief feels a bit like hypomania. I engage in some magical thinking: maybe if I spend thousands of dollars and leave *right now*, I'll make it somehow! And once I think that, my mind jumps a few steps. Maybe I'll get to see him one more time before he dies. But I know this is just regret for not being in regular contact with him, that these hopes aren't real.

I go for a long walk. It's autumn, and the sharp air reminds me it's spring in Brooklyn, where my family are mourning. The distance feels pronounced, poignant.

I notice a sign stuck up at the local tennis courts that says, *WHEN DO I BEGIN LIVING?* I don't know if someone wrote it as a cry for help and meant it as a genuine, existential question or if it's some kind of marketing ploy. There is no way to tell anymore. I feel that my grief over many loved ones has removed layers of skin, as though I have been excoriated.

But this time my grief doesn't lead to a manic episode. I continue to take my antidepressant and antipsychotic every day and see my therapist every fortnight. This is not an ode to Big Pharma, psychiatry and psychotherapy. It's an acknowledgement of my brain chemistry, my DNA and my history.

Mood

* * *

Rachel and I return to Hawaii at the start of 2020, before we know about the pandemic. She has recently graduated with her PhD and the trip is partly to celebrate her becoming a doctor.

We go out for drinks and watch the sunset from one of the beachfront hotels, a block over from where we're staying above a gay karaoke club. I suggest an illicit swim in the hotel's adults-only infinity pool. We joke, swim and kiss. When the night has spread around us, obscuring even the magnificent Diamond Head, I turn to Rachel.

'I'm so sorry. For everything.' For the first time, perhaps in my life, an emotional conversation doesn't feel forced or stilted. The words roll out and I'm shocked: by how much I mean them, by how earnest I am. I haven't felt that way in a while. 'I want you to trust me again. I want to rebuild what we have. I want to make new vows and make sure I don't break them. I never want to hurt you again.'

Rachel takes my hands. Perhaps it's the combination of the soft night air, the sunset, the calm she feels in Hawaii and her love for me – despite the way I have hurt her. But she seems to recognise my sincerity. She agrees to try again. We both tear up.

When we're home, we work on our mental health individually, with therapists. We put a lot of time and effort into addressing the issues in our marriage. Mental illness, it seems, can bring up all sorts of previously unaddressed issues, as well as producing new ones.

Rachel tells me she feels like she's only now beginning to grapple with everything that happened. 'The way you treated me, at times, was like you hated me. Like you wanted to destroy me.'

Starting over is too weak, too clichéd, to describe what comes next in a relationship where mental illness has led to emotionally abusive behaviour. The first step was my sincere apology followed by behavioural change.

I address my anger during therapy. I learn how to redirect it into other things, like my writing and creativity. There are times when writing saves me and times when I can't open a document. The thought that I might let my fears stop me, the way I used to, fills me with dread. So I push through, even if it takes me to a dark place. The idea of possibly hurting myself to write a book about recovery and healing strikes me as so typically me.

Sex is another great way to expend intense manic energy. I also learn to direct my anger at the system – the systemic, structural issues that make it so hard to live with mental illness and disability – instead of at Rachel.

I learn how to calm down and not catastrophise during our fights. I learn how to address my mistakes after I make them. I learn how to pause and critically reflect if someone tells me how I should feel about something. I learn how to be more present, even if I'm still erratic at times. I learn how to control myself, to straighten out my boundaries and remind Rachel of them if I think they're going to be broken. I make a promise to myself that I am safe, that I won't be hurt or abandoned, that I don't need to make Rachel feel unsafe to have a sense of control and security.

I rebuild friendships and relationships with people I hurt, alienated or rejected during my worst episodes of mental illness. I'm so much better, now, at engaging with emotions. Even if they're not always obvious to me, I study their shapes like a Rorschach test and attempt to identify how I'm feeling. The most elusive ones are anger and sadness; there is so much to them – layer upon layer – and it can be hard to work out what I'm seeing.

I'm more open than I've ever been – not that that's a yardstick of mental health. I have limits and boundaries. I try not to step over other people's limits and boundaries, and don't always manage to do so, but I try again the next time.

Cameron and I work on our friendship. We avoid certain topics for months before we're ready to return to them. We're most cautious about mental health, about relationship advice, about overstepping the lines of friendship. Our friendship becomes fun and playful, like it used to be, but now with boundaries in place. I'm still wary that my symptoms might return, but I stop tensing up around him.

I apologise to Sharon for forcing her to be in the middle of my relationship with Rachel during some of my manic episodes.

'You don't have anything to apologise to me about, Roz,' she says. 'I will always be here for you, no matter what.'

I realise she has never judged me. I try to become more like her in that way.

Shortly afterwards, Sharon comes out as queer. She posts on Facebook about being bisexual, and people think she is making some sort of statement about her marriage and ask if she and David are still together. They are.

People in my life who know her ask me the same question.

'Yes, they are still together and doing very well,' I reply.

'So what did her message on Facebook mean?'

'She wants to be honest about who she is.' No matter how many times I say it, some people don't understand that sexuality is about identity, and that it isn't dependent on who you are currently in a relationship with.

Sharon tells me and Rachel how grateful she is towards us. We argue the gratitude should run the other way, that there is no way to repay her generosity and the leap of faith she took with us. She shakes this off gently. She says she is so glad she knows us and we give her courage.

* * *

Sometimes, writing this book feels like covering myself with the weighted blanket I finally ended up buying: like it's slowly pushing all the air out of me, leaving me flat, but relieved and less anxious. I work on it late at night, long after I should have gone to bed. At other times, writing feels like I am delivering electrical shocks to my heart.

John tells me sleep deprivation can lead to psychosis. After that, I try to be more careful about how much sleep I get.

Sometimes, I'm tempted to become manic again. I know what I need to do to induce a manic or hypomanic state. It's appealing because I make connections between things I don't normally see. I become extra metaphoric and poetic. Writing in that state is electrifying. My heart beats so fast as the ideas flow and I become hyperaware of my fingers on the keyboard.

I miss the grandiosity and the occasional narcissism. As someone who was bullied at a young age, being cocky and confident is startlingly different to my usual feelings.

And I am delighted – smug, really – when that familiar feeling returns of wanting to connect with others again. I try to find that feeling even when my mood isn't elevated, but it isn't quite the same. At least I no longer hold back what I want to say.

Except I still don't really know how to say no. I go out for tapas with a new friend and she chooses the dishes since she's been there before. She knows I'm vegetarian but I mention I sometimes eat fish, forgetting to specify I don't eat other seafood. She runs through the order with me. 'Definitely a serve of the salt and pepper calamari; it's incredible here.' She looks to me for my okay.

'Yep, that sounds good,' I say, hating myself for my passivity.

When the food comes, she notices I'm not eating the calamari. 'Do you not like it?' she asks.

I'm so afraid of upsetting her, I say, 'Oh, no, I forgot to eat it!' I press my fork in and bite into the rubbery texture.

Later, I think about how little I prioritise my preferences, how I view them as less important than anyone else's.

I'm still afraid of causing conflict with my family, in-laws and friends in case they punish through silence and distance. Abandonment and rejection are the worst forms of punishment to me. But our relationships have grown and evolved so much. I can set boundaries, albeit very timidly and hesitantly, and people stick around.

Dara taught me not to trust myself or others. It's time to let go of that.

I try to apply a small amount of how I feel when I'm manic, when I'm convinced of my own greatness. It's funny; when I'm depressed, I put people at a distance, and when I'm manic, they watch me warily from a distance. There's always a pane of glass between us. It's hard to find a middle-ground, but I'm getting there.

* * *

I start to think of mental health and mental illness as another binary that doesn't work for me, along with the gender binary and being gay or straight. I realise my anxiety, depression and mania protect me. They help me determine whether I want to take flight or fight. Sometimes they push me out of my shell and remind me to free myself from constraints, while other times they serve as my hiding place, my excuse not to show up.

Bipolar disorder used to be called manic depression. It's no longer treated as two polar opposites. Some people experience rapid-cycling, while others, like me, experience longer periods in one mood state.

Borderline personality disorder might also be renamed; I keep coming across articles urging psychiatrists to rename and reclassify it as an identity or mood disorder due to the stigma associated with personality disorders. There's talk of renaming it complex PTSD or another name that acknowledges it stems from trauma rather than a flawed personality. The name added to my distress when Susan first dangled the diagnosis in front of me. It no longer means much to me, but people's reactions still hurt. Every time I see a new doctor, I question how much to tell them. If I mention BPD, I know their body language may change. When I list an anti-psychotic along with other medications, they may flinch. It's best to let my embarrassment fade and think, *Let them flinch. Let them wonder how my mood and personality disorders play out. I don't owe anyone answers, information or shame for being the way I am.*

Our society – due to colonisation, neoliberalism and capitalism – doesn't value the beauty, complexity and nuance in those of us who are mentally ill, disabled and neurodivergent. Now I know, finally, that we aren't the ones who need to change.

* * *

I get three more tattoos before finishing this book. If the first tattoo was in honour of Rosie's arrival and the second for Opal's, then the third is for my marriage, which has survived despite all odds. I have the rainbow lorikeets from our wedding invitation tattooed on the back of one arm, in technicolour. It's a physical reminder of our relationship, what we've been through.

In 2020, in between two lockdowns during the pandemic, I get my fourth tattoo. This one is for me. It's a botanical drawing of jacaranda in its different stages of growth. There are the leaves, the seed pod cracking open, the buds and then one perfect flower. The tattoo represents the jacaranda tree in my childhood home in Sydney, and also its native South America, where some of my family migrated to from Ukraine.

It's a nicer plant metaphor than one I heard growing up: the antisemitic overtones of the weed 'wandering Jew', *Tradescantia fluminensis*. The wandering Jew is a beautiful weed, with green, heart-shaped leaves, purple stripes and a silvery sheen. It's thick, persistent and invasive. It survives in warm temperatures. Plant guides mention that 'as its name suggests' it loves to wander but it isn't tolerant of the cold and will die in the freeze if left outside.

My mother-in-law once came over and told Rachel and I that we should rip out the weeds in our courtyard daily, that it would be good exercise and would keep our garden looking well-maintained.

But I relate to the weeds: growing between cracks, desperate, surviving *despite* or in spite, like my family in Romania, Ukraine, Uzbekistan, Siberia.

To me, jacaranda represents triumph, joy and flourishing. It's a testament to my life and my family history lived here and there, growing seedlings and blooming bright flowers in unexpected places.

At a writing workshop, I talk about being the 'wandering Jew'. A writer says to me: 'Maybe you *don't* belong anywhere. Maybe that's okay. Maybe your body is the only place you belong.'

The concept makes it easier to breathe, to understand myself. I don't have to work out whose stolen lands and waters I belong on. The person who says this to me is a migrant on different stolen lands. They're right. I love the sea because my body is mostly water. My veins are the only map I need to make sense of. I will continue carrying this body forward – even when it aches or loses touch with reality – because of guilt, and love, and a surprising sense of hope.

In early 2021, celebrating the freedom of being out of lockdown and Trump no longer being the president of the United States, I get my fifth tattoo: a hand-poked one. Madison Griffiths, a queer writer, does it for me. It's her own design from her flash collection of new tattoos and it says: *A TRUE STORY.*

Once she's finished, I look down at my thigh. It looks gorgeous, with my newest tattoo so close to my first, the Audre Lorde quote. They are perfect. I relish using that word now. No one is going to tell me not to use it again. Sometimes, art – like nature – is flawless.

In 2022, I pause my tattoo journey. A year earlier, Rachel and

I started the process of trying to conceive through a fertility clinic. I became pregnant with our first baby. I learn that once you carry a baby, their fetal cells stay in your blood and tissues for years, if not life. I've indelibly marked myself with this child, or he has marked himself on me.

While I'm pregnant, John tells me that I no longer meet the criteria for borderline personality disorder. I'm elated, then cry for days. I don't know which part of the journey 'fixed me'. I want to take credit, for obediently consuming my medication and turning up fortnightly for therapy sessions, but I also think that stepping out of the fire – of teaching, of facing my traumas – has made the most difference. Finally, I realise it doesn't matter what helped. The causes aren't what I was searching for. I lie to my delivery hospital about my mental health history, not wanting myself and our baby to be psychopathologised before he's even born. John nods at this, not judging, and I feel safe – out of the hands of institutions.

I have such a strong desire for control. When I clean the house and vacuum dog fur out of carpets, I want the cleanliness to last and wish living didn't produce so much mess. Sometimes I try to donate or throw out household items that we need, or attempt to use up every product in the pantry rather than buy more, and then wonder if I am seeking out emptiness because I fear it.

My relatives survived the war and starvation by hiding and eating dirt. My body has always known fear, and I still have a tendency to try to expose myself to my deepest fears to heal myself. Then I remember I have faced, and survived, many things that scare me. I can make things dirty again. I can cope with conflict, with life's moods, with not having control.

I am lucky to live a life in which I can lose touch with reality, and my sense of self, and things can still work out okay.

Even though my mental health is fairly stable now, my dreams leave me feeling lost sometimes, forced into places where I don't feel safe. I'm still a teacher and I'm unprepared for my classes, then reprimanded and humiliated in front of my students. I have terrifying, violent Holocaust dreams where I don't manage to hide in time. When I wake, I remember that as a teenager, I had a plan for where to hide in case Nazis turned up at our house.

Rachel listens to my dreams and tells me they aren't real, even if I insist they are. As she holds me, I feel my tension and fear disappearing.

When I get out of bed, Rosie and Opal wake up, stretch out their long limbs, and greet me. The beauty and steadiness of their faces bring me back.

Watching the dogs reminds me to appreciate nature: the sunshine, the wind blowing us about, and every blade of grass, even if it's about to be peed on. The smells and the landscape around us are equally fascinating to them whether we're walking in a neatly manicured park, at a dog beach reeking of seaweed, or along a busy road. On these walks, I think about rescue: what it means to rescue dogs and what it feels like as a human who often needs rescuing.

The dogs help me figure out other things – things I didn't expect them to teach me. I learn how to be firm with Rosie when she tugs us in the wrong direction or Opal when she gets too excited with other dogs, even though I want to give into their whims. My relationship with them is safe, so I can explore what it means to give in sometimes, but to push back at other times. I learn to be more consistent and to have a routine: for my health and for theirs.

I don't know what things will look like next season or year, but Rosie and Opal put a stop to ruminating on it. Who cares? There's tan bark to pee on. There's a bum to sniff. There's a possum up that tree. There's a cat hiding under that car. There's a stranger to demand pats from, and there's another stranger to slink away from, throwing them a look for daring to come on too strong.

And there'll be another walk, later.

Acknowledgements

Mood was written on the unceded lands of the Wurundjeri people of the Kulin nation. I pay my respects to their elders, past and present.

When I started writing a memoir, I believed it to be a solitary activity – a lone figure looking out at the horizon. As *Mood* started to take shape, I realised that without the communities I belong to, there is no horizon.

Thank you to the many writers and arts professionals who have supported and encouraged me in the development of this book: Jessica Bellamy, Sharon Angelici, Jasper Peach, Matilda Dixon-Smith, Jax Jacki-Brown, Domi Shoemaker, Kel Butler, Sam Van Zweden, Kate Cuthbert, Melissa Cranenburgh, Sam Elkin, Billy-Ray Belcourt, Maria Tumarkin, my colleagues at Archer Magazine and drummond street services, and the writers in my Chamonix and Tin House writing workshops, the 2022 Book Gang and the 2023 Debut Authors group. Thank you to Kate Richards, Cheryl Strayed and Anna Spargo-Ryan for endorsing this book with such beautiful words. To the members of my writing group, Anna Kate Blair and Alexandra O'Sullivan (and, for a time, Anna Kiss-Gyorgy): thank you for your friendship, insights into my work, and the sense of community as we share our writing and lives.

Working with Nadine Davidoff was critical to completing *Mood*. Nadine's detailed structural edits and revisions helped me fine-tune my manuscript and build the confidence to send it off to publishers.

I am still pinching myself that I got to work with Jo Case as my editor. Jo, who was interested in my manuscript from the day it arrived at Wakefield Press, has contributed an enormous amount to this book through her thoughtful edits, questions and provocations. This is a deeply personal story, and Jo was gentle, respectful and meticulous – all the things one wants most in an editor. I'm also incredibly grateful to the team at

Wakefield Press, including Jesse Pollard, Julia Beaven, Maddy Sexton, Michael Bollen, Polly Grant Butler and Poppy Nwosu, for their support, enthusiasm and attention to detail during the publication process, and to Duncan Blachford of Typography Studio for designing a beautiful, striking cover for *Mood*.

Thank you to the organisations that allowed me to develop and sustain my creative practice, including the National Young Writers' Festival, the Emerging Writers' Festival, Express Media, Melbourne City of Literature, Merri-bek Arts, Tin House Workshops, Kill Your Darlings, the Wheeler Centre and Writers Victoria. *Mood* was supported by grants (including Covid-19 emergency relief funding) from the City of Melbourne, Creative Victoria, Australia Council for the Arts and the National Assistance Program for the Arts.

In addition to the creative communities that sustained my practice, there are many others who made the research and writing possible.

To my colleagues at La Trobe University, where I completed my PhD at the same time I wrote *Mood*, and those I have worked with and consulted at other universities, libraries, archives and community organisations: thank you for deepening my understanding of mental health and wellbeing in marginalised communities, and for the vitally important work you do.

To Radhika, Karyn and John: thank you for helping me figure out important parts of myself.

My past students played a significant role in my life and are an important part of *Mood*. I'm grateful to them for teaching me so much, even when I wasn't ready or able to learn it all.

To my late grandparents and friends: I think of you constantly. Regardless of how much of your story is in *Mood*, the entire book is suffused with you. I miss you all.

To my extended family, including my in-laws, Wisconsin family, and friends: thank you for your love, generosity and support.

To my parents, Nella and Des, and my sister, Jessica (again): thank you for always encouraging my curiosity, eccentricity and creativity. I'm so grateful for you.

To my greyhounds, Rosie and Opal, and our many pet rats: you have shown me what it looks like to have strength after adversity. Thank you for trusting us, even though other humans mistreated you.

To my baby, who I will call K: I hope you don't mind that so much of your mama (and your mommy) is in this book. I am so amazed by you – your impressive communication skills, sense of humour and persistence. I can't wait to hear your stories and ideas as you grow.

Finally, to Rachel: you're my safe place. Thanks for letting me be yours.

Wakefield Press is an independent publishing and
distribution company based in Adelaide, South Australia.
We love good stories and publish beautiful books.
To see our full range of books, please visit our website at
www.wakefieldpress.com.au
where all titles are available for purchase.
To keep up with our latest releases, news and events,
subscribe to our monthly newsletter.

Find us!

Facebook: www.facebook.com/wakefield.press
Twitter: www.twitter.com/wakefieldpress
Instagram: www.instagram.com/wakefieldpress

www.ingramcontent.com/pod-product-compliance
Lightning Source LLC
Chambersburg PA
CBHW030826230426
43667CB00008B/1389